D0966813

Praise for *Customer Capitalism*

"*Customer Capitalism* provides an original and potent model for business success. A book that finally puts the nail in the coffin of product-driven capitalism and outlines a whole new way to grow a business and own a market."

Philip Kotler, S.C. Johnson & Son Distinguished Professor of International Marketing, J.L. Kellogg Graduate School of Management, Northwestern University

"In her innovative book, Sandra Vandermerwe shows how organizations can enjoy benefits of increasing returns if they understand and use the principles of customer capitalism. They must exist for customers rather than for products and create value in the 'customer space' rather than the 'corporate space'. Most significantly they have to combine technology with imagination, and cultivate an ability to anticipate, rather than react."

Professor John A. Quelch, Dean, London Business School

"In *Customer Capitalism* Sandra Vandermerwe provides an alternative business model which is proving to revolutionize business performance. All stakeholders can enjoy a new era of increasing returns by adopting the principles described in the book, whereas simply continuing to improve existing business will not deliver outstanding returns."

Jeff Cox, Monsanto

"This book is immensely readable. It should find its way on to the shelves of every business leader who wants to understand and apply the principles of customer-centered organizations.
Sandra Vandermerwe introduces some ground-breaking material on the 'new world' concepts of customer-centered organizations and growth. She illustrates with short case studies how many organizations have transformed their future prospects by applying the principles of customer value to everything they do."

John Bale, Andersen Consulting

Dedication:

to Woody Red Vandermerwe

who sat through the entire writing of this manuscript

and has given me nothing but increasing returns...

CUSTOMER CAPITALISM

The new business model of
increasing returns in new market spaces

SANDRA VANDERMERWE

NICHOLAS BREALEY
PUBLISHING

LONDON

First published by
Nicholas Brealey Publishing Limited in 1999

36 John Street
London
WC1N 2AT, UK
Tel: +44 (0)171 430 0224
Fax: +44 (0)171 404 8311

1163 E. Ogden Avenue, Suite 705-229
Naperville
IL 60563-8535, USA
Tel: (888) BREALEY
Fax: (630) 428 3442

http://www.nbrealey-books.com

ISBN 1-85788-241-5

Library of Congress Cataloging-in-Publication Data
Vandermerwe, Sandra.
    Customer capitalism : the new business model for increasing
returns by becoming the customer choice / Sandra Vandermerwe.
        p.   cm.
    Includes bibliographical references and index.
    ISBN 1-85788-241-5
    1. Customer services. 2. Target marketing. 3. Capitalism.
I. Title.
    HF5415.5.V357   1999
    658.812–dc21   98-56043
                                                                    CIP

British Library Cataloguing in Publication Data
A catalogue record for this book is available from the
British Library.

Printed in Finland by WSOY.

Contents

Acknowledgments

As we know, all books are shaped by conversations and discussion, the spark of an idea at a meeting or in a boardroom or classroom, by the books of the 'grand masters' and writings from management and economic theorists, consultants and the business press. This one is no exception. It represents the coming together of many disciplines, ideas from academia and business, and evolving and converging management, economic and financial theories, as together we search for new constructs to take corporations into and through the next millennium.

Much of my work began in the 1970s when I wrote my doctorate, 'The Influence of the Marketing Concept on Company Performance'. I was convinced that customers were not the exclusive domain of the marketing function, but were the key to a corporation's sustainable success. So began a 25-year journey straddling the disciplines of marketing and strategy, to drive the customer message by word and mouth, whenever and wherever I dared.

Quite naturally this led me into services in the 1980s, inspired by Juan Rada (the then Director General of IMI, later to merge with IMEDE to become IMD). He, like me, believed that services had become the core constituent in customer value in all industries and soon would, therefore, be the wealth generator for both corporations and economies. From research spanning several years in this field came my book *From Tin Soldiers to Russian Dolls: Adding Value Through Services*.

The inevitable next step? To figure out how corporations – both in manufacturing and the service sector – fundamentally change, from just making and selling their offerings to become enterprises who know how to accomplish the intricate and longer-term goal of 'owning' the customer relationship. Exposure to top global corporations at IMD and a dedicated project in this field there culminated in the mid-

1990s in my next work, *The Eleventh Commandment: Transforming to 'Own' Customers.*

This book is an extension of that work. Its prime concern is how corporations achieve ongoing superior offerings for customers and benefit over time from this investment. But our new economic world – call it what you will: the digital age, the wired society, the networked era, the knowledge economy – is such that it makes it possible (and indeed necessary) for an enterprise to deal differently with customers from at any other time in our history. It eradicates once and for all the irrelevant management theories and frameworks inherited from old capitalism and makes vital an alternative, more appropriate business model, which I call customer capitalism.

Many individuals have contributed in very specific and special ways to making this book on customer capitalism possible. The executives themselves who, rich in minds and settings, have given so generously: sharing their ideas; hearing and refining mine; partaking in case studies; engaging in research projects; giving interviews; and inviting me into their boardrooms, discussions and workshops to participate in the demanding task of formulating their thinking and strategies for a new and exciting millennium.

Some of these executives I have mentioned by name in the book, others I have not, so as to preserve their privacy. All are part of a process of application-driven enquiry and analysis, which form a body of research I call 'research of new practice'. It is built on the insights and actions of people who do not just reflect on existing theory, but help invent and articulate the new as they go along. My grateful thanks to them. I hope I have represented them well (though the responsibility for interpretation of course rests solely with me).

In particular, I should like to make special mention and thank three executives and their companies who knew and trusted me enough to provide the funds necessary to pursue this project: Andrew Creasy, from IBM; Sarah Galbraith, of ICI Fluorochemicals; and Ian MacMillan, from Northumbrian Water (now part of Compagnie Lyonnaise des Eaux).

Marika Taishoff, Senior Research Fellow, has worked with me on and off for nine years both at IMD and Imperial Management School, and credit is due to her for many of the case studies that we have written together mentioned in this book, and for her conscientious research that has formed the background for this work.

Grateful thanks are also due to those who read early drafts of my work, particularly Sue Birley, Professor of Entrepreneurship and Director of Research at Imperial Management School; Michael Hobbs, an Imperial MBA and British Telecom executive; Professor Andre Vandermerwe; and Nick Brealey, a publisher unafraid to push (and keep pushing) his authors to perfect the final product. I would like to thank Sue Coll for her work on the manuscript and Sally Lansdell for editing and designing the book. And to Deborah Sharp and Annie Johnstone for support, and Justin Welford and Norman Murray for diagrams and computer assistance respectively, I am also indebted.

Essential to writing a book of this nature is an institutional base – a place where rigor is appreciated as much as innovative thinking. I am blessed with such a place at Imperial Management School, and with a Director, David Norburn, who is equally concerned with academic excellence and practical relevance. He is a person who understands the nature of that particular beast who seeks to invent rather than just report. Thank you, David.

But most important is the support that comes from those wonderful family and friends around you who spur you on when times gets rough, who tolerate late dinners or no dinners at all, and anguish with you twixt the constant bouts of elation and despair.

And, despite it all, go on loving you...

Sandra Vandermerwe
London, March 1999

CHANGING THE BUSINESS MODEL

JEFF BEZOS PROBABLY HADN'T FIGURED ON SORE KNEES AND AN ACHING back when he decided to leave his high-powered job to begin an entirely new career and business. Just 30, he had until then followed the whizzkid's classic path: a *summa cum laude* Princeton University graduate in computer science and electrical engineering, the youngest ever senior vice-president in a Wall Street investment bank, and fast becoming one of the city's leading money and hedge fund managers, he was seemingly destined for the corporate fast track. And yet in 1994, everything changed.

During a casual read, Jeff Bezos came across a startling statistic to do with the Internet: usage of the new medium was growing at 2300 percent a year. His reaction was quick and decisive: *'It was my wake-up call.'* Anything that was growing that fast was going to be an opportunity for market creation and growth.

Thanks to the bonuses he had made in his brief yet successful Wall Street career, Bezos decided to quit his job. The next few months he spent studying the key factors necessary for success on the Net. He soon narrowed his list down from about 20 potential products to just two: music and books. Possibly because he loved reading, possibly because his wife was an aspiring novelist, and definitely because of the innumerable hassles encountered by customers at any traditional book retail outlet, he chose books.

He called the business – what he intended to be the world's biggest bookstore – after the world's longest river. Using some of the $11 million he had managed to raise thanks to his contacts on Wall Street and through his intensive networking among West Coast venture capitalists, he set up his headquarters in July 1995 in a 400 sq. ft. storeroom, three floors above an art gallery in a slightly seedy street in Seattle. It was furnished with a refrigerator-sized box running the computer hardware for the Amazon.com Web site. Bezos and his workers would kneel on the floor, late into the night, packing books to ship off to their growing number of customers – hence the sore knees and aching back.

From the outset, Bezos's objective was to build an online store that was customer friendly and easy to navigate. The idea behind Amazon.com was not to replicate, or even do better, on the Web what 'bricks and mortar' bookstores did: sell books. None of the traditional outlets had the goal of having every book in print in stock – a concept Bezos visualized for Amazon from the very start, a cross between a library, an information bureau and a retail store. He wanted to provide a different and enhanced experience for customers and thus get as many as possible back again and again. So the immediate priority was to identify and remove the hassles of book buying, including getting to the store; looking for a book; waiting to be served; standing in a line to pay; waiting weeks for out-of-stock books; lack of feedback and follow-up when these books did arrive; and, last but not least, paying inflated prices for physical and personnel infrastructures.

Bezos was determined to show that being online did not mean less service – it meant more. *'If you make customers unhappy in the physical world, they might each tell six friends. If you make customers unhappy on the Internet, they can each tell 6000 friends with one message to a newsgroup. If you make them really happy, they can tell 6000 people about you. You want every customer to become an evangelist for you.'*

Amazon sought to get to know individual customers better. Employees were trained to spend as much time, money and energy on service and building relationships as they did on selling and shipping books. They were encouraged to go to greater lengths to exceed expected standards when a customer needed assistance on, say, a queried title, a mistaken address and so on. When a customer wanted help, the humans took over from the machines – 20 percent of Amazon staff did nothing but answer queries from the e-mail center.

'We want Amazon.com to be the right store for you as an individual,' commented Bezos. *'If we have 4.5 million customers, we should have 4.5 million stores.'*

Because Amazon had effectively done away with activities and expenses that were not adding value to the customer experience – looking for prime sites; decorating, redesigning and promoting them; as well as a huge administrative and sales staff – it was initially able to take 30 percent off the price of selected hardbacks, and 20 percent off paperbacks. But while being able to offer books for less was an important element in the Amazon strategy, it wouldn't be enough to ensure that customers came back to the site over and over again. To achieve that, customers had to feel that they were getting superior and personalized value. The Amazon.com site went beyond being an extensive catalogue. Typically, a brief synopsis of the book would be included, as well as reviews – from leading journals, such as *The New York Times*, as well as from other readers. Visitors to the site were encouraged to write and submit reviews of books they had read.

Bezos's intention had always been to grow the market, rather than just cannibalize existing sales. When customers looked up a book on the Amazon site, they were told of two or three other titles purchased by other people who had bought the same book. Customers were signed up through a personal notification service, called 'Eyes', which meant that they could indicate what kinds of book – either in terms of subjects or authors – they liked to read. They received regular e-mails with reviews of what Amazon's editors considered 'exceptional' books in these categories. Customers could modify or add to their personal reading profiles whenever they wanted by e-mailing the customer service desk. Paying for books was done by entering credit card information, which was specially encrypted to ensure privacy and security.

Bezos also pioneered the concept of an 'Associates' program. He knew about networking effects, one of the precepts of the modern economy, and that the value of an infrastructure increased exponentially as more members joined it who produced customer value. And that meant more – for everyone, including customers. The objective was to get as many others as possible to join the Amazon network, rather than to keep it proprietary. That way, customers could find exactly what they wanted irrespective of its location on the Web, and get to that site quickly and seamlessly at the click of an icon. For example, for readers interested in cooking, Amazon provided a direct link to Starchefs, which specialized in books for gourmets. Through this collaborative concept, Web site owners also recommended books to be purchased at Amazon.com, in return for which they earned referral fees of up to 15 percent. By the beginning of 1999, the number of Associates had grown to 200,000.

In the second half of 1998, Amazon spent $250 million on purchasing two Internet companies: PlanetAll, a provider of highly personalized online services for 1.5 million subscribers that enabled customers automatically to update their address books, calendars and reminders on a minute-for-minute basis; and Junglee Corp., a maker of database systems which let customers find any kind of merchandise on the Net, and which shared its revenues with the portals that co-branded its services. The Junglee technology enabled Amazon to stretch its brands even further into e-merchandising. The PlanetAll connection gave it access to the names and addresses of people to whom Amazon customers may want to send such merchandise, for example as gifts.

Amazon also formally entered the European market with the launch of two new Web sites, one in the UK – Amazon.co.uk, following its acquisition of Bookpages – and the other in Germany – Amazon.de, after acquiring Telebook. Bezos explained his thinking: *'We want to make it possible for anybody in the world to order a German-language book, a Japanese-language book – not just an English-language book. So we need to have local customer service operations, local distribution centers, to really service those markets as if we were a local company there.'*

One of the drawbacks of an online bookstore like Amazon.com was that it cannot offer comfy sofas and cappuccinos to those who browse through its virtual aisles. So Bezos determinedly set about finding innovative ways to enhance the overall customer experience. For example, an agreement in July 1997 with Pulitzer prize-winning author John Updike entailed Updike's writing the beginning of an original story (entitled 'Murder Makes the Magazine') exclusively for Amazon. Over the next 44 days, visitors to the site could write and submit their own suggestions for continuing the story. The writers of paragraphs selected by the Amazon editorial staff to continue the story each received $1000. In all, 400,000 people participated.

Hand in hand with such 'fun' initiatives, Amazon.com continuously enhanced and upgraded its customer interface technologies and infrastructures. It launched a 'recommendation center' on its Web site, offering individuals personalized book recommendations based on their specific profiles and interests and on the ratings of other customers. Since many people didn't know precisely what they wanted to read next, an 'If you like this author' selection gave them a suggested list of other authors. Bezos and his team also began working on highly sophisticated systems that would help individuals find the precise books that *would change the world for them. If you can do that you are creating real value,'* he said.

Amazon developed and launched a technology called 1-Click, which gave customers the ability to make purchases with a single click of the mouse, eliminating the need for them to give order information every time. Bezos claimed that 1-Click represented a *'new standard for ease of buying on or off the Web'*, irrespective of product.

In another innovative application of technology, Amazon began work with a company called NuvoMedia on a handheld device allowing readers to download the books they wanted directly from the Web.

In June 1998, its presence now firmly established in the marketplace, Amazon expanded into music. More than 125,000 CDs were offered, ten times the selection of the average music store, at discounts of up to 40 percent. Music fans could search by CD title, artist, song title or label, and listen to more than 225,000 songs. There were expert and customer reviews, interviews with artists, essential lists, news and an updated index of the hottest CDs. A few weeks later, at customer request, the site was expanded to include 42,000 classical and opera CDs.

Also based on demand and feedback from customers, the company launched a 'mini store', aimed specifically at children, called Amazon.com Kids. This featured a catalogue of more than 100,000 books for children, teens and their parents. In addition, the mini site had in-depth articles, reviews, interviews, and special search and recommendation services.

Bezos was determined to build what he called a '*literary stock market*', from which both readers and writers could benefit. Authors, accustomed to getting royalty statements once a year from publishers, could check to see how their new book was doing on a daily basis from a globally assembled listing, continually updated. Students and others seeking information could use Amazon as a reference site.

Bezos follows the mantra of 'GBF' (Get Big Fast). He explains: '*This is a scale business. And what happens is that the fixed costs of doing this business are very high, and the variable costs of doing this business are extremely low. As a result, our major strategic objective has always been GBF. At the same time, we are investing significant amounts of money in advertising and marketing in order to introduce ourselves to as many customers as possible, as soon as possible ... We spend marketing dollars at a level which is disproportionate to a company of our size. And we do that because we believe this is a critical ... time where, roughly speaking, maybe a dollar spent on advertising today is worth $10 spent on advertising next year.*'

Amazon is able to boost sales simply by persuading more people to visit its online store, rather than having to follow the normal retail route of opening new outlets. As chief financial officer Joy Covey explained: '*I don't think we could have grown a physical store base four times in one year.*'

Throughout 1997 and into 1998, Amazon worked on several levels in order to achieve this 'GBF' growth objective. It also began tapping outside sources of finance. In May 1997, it went public with an initial public offering of 3 million shares at a price of $18 per share. By early August, the price had jumped to $28.75. A few months later, Amazon negotiated a $75 million, three-year credit facility from a bank consortium led by Deutsche Morgan Grenfell.

By the first quarter of 1999, Amazon had become the third largest bookseller in the US in revenue terms, and the leading online shopping site. It had also become the number one bookseller in the UK and Germany. It had 6.2 million customers in over 160 countries, with 64 percent repeat buyers. Its share price had sky-rocketed by 1300 percent in 12 months and, though it had not yet reported its first dollar of profit, investors had put its market value at $11 billion, much higher than many of the traditional 'greats' of retailing.

Notwithstanding the enormity of competitive reaction on a global scale to Amazon's revolution, a *BusinessWeek* article in December 1998 commented: *'Even though Amazon is still a long way from making a profit, its basic economics suggest the upstart will someday look more like a fat-cat software company than a scrambling-for-profits retailer. Once Amazon gets enough customers and sales to pay off its initial marketing and technology investments – and as that technology pays off in falling ... costs – additional revenue drops to the bottom line.'*

The Amazon story is yet to be fully played out. But it is what underlies it that illustrates the potential power of customer capitalism...

CHAPTER 1
THE TEN PRINCIPLES OF CUSTOMER CAPITALISM

JEFF BEZOS IS ONLY ONE OF MANY LEADERS IN A VARIETY OF industries who are confounding traditionalists by making money (and history) using a business model that is radically different from that of the past. These individuals force us to open our eyes to the fact that traditional capitalism is no longer viable: there is a new set of market and economic dynamics which we must understand and learn to work with. If we don't, we risk being left behind.

Overturning the theory

The experiences of these entrepreneurs and new corporate leaders transcend the economic mindset of traditional capitalism, which programmed managers to think and behave in a particular way and which brought about plenty of short-term rewards but led, eventually, to diminishing returns. Instead, these new leaders use the principles of customer capitalism to look for *increasing returns* – positive, disproportionate gains over time – by becoming *the* customer choice on an ongoing basis, so ensuring a compounding competitive advantage and sustainable growth.

The traditional capitalism model was good when the art of making and moving more products and services – the 'core items' – was what mattered. But it is hopeless today in a world where the balance of power has shifted from producers to customers – customers who know more, care more, demand more and participate more. And while traditional capitalism made annual profits for firms and institutions, it was just not a formula for building enduring competitive strengths.

Not that traditional capitalism didn't make corporations more efficient – it did. But it did so by the classical means of cutting the costs of producing and distributing volumes of core products or services, rather than giving customers the value they were after. Even in the 1990s, when corporations got serious about trying to radically transform themselves, they were still caught in traditional capitalism thinking. They used new sophisticated tools, but only to pull down costs so that they could show even better short-term results – exactly the wrong thing to do. This is why so many companies in the *Fortune* top 1000 improved their margins between the mid-1980s and 1990s, but fewer than 40 companies actually grew their total shareholder value by more than 25 percent.

STEALING
TO GROW

Part of the problem was that with the traditional model, growth meant doing more of the same thing. This inevitably meant stealing customers from others who were also doing more of the same thing, which created an irresistible argument for stealing still more. Alternatively, it meant buying growth through mergers and acquisitions, often in businesses unrelated to a corporation's own. Neither course of action did anything to bring about the multiple benefits that can be gained from a company's long-term associations with customers.

In transactional fashion, the core items – whether insurance policies or personal computers, airline tickets or automobiles – were bought and sold along linear chains. This involved a continual counterbalancing of demand and supply, which invariably reduced strategies to price. Even differentiation strategies, which sought to distinguish corporations, became so easy to copy and so product driven that ironically customers had no incentive to stick with any particular firm or institution.

The result? Huge replacement costs were incurred as customers exited for newer and fresher pastures, which meant that other customers had to be acquired if firms were to reach market-share targets. Energy and resources flowed into this acquisition, instead of into the genuine customer origination that was needed to build and grow markets. This practice further dissipated prospects for growth, corporations had to continue to cut costs in order to show annual improvements, the future was sacrificed even more, and returns worsened.

Classic diminishing returns – for everyone.

Thus many of the companies we thought were doing well and praised in the 1970s, 1980s and early 1990s simply disappeared or experienced a deterioration of their value in real terms. And several that currently have the highest sales and assets (previously thought to be *the* measure of success) do not have the highest market capitalization, and are not the ones that are growing or that investors are supporting and pushing into the limelight.

Of course, the financials of these traditional companies often looked good at the time – by conventional standards, that is. This is why many corporations who were considered successful or 'most admired' by European financial magazines and appeared at the top of the *Fortune* 500 now don't appear at all. As it turns out, only 30 percent of those that were on these listings in the 1970s still feature. The rest are new entrants who leapt on to the scene, lapping up the big new opportunities.

The promise of customer capitalism

Customer capitalism does what the old capitalism could never do – it gives the corporation a sustainable edge. Instead of the diminishing returns inherited from old minds and logic, customer capitalism means that the new enterprise can gain from the compounding characteristics of our new economy. Over time a corporation's advantage continues to accumulate, amplify and multiply.

CUSTOMER 'LOCK-ON' There is a singular reason for this. With customer capitalism, customers 'lock on' to a corporation. The customers become an 'installed customer base', a group of people who want the firm or institution *as their dominant or sole choice on an ongoing basis*. Not only do they do business with the corporation in ways different from the past, but they do so over time, even over a lifetime. This differs from the days where a customer would flit from supplier to supplier seeking the best deal, which typically meant the lowest price (though not the best long-term result) given that most corporations worked in the same conventional way.

So with customer capitalism it is not the product that keeps competitors out, nor is it the technical standard or the technology that protects an organization from rivals, but rather customers who lock on to a company or institution and become the barrier to competitive entry.

PRODUCT 'LOCK-IN' IS NOT ENOUGH Customer 'lock-on' is very different from the product 'lock-in' that traditional management dreamt about, or legislators feared, where customers had no choice because there was only one supplier or because they were captive yet disenchanted by the way an industry operated, or the switching costs of moving to something preferable were too high. It also differs from the product 'lock-in' that the new economists, most notably Brian Arthur, analyst of increasing returns at Stanford and Santa Fe Institute, talk about. This is based mostly on products and their technical standards which once established – whether by strategy or by chance – give the customer little or no option, and give the corporation quasi-monopoly powers for as long as that particular technology wave lasts.

Of course, in all these cases, corporations did get ahead and continue to do so. They may even benefit from increasing returns for a while. However, what such corporations lack is what it takes to get customers to lock on, i.e. to motivate customers to want to do business with the corporation on an ongoing basis because they have good and sufficient reason to do so. Without this these corporations are unable to sustain their position on a longlasting basis, because this achievement can only be accomplished by customer capitalism.

The 10 principles of customer capitalism

The discipline of moving from traditional capitalism to customer capitalism begins with an understanding of a set of principles along key strategic dimensions. These direct resources, energy and priorities and form the backbone for the competitive strategies of the new enterprise. As the chapters unfold, these principles, together with many examples and case studies, will be dealt with in detail. They are summarized in Table 1.

THE
STRATEGIC
BACKBONE

1. The aim of the enterprise is to fundamentally transform itself

Traditional capitalism gave corporations little incentive to do anything other than what they did best, basically make and move their core 'products or services' (remember 'stick to the knitting'?). The object was to retain equilibrium and the *status quo* rather than to invite in disruption.

But without disruption there can be no new markets. And without new markets there can be no real growth. Sadly, therefore, conventional players could only continue their sterile battles with others who were doing what they were doing (or rather not doing), while new entrants took the exciting opportunities and new wealth by storm, as the examples in this book will illustrate.

With customer capitalism, the new enterprise moves *outside* of itself in search of the future. Driven by the challenges of an immaterial world, information and knowledge rich and globally connected by high-tech, it proactively opens up

	TRADITIONAL CAPITALISM PRINCIPLES	CUSTOMER CAPITALISM PRINCIPLES
1 **AIM**	Maintaining the status quo	Fundamentally transforming
2 **LEADERS**	Replicating and improving products and/or services	Finding new ways of doing things for and with customers
3 **INNOVATION**	Inventing new technologies	Originating for and with customers
4 **OBJECT**	Optimizing margins on unit transactions	Maximizing the time value of customers
5 **MEANS**	Increasing market share in product/service categories	Dominating activities in market spaces
6 **VALUE**	Making and moving more core items	Linking benefits in an ongoing integrated experience
7 **TARGET**	For markets and average customer	For individual customers in an ever-increasing, ever-lucrative installed base
8 **UNIT OF COMPETITION**	By units/companies/ countries/industries	With win–win for all contributing players in new enterprise spaces
9 **RESOURCES**	Relying on the scarce tangibles	Relying on the abundant intangibles
10 **SCORE**	To make set ROI, ROA ROC targets	Creating market and accumulating a sustainable advantage

Table 1 Principles of traditional and customer capitalism

new ground, changing not just the playing field but also the key players and the game itself. It seeks to create whole new markets rather than just take share from those that already exist, a strategy fundamental to exploiting the new dynamics of increasing returns.

2. Leaders find 'new ways of doing things'

With a revolutionary mindset and equipped with the tools and tempo of customer capitalism, leaders are on the lookout for the next big breakthrough so that they can keep offering customers exactly what they want, bringing them back again and again – even if it means building obsolescence into their current way of doing business. They recognize that customers can't necessarily express what they want because they haven't experienced it yet, and realize that the ability to anticipate rather than react is vitally important.

BUILDING IN
OBSOLESCENCE

Unlike their predecessors, managers using customer capitalism positively refuse to emulate what exists – in fact, they actively try to make it irrelevant. Restless and relentless, they deliberately destabilize in order to expose new opportunities. They look beyond improving existing ideas, products and services, and instead look for 'new ways of doing things'.

The distinction between the 'core items' of traditional capitalism and customer capitalism's 'new ways of doing things' is that the former can never get results to customers, whereas customer capitalism can. This is why the revolutions we see today are not just about core items with an edge – i.e. the loan, the books, the cars, the medical supplies, the groceries, the insurance policy, the credit card. They are about Amazon's *new ways for customers to discover information and knowledge,* or Mercedes' *new ways for customers to move around,* or Baxter's *new ways for customers to preserve and prolong their health and wellbeing,* or Peapod's *new ways for customers to manage their daily home supplies and chores*. The principles of customer capitalism can also be seen in Direct Line's *new ways for customers to cover and handle their auto risks* and Mondex's *new ways for customers to pay globally for their small-ticket purchases*.

The new enterprise seeks to become the standard for these new ways of doing things with both existing and new customers by gathering market momentum. This is achieved by getting a critical mass of customers whom others follow. As more individuals see and use and get value from a new way of doing things, it becomes more prevalent, making it and the brand infectious to others. As one publisher put it, *'When people think of ordering a book online now, they think of Amazon.'*

3. Innovation means originating for and with customers rather than just inventing new technology

It wasn't that Baxter Renal invented a new technology (though it spends a fortune on R&D) that made it the standard for renal patients today. It's that it originated for customers, creating a totally integrated care system to prolong the quality and length of their lives. Nor did Tim Jones and Graham Higgins, the originators of Mondex, invent a new technology. They combined different pieces that already existed. And Amazon didn't invent anything – in fact Jeff Bezos knew very little about technology or books. The wholesalers which supplied him could have done exactly what he did – but they didn't.

So with customer capitalism the leaders are not necessarily those who invent or own a new technology. In fact, a negative correlation has been found between the number of patents that corporations held in the past and the number of new market opportunities that they opened up. Leaders 'see' the market opportunity and make it happen. They ask: How do things interact? What's happening that could influence what? Where can that lead? They see the dynamics of behavior and how people influence people, and events influence markets, and technology influences all of these to open up new opportunities. They are able to detect future changes before they happen, and understand them when they do, making sense of them in a way that others cannot see at first.

4. The primary object of the enterprise is to maximize the time value of customers

With customer capitalism, every customer is an investment and, like any other investment, every customer has a time value. This way of looking at the situation is quite contrary to the past way of making money on the margins of the discrete core items. This forced managers to push volumes to get costs down, only to ride the diminishing returns treadmill.

CUSTOMERS AS INVESTMENTS

This book argues that a fixation on margin actually damaged a firm's (or an industry's) ability to compete durably. The reason is that it worked in exactly the opposite direction to motivating companies to invest time, energy and money in building the relational, infrastructural and intellectual assets needed to achieve longlasting and exponential customer rewards. Apart from this, the whole notion and significance of margins become obsolete once offerings become more knowledge, information and idea dependent, which they now irrefutably are.

Success through the time value of customers is what amasses the potential for high-quality cash streams – the key strategy emanating from the principles of customer capitalism. Maximizing these value streams means:

➡ attracting new customers – making the installed base ever larger
➡ keeping customers longer – extracting their time value
➡ enhancing value per customer – making the installed base ever lucrative.

This can only happen if both the company and the customer are better off in the long term through the achievement of two reciprocal, inseparable and simultaneous goals:

the lifelong value of the corporation to the customer
and
the lifelong value of the customer to the corporation.

To get increasing returns, the new enterprise must accomplish both of the above, and the following chapters will show how. One without the other and it is back to traditional capitalism and diminishing returns, competing with the old formula based on product specification, price cutting and increased push and pull through distribution and promotion – all too easy to emulate and, however good, not good enough.

And traditional capitalism would have us tracking progress with static indicators such as market share, customer satisfaction, retention and brand loyalty, all of which tell us more about past, discrete purchases than about potential for exploiting future opportunities.

5. Dominating activities in 'market spaces' achieves the time value of customers

Belief in market share was (and still is) seriously dangerous, because it hides rather than exposes the real opportunities for new breakthroughs, and the competition. It may have helped present a view of competitiveness within static product/ service areas in the past, but it never produced perspectives for getting customer results. And it is results that customers want, not the core items.

Customer capitalism shifts the classic product/service categories away from market share into new dynamic 'market spaces', which is where the cornucopia for adding customer value lies. A market space is an articulation of the results that customers want, a framework for doing business that is dynamic instead of discrete like the product or service categories that traditional capitalism used. Compare, for example, cars vs *personal mobility*, loans vs *lifelong event cash managing*, personal computers vs *global networking capability*, dialysis bags vs *renal sufficiency management*. The market spaces become the new broader playing fields or 'activity arenas' in which the new enterprise competes through customer capitalism and where opportunities multiply rather than just add up.

Don't misunderstand: corporations can, and have always been able to, make money from discrete products or services, but however innovative, they are still only products or services – the core items – discrete and vulnerable to better or cheaper ones when these come along. The new customer capitalism model is more ambitious since it pushes corporations to articulate market spaces (existing, emerging *and* imagined) and then to dominate activities within them to produce customer results that are superior in both content and contact terms. This is what brings customers back again and again, giving the new enterprise a deeper, broader, longer and more diverse share of their spend.

6. The source of value is the linking of benefits in an integrated customer experience

The new enterprise needs to become indispensable in getting superior results to customers in these market spaces. This can only be accomplished by those who deliver a totally integrated experience to customers, and it must happen throughout the customer activity cycle, a methodological tool presented in this book.

BECOMING INDISPENSABLE

A totally integrated experience was a feat that old capitalism could seldom, if ever, achieve. It pushed more and more discrete products or services through the system and could never produce the required linked benefits, no matter how good the products or services were on their own. Consequently, there were interruptions at critical points in the customer activity cycle and huge value gaps were created. The result was that access points were opened up to innovative newcomers who established vital links with customers, building reputation and trust and finding ways to do more business with them in a different way.

Compare the old IBM with the new and you have a classic case. Having confined its thinking and strategy to core items like personal computers and mainframes, it missed the broader market space, *global networking capability*. So in the 1980s its biggest competitors became service companies like consulting (Andersen Consulting) or software (Microsoft or EDS) or others outside of its industry or new entrants like Cisco which filled the value gaps and got into powerful positions, enabling them to accumulate advantage and customer capital. Today IBM and its partners offer all activities at every point in the customer activity cycle, in order to link benefits for them rather than just provide the core items that customers can get from any other supplier. And that's why it is now getting customers to lock on.

CONVERGING ON CONVERGENCES

Another reason that outsiders got into critical points in the customer activity cycle was that the old business model programmed managers to extend their strategies within trends inside their industry. In fact, many of the new market spaces, from which results for customers come and where new markets and opportunities are thus to be found, came from the convergences *between* industries, as the chapters and examples in this book will demonstrate.

The medical arena, or the *total wellbeing and life extension* market space, is a classic example. None of the new opportunities stems only from existing industries: they come from the convergence of several, like pharmaceuticals, biogenetics, food, information technology, healthcare, fitness, cosmetics and nutrition; and from the growing numbers of new customers willing to pay not to become ill.

7. Individuals form an installed customer base that becomes ever increasing, ever lucrative

Given the criticality of the time value of customers, the target for strategies based on customer capitalism is no longer the mass market 'out there', nor one particular chunk or segment of the market. The simple reason for this is that no customer fits one single market or segment any more, nor can one product or brand satisfy the diversity, let alone the longevity, of an individual customer's life.

It is individuals, each with their own set of preferences, that customer capitalism targets. It is they who form the installed customer base, i.e. **those people who want the firm or institution as their dominant or sole choice on an ongoing basis**. Customer capitalism sets out to to grow this installed customer base, rather than just cater to customers as transactional purchasers who come and go. Once a company does this, it gets a broader, longer, more diverse and deeper share of customer spend.

THE INSTALLED CUSTOMER BASE

However, the installed customer base can only become larger and more lucrative if the enterprise is continuously innovating. Offerings are personalized to suit the evolving, unique and multiple needs of individuals, as opposed to only providing what the firm makes or has in stock at that moment in time. This strengthens the bonding that enables the corporation to be proactive, and the offerings to be more precise – this is what gets customers to lock on. It also makes it very difficult for others to gain access to these customers, no matter how compelling their offerings may be.

8. The 'enterprise space' becomes the new unit of competition with win–win the goal for all contributing players

Separations and silos were the hallmark of the traditional capitalism model so that divisions, units, companies and countries could be kept accountable and accounted, but this method had no benefits for customers for whom value is in the results. Results, like being constantly mobile or extended survival and wellbeing, come unequivocally from the linking of benefits to form an integrated customer experience produced by the interconnections between divisions, units, firms and their offerings.

Results can only happen across company, country and industry boundaries, or in new 'enterprise spaces', to use the language of customer capitalism. Old industry product-bounded distinctions may have accounting or technical significance for corporations, and legislative significance for governments (for example deciding on what is or isn't a monopoly), but they are discrete product representations and quite irrelevant for lifelong customer relationships and sustained corporate competitiveness.

With customer capitalism no one can win alone. The interactions of other players in the enterprise space delivering their part of the customer experience are not only significant but crucial to success, as the cases in this book will demonstrate. The enterprise that seeks exponential rewards actively looks for participating players – what Andy Grove of Intel calls fellow travelers – with whom to connect. Working together and sharing resources and responsibility for an integrated customer experience and the resulting exponential rewards, the various players become an enterprise space, the new unit of competition for the modern economy.

9. The integrated customer experience is essentially achieved through intangible resources which are abundant by nature

Today it is overwhelmingly the intangibles that are driving growth and prosperity, in complete contrast to traditional capitalism where it was the scarce resources that produced the wealth. This fact was powerfully placed in an economic context in the mid-1980s by Paul Romer, professor of economics at Stanford. In his New Growth theory he argued –

and for the first time gave evidence to support the fact – that it is the ideas, not the items, which generate growth and increase returns on investment.

For managers, the significant point is that these intangible factors – ideas, knowledge and information – are *the* high-value ingredient in today's offerings. They differ dramatically from the scarce productive resources of the old era, in that they *grow* the more they are used and shared, instead of being depleted. Not only do they grow but, if kept alive, these intangibles will never become obsolete. As they augment in value they become the platform for building standards for the new ways of doing things on which other standards can be built. This is what makes whole new markets, with infinite possibilities for both customer and corporate value, an ongoing and exponential phenomenon today. Grow
as you
use

So the prospects for economic growth, market creation and positive disproportionate gain are far greater with customer capitalism than with traditional capitalism, if a firm knows how to harness and mobilize these intangible resources to produce the ongoing results that customers are after. Moreover, as the enterprise learns to use new networked technologies over a wider variety of customers and circumstances, not only does the quality of the offering go up, but costs go down. In addition, all of this can be achieved without any of the formidable tradeoffs of traditional capitalism, as the following chapters will illustrate.

The economics change with customer capitalism. As abundant intangibles dominate, and as the use of technology proliferates, the notion of marginal cost features much less, if at all, in the financial algorithm. The economics reconstruct from being mainly dependent on volume to get economies of scale *up* to push marginal costs *down* to generate profits per unit. **Instead, the intention is to generate ongoing and growing high-quality cash streams from ever-deepening and expanding relationships with** New
economies:
skill, stretch,
sweep, spread

individuals in the installed base who lock on to an organization. The corporation can thus achieve leverage by increasing revenue through the longevity, depth, width and diversity of customer spend and through decreased costs thanks to the new economies of customer capitalism – namely skill, stretch, sweep and spread – to generate positive disproportionate gains and increasing returns.

10. Scores are based on whether an enterprise has accumulated a sustained advantage with customers and potential for growth

INVESTING
FOR THE
LONG TERM

Look at how today's corporate leaders and investors rate performance and you will see that the spirit of customer capitalism is making its mark. Horizons are getting much longer and gone are concerns with history. The traditional capitalism approach has been replaced by the recognition that in times of fast change, data about the past is no indicator of future potential.

This book looks at how to score for customer capitalism. Previously, scores on performance were designed as lag indicators and were reflective in nature. Past indicators measured and tracked for an era of managers who understood and were reliant on scarce, tangible resources. Customer capitalism needs scores based on the true customer value producers – the intangible aspects of a company. It also needs more than share price performance – which many firms artificially maneuvered around, compromising their long-term potential – or short-term profits.

With customer capitalism, the enterprise endeavors to compete durably for customers not just today but also well into the future, and assesses itself accordingly. Investors are now hungry for information that will give them this perspective on a company. Increasingly, they see the correlation between a corporation's true worth and ability to grow in and with the future, and the relational, intellectual and infrastructural assets it possesses to both *give and get* long-term customer value.

Moreover, they are increasingly prepared to support those enterprises that go beyond the obvious, demolishing old beliefs and outdated ways of dealing with customers to achieve this quest, in preference to those companies that possess tangible assets or just produce short-term profits.

The six loops of customer capitalism

Once the 10 principles of customer capitalism drive strategy, six positive reinforcing loops go into action. What is important about these loops is that they operate according to the law of increasing rather than diminishing returns and therefore they bring about the exponential opportunities that the new enterprise seeks.

GETTING CUSTOMER LOCK-ON

Loop 1: relationships loop
The more relationships with customers strengthen, due to the superior value customers receive because the corporation knows and suits their unique needs, the greater the depth, breadth, length and diversity of their spend, which reinforces the relationship, and their spend...

RELATIONSHIPS

CUSTOMER

Loop 2: intangibles loop
The more dominant intangibles – ideas, information and knowledge – become in offerings, and are used, reused and shared, the more they grow and appreciate in value, enhancing the offerings, increasing their use and reuse, and their value still further...

INTANGIBLES

CUSTOMER

Loop 3: networks loop
The more people and machines are connected by a particular technology to form the infrastructure that produces a superior customer offering, the more these networks gain in exponential value, making them more attractive to still

NETWORKS

CUSTOMER

more customers, pushing up their value and the value of individual nodes within them.

Loop 4: players loop

The more players that supply, support and service the offering, the more customers get the linked benefits that produce an ongoing, standard-setting, integrated experience, which attracts more customers and spend and draws in still more participating players...

Loop 5: developers loop

The more prevalent a new way of doing things becomes, the more developers respond by innovating with extensions, upgrades, new applications and new inventions to ensure that customers keep getting an enhanced and integrated experience, and so spend more, causing more innovation, which attracts a bigger market, multiplying and accelerating the rate of innovation and applications still more...

Loop 6: costs loop

The more relationships between the corporation and the customer strengthen, and resources between the various players, networks and developers are shared, the more intangible resources – ideas, knowledge and information – flowing between company and customer and company and company are used and reused, the more the cost of doing business goes down. And the more abundant resources dominate offerings, the more the cost of those offerings inverts...

Success breeds success

As we can see, each of the six positive reinforcing loops contributes to getting increasing returns. Each has potential, but on their own none can increase the fame and fortune of an organization in the long term. It is only when all six loops are managed together as one interlinking, reiterative system that corporations can get customer lock-on. Then the real forces of the new market and economic dynamics of customer capitalism come into play, with all of the explosive potential to produce the multiple and exponential rewards of increasing returns.

Figure 1 The six positive reinforcing loops of customer capitalism

The ability to work with this looping mechanism in one, all-encompassing strategy is what sets the new enterprise ahead and, once ahead, further ahead still. This giant feedback effect, an interactive process as found in any complex system such as biology, nature or quantum physics, becomes self-sustaining, characterized by compounding rather than linear outcomes.

ONE ALL-ENCOMPASSING STRATEGY

In other words, success breeds success. Unlike traditional capitalism where benefits increased linearly and only up to a point, customer capitalism ensures that rewards can multiply. The difference is, as Kevin Kelly of *Wired* so cleverly puts it, between '*a piggy bank and compound interest*'.

Infinite possibility is the promise for those new enterprises that understand the principles of customer capitalism and make the six reinforcing loops central to their strategy. Advantage accumulates as customers lock on, and this is what makes it so potentially difficult for competitors to copy and therefore dislodge them – unlike conventional strategy based on traditional capitalism.

The good news – and the bad

But, as Brian Arthur points out, while the positive loops of increasing returns reinforce success, they also aggravate loss. This is bad news for those not working with the principles of customer capitalism, or those who start off well but fail to continue to deliver ongoing value to customers. Mistakes drag them into a descending spiral from which it can be extremely difficult to recover, if indeed it is possible at all.

CLASSIC CASES   Steve Jobs, who popularized the personal computer and the use of icons, failed to extract the ensuing value from the market. Apple may yet recover, but years have been lost because Jobs, despite his genius, misread the needs of his customers. With the typical logic of traditional capitalism he kept his technology proprietary, hoping to dominate market share and build his empire, which was mainly positioned for the education and desktop publishing markets.

But what Jobs did not see was that if Apple's products and technology were not connected with others so that customers could get one high-quality, integrated experience at home, work, school and play, these customers would not be able to function effectively and he would lose them. This is exactly what happened. Apple went into a negative spiral, making the company only a marginal player in the massive personal computer market that ironically Jobs helped invent.

To use the jargon of increasing returns, a negative loop entered the system: as fewer and fewer customers wanted the machines because they couldn't be used with anything else, fewer and fewer retail players stocked them, and as fewer and fewer developers invested in them, fewer and fewer consumers wanted them, and so on and so forth. THE DOWNSLIDE

Of course, as we know, the reverse happened to Gates, accounting in no small way for Microsoft's success in the past. In contrast, Gates licensed his operating system, making it so well known that as more and more systems used it, more and more people and computer manufacturers wanted it, meaning more and more were available and bought by customers, so more and more players were drawn in, more developers were committed to innovating for it, and more customers were attracted. This meant that benefits went up and costs went down, and momentum kept building in an upward spiral. And with his capabilities in networking, Gates is intent on becoming a multifaceted gateway for new ways of doing things in the future, rather than just relying on software (i.e. product lock-in) – locking on customers, households and businesses – in a wide variety of new market spaces.

This book answers these questions

The new enterprise understands the principles of customer capitalism and how to use the new market and economic dynamics of loops to get exponential growth and enduring competitiveness. The new enterprise also knows how to change from what it has done well in the past. It looks for answers to the following questions, answers which this book sets out to help it find:

➡ How do we relate the principles of customer capitalism
to our business?

➡ How do we activate the six positive reinforcing loops of
customer capitalism to get customer lock-on?

➡ How do we fit all of this together into one new, all-
encompassing strategy, to get increasing returns?

If it answers these questions, the new enterprise can get
ahead in a way that makes it difficult for others to catch up.

Any and all organizations can get the exponential effects
of increasing returns. They don't have to be big, they don't
have to invent anything – but they do have to escape the
traps of old conventions and originate for customers rather
than just invent technology; create value in the 'customer
space' (so to speak) rather than the 'corporate space'; use
time, money and energy to build markets and new market
spaces rather than take share from others in the same
product/service categories. Most significantly, they have to
combine technology with imagination, and cultivate an ability to anticipate rather than react.

No short-term thinking will do. Traditional capitalism
programmed the corporate mindset to take the short view,
making money early on and quickly before competition
invariably and predictably set in. The new enterprise must
take the long view to build customer capital at an exponential rate, and make the moves to accumulate an advantage
today for tomorrow's business – the ultimate outcome of a
sound approach to customer capitalism.

PART ONE

NEW WAYS OF DOING THINGS

CHAPTER 2
PUNCTUATING THE EQUILIBRIUM

EARLY IN 1995, WHILE MANY RETAILERS WERE STILL LOOKING AT how to improve existing stores within the existing industry and legislative structures – attempting to do better than others doing exactly the same thing – Jeff Bezos had quite a different idea, as we saw in the Prologue. He believed that he could do something that traditional retailers couldn't.

Could he?

It seems so. Amazon, though it may not yet have shown a profit in some of the conventional accounting ways, has all of the potential precursors for increasing returns. Losses as a percentage of sales have steadily gone down, and some analysts say that had it not been for Amazon's huge investment in marketing and acquisitions to build critical mass and enhance and expand its customer offering, it could have shown a profit long ago.

Amazon's retail site is the most heavily trafficked on the Web, with half a million daily visitors and over six million customers, growing by 50 percent every quarter, many of whom (to the tune of 65 percent) are regular repeat buyers, a figure also increasing rapidly. Its rate of customer acquisition has also been growing: whereas it took the company 27 months to acquire its first million customers, it has taken it increasingly less time to acquire the next four million. It has been generating sales at an average annualized rate of $1 billion and is growing at over 30 percent every three months. Most interestingly, Amazon's share price has soared exponentially, as has its market capitalization, as it continues to attract customer and investor funds. And it is stretching its brand further afield into CDs, videos, computer games, gifts and healthcare.

Bezos followed the natural progression of customer needs in the global electronic information environment, which is growing faster and vaster as we speak. Why, he asked himself, should customers have to wait weeks for books, have hassles getting them and pay inflated prices for infrastructures that were doing them no favors? How could he benefit from customer capitalism, rather than trying to compete with a business model long outdated? Could he get customers to 'lock on' and make him their dominant or sole choice on an ongoing basis? And, working with the new market and economic looping dynamics of customer capitalism, how could he leverage from positive disproportionate gains? In other words:

- ➡ How could he get the books and services the customers wanted to them in a superior way, thereby building **relationships**, getting customers' trust and gaining a deeper, broader, longer and more diverse spend?
- ➡ How could he build an infrastructure through his **networks** that was substantial enough to enhance the customer experience, thereby increasing the number of customers and the value of the networks, producing more customers and more spend?
- ➡ How could he share **intangibles** – ideas, knowledge and information – to deliver a superior offering, so attracting more customers and spend, increasing the value of his intangibles still more and decreasing their cost?
- ➡ How could he get more **players** (retailers, publishers, other websites, couriers etc.) to link customer benefits, thereby increasing the value of his offerings, attracting more customers, more players and value all round?
- ➡ How could he get **developers** to invest, so enhancing applications, to attract more customers and spend, and therefore more and more innovation?

➡ How, through all of the above, could he bring the **costs** of doing business with customers down?

'Seeing' the new markets

Bezos *punctuated the equilibrium*. This is a term borrowed from evolutionary biology to describe a break with patterns or norms, in which things change so radically that what worked in the past is just no longer relevant. What exists at the time of this change either makes the necessary adjustment or disappears, since the characteristics needed to be a winner on one side of the punctuated equilibrium are very different from those on the other. Unless the species is able to adapt, it is wiped out.

History is full of examples, the classic one being dinosaurs: having been the prime species for 130 million years they suddenly became extinct, whereas mammals adapted and prospered. Economic history also has points of punctuated equilibrium, the Industrial Revolution being the obvious one. After thousands of years of agricultural dominance, the steam engine created a new economic pattern. Similarly, the automobile transformed living and working patterns and ideals (though ironically, automobiles are now fighting to retain dominance in a new reality, to be discussed later). Today we are in the midst of a new massive punctuated equilibrium driven by the likes of interactive technology that we haven't even begun to comprehend fully.

WHAT IBM
COULDN'T SEE

Why did IBM lose its lead in the computer industry in the 1980s and then go on to make the biggest loss in US corporate history? Because no one in the company really 'saw' a new market, concentrating as they were on beating others who also didn't see it. As far back as 1940, IBM had the technology and the resources, it even had the customers ('no one ever got fired for ordering an IBM'), but the then chairman had declared that the world would only be able to absorb five computers at the most. He couldn't visualize the future and therefore he couldn't make it happen.

Even in the early 1980s, IBM executives still underplayed the significance of the new market: 'good for 75,000 PC units' is what top management said, although by 1984 IBM itself was using that amount internally! Compare that to the plaque put up on the entrance to Microsoft's headquarters that reads 'a computer on every desk' (running Microsoft software); this may soon have to be changed to read 'an MSN network on every desk'.

Back to our cyberspace book entrepreneur. He 'saw' the market. He got access to millions of books (a store would need 40 miles of space in order to equal Amazon's stock) and he had low overheads that translated into discounts of up to 45 percent on bestsellers.

But Bezos went further. He used the positive reinforcing feedback loops of customer capitalism to sustain competitiveness and didn't just cut prices because its overheads were lower. The more customers bought, the more access to books they got, the larger the networks grew, the more its value increased, the more it was able to access and share ideas, information and knowledge, the more customers were attracted. So more suppliers, players, developers and customers came on board, drawing in more customers and spend with decreasing costs of doing business, so the more competitive it became and so on.

From nowhere, book retailing became a global industry.

CHAPTER 3
THE POWER TO REVOLUTIONIZE

THE BURNING QUESTION THAT ONE CAN'T HELP ASKING ONESELF is why didn't this innovation come from traditional bookstores? Why did established retailers wait for customer momentum to build for Amazon, heading them towards the threshold of compounding increasing returns, before they made their moves?

THE BATTLE
OF THE
BOOKS

Barnes & Noble, the largest US book retailer with over 1000 outlets spread across the nation, set up its Web site two years after Bezos had established his. In the spring of 1999, German-based Bertelsmann, the global media and publishing conglomerate with one of the largest direct bookclub operations in the world, launched a European Web site called BOL in Germany and the UK, followed by the Netherlands, France and Spain. To get into the US, it had bought 50 percent of the Barnes & Noble Web site for $200 million.

The battle is still being fought, but the point is that traditionalists stuck to conventional wisdom, copied what newcomers did and tried to crush them with size, buying up outlets fighting a traditional distribution war. But the war wasn't traditional and by the time they reacted, Amazon had enough leeway and customers to withstand the initial onslaught.

Typically, discounting had caused massive price wars, but these had no added value for customers. While traditionalists kept selling books cheaper or putting in marginal improvements to try to entice people into their stores, what customers needed, and what would set up positive reinforcing loops of customer capitalism, was a whole different experience. Customers wanted the hassles taken out of buying. They wanted to be able to get what they wanted, when they wanted it, preferably from one source, rather than having to buy what stores had in stock at that moment in time, wait or do without.

What is also interesting is that not only did none of these traditional megastores lead the electronic bookselling revolution, they didn't fully exploit the counter-revolution either. This counter-revolution began in the US; Borders, another newcomer, rose to take the prime spot. The new trend goes by the name 'cultural superstore', and has quickly spread from the US into Europe and Asia. Bookshops have become social centers, complete with cafés, comfortable seating areas, music sections, desks and *crèches*. In addition to a broad range of books, magazines and periodicals, they sell videos, music and computer games. They have musicians playing and writers reading from their works in these new literary salons. Bob DiRomualdo, CEO of Borders, explains:

THE COUNTER-REVOLUTION

> *There was a classic mismatch between supply and demand: the population was becoming better educated, but the book assortment available to them was thinning out ... as specialized stores fell by the wayside and the larger operators standardized their selection (and the way they operated).*

Notwithstanding its move on to the Internet, Borders has not only grown multifold since its inception, but has rapidly spread globally in a business long considered to be highly localized. It expects to have 450 stores by the year 2003, designed to appeal to the reading and music tastes of the over-30s. It installs listening posts and stocks more vintage jazz, rock, New Age and classical music than its teen-oriented competitors. *'We'll never be the coolest place to buy music,'* remarked DiRomualdo. *'That's why it works.'*

This brings us to the first principle of customer capitalism (see Table 2). To unleash the positive looping mechanism and power of increasing returns, **the new enterprise aims at fundamentally transforming instead of maintaining the status quo**, the mainstay of the traditional capitalism model.

	TRADITIONAL CAPITALISM PRINCIPLES	CUSTOMER CAPITALISM PRINCIPLES
1 AIM	Maintaining the status quo	Fundamentally transforming

Table 2 Principles of traditional and customer capitalism

DRIVING THE REVOLUTIONS

It was Peter Ellis of Auto-by-Tel, offering an online connection between vehicle buyers and sellers, who revolutionized auto selling. How was it possible that traditional dealers and manufacturers in the US and Europe were forced to copy an unknown operator in order to hold on to their customers?

New retail home-shopping is another example. Why is it that the traditional supermarkets kept on replicating their current retail practices with some incremental add-ons, trying to win people over with price and promotional loyalty schemes, rather than riding an electronic wave that should have been a natural extension for them, one ridden successfully by outsiders like Peapod and Streamline (both from the US but now in world markets) or being pilot tested by manufacturers like Nestlé, the Swiss global giant, in Switzerland, or Unilever, the Anglo-Dutch megacorporation, in Malaysia.

How come Encyclopaedia Britannica, one of the best-known brands in the world which had completely dominated its industry, allowed such complacency to set in that CD-Roms came from nowhere and devastated its business?

Reportedly, it never took Microsoft's Encarta seriously, considering it an inferior toy, but customers loved it. It proved more or less perfect for parents who could get it cheaply and easily and persuade their PC-prone children to use it. In addition, there was the added benefit of its being multimedia learning: kids could have more fun from the personalized system, which is what they wanted. Clicking on 'Mozart', say, allowed youngsters to read the composer's biography, see the inside of the house where he grew up in Salzburg and also listen to some musical excerpts of their choice.

This all goes to show that technology in itself has no power to revolutionize – only people and organizations do. Robert Solow had won the Nobel prize in 1987 by showing that technological innovation was at the heart of economic growth, but it was only when Paul Romer came on the scene that the point hit home: technology wasn't 'somewhere out there' – someone actually had to take the technology and turn it into a new market, as the examples show, if the kind of growth that the new economists were talking about was actually to manifest itself.

TECHNOLOGY CAN'T CREATE REVOLUTIONS

The *Asian Wall Street Journal* tells a wonderful story:

It's 1995, and an aide to the top dog of a large Regional Bell Operating Company (RBOC) in America's Midwest has arranged a meeting between his boss and a Silicon Valley rising star, John Chambers, CEO of Cisco Systems. Here's how the aide describes the meeting: Mr. Chambers talks excitedly about the future of data communications and the Internet, growing ten-fold every year. The RBOC head listens uncomfortably. The more enthusiastic Mr. Chambers gets, the more dour and agitated grows the telco man. Finally, Mr. Chambers leaves, and the RBOC chief turns a grim eye to his aide: 'Why in God's name did you bring him here?'

The rest is history. Cisco, barely 10 years old, is now a quintessential high-tech innovator, world leader in Internet networking solutions, and cited by *Fortune* in March 1999 as the third most admired company for long-term investment value, 14th overall, and appearing more often than any other top-ranked company over all admired categories. In contrast, most telecoms only have growth rates of between 7 and 13 percent in the new multimedia data traffic over the Net, the fastest-growing telephony medium.

CHAPTER 4
BECOMING *THE* STANDARD FOR NEW WAYS OF DOING THINGS

IN THE LATE 1980S, DESPITE HAVING FAILED TO TAKE A LEADING role in either credit or debit card products, NatWest, the largest bank in the UK, made a decision to look at smart technology to create an alternative form of payment. Its top management decided that rather than wait for someone outside of the industry to do it first, they would assign two corporate entrepreneurs, Tim Jones (now CEO of the UK bank) and Graham Higgins, to the task. What evolved was Mondex, the global multicurrency electronic purse.

A new market for this new way of payment would come, they surmised, from the sudden rise in electronic shopping and the Internet ('*It's still relatively easy to shop on the Internet, but difficult to pay,*' as one executive put it). It would also come from creating a new way for people to buy and sell in low quantities. The key to Mondex was that it enabled person-to-person cash transfer – it allowed money to flow between individuals. This would eliminate the frustrations experienced by customers who never seem to have the correct change for taxis, news-stands or flower stalls.

THE DEMISE OF CASH?

With 90 percent of the world's payments still in cash and most transactions under $10, Mondex could be an alternative to cash and other existing payment methods. Value is transferred directly between individuals, say from customer to store, friend to friend, spouse to spouse, spouse to child, or child to Disney – for a ride or a game on a Web site. Money can be sent down the phone line to a friend, supplier or creditor. The Mondex purse contains up to five different currencies that can be held in different pockets on a standard-sized plastic card. It is immediately acceptable – no checking or credit rating is needed, giving the person carrying it total privacy. Cards can be locked and unlocked using a personal code. Loading, reloading and unloading money value are done directly from bank accounts, cash machines, public telephones, telephones in the home or office, PCs, digital TVs, other electronic appliances and the Mondex terminal.

Beyond the core items

MONDEX
JUMPS
OUT OF
THE BOX
The credit and debit cards that so radically changed society and customers' lives had involved money being borrowed from a financial institution or being retrieved from an account. Mondex was to be a self-standing store of cash value that could be filled up or spent without going through a bank or credit agency's computer to supervise the process. The intention went beyond creating just another core item. The goal was to become *the* standard for a *new global way of paying for small-ticket items*. The key to the breakthrough came 'in a flash' when Jones and Higgins realized that Mondex had to break from the *status quo*, based on account-ability. Tim Jones remarked:

> *It was like everyone was bouncing around in a bubble, and suddenly, when we went outside of the bubble, we could see it clearly. Like cash, we would have no centralized record of transactions. Up until then, all payment cards and systems were accountable. Bankers had grown up to account for everything. But as long as funds didn't grow, who needed this? The myriad of trans-actions in the accountability system offered no real added value to customers. And it cost the banks and merchants plenty.*

With the mind and spirit of customer capitalism, the executives set out to grow their new way of payment exponentially, making it available across the world to ever-growing numbers of globally mobile customers. Unlike others such as Proton, the Belgian multibank conglomerate, and various other smartcards like VisaCash, which had stuck to accountability and single national currencies, Mondex would fundamentally alter the system – it would be global with no centralized records. In other words, unlike competitors where transactions involve at least five parties – purchaser and bank, retailer and bank, and the settlement agency – Mondex would enable person-to-person cash transfers anywhere in the world. Mondex transactions are also a fraction of the cost because the security is in the chip, so the costs associated with the central accounting systems of traditional cards do not exist.

In food retailing, Peapod and Streamline did the same as Mondex. They didn't just invent a new product or service or improve the existing core items – they created a standard for new ways of doing things and fundamentally altered the nature of the customer's daily provision-shopping experience. They went beyond conventional marketing notions of home delivery, alternate channels, electronic mail ordering, supply chain management, promotion, or offering home delivery for products that they have in stock at that moment (what most retailers still do). Instead, they transformed the way customers shop. They concluded that their customers were too busy to put up with the time (today's real scarce resource) and hassle of getting their staple shopping or other chores done.

Peapod was the brainchild of entrepreneur brothers Andrew and Thomas Parkinson, who 'saw' a new market in the combination of the statistic that 60 percent of customers in the US did not want to shop in the traditional way and at the traditional time that stores were open, and advances in new electronic technologies. Also customers did not want to go from store to store to get their full complement of requirements. In fact, people actively disliked grocery shopping, ranking it second to last in a list of 22 daily activities. This was a sentiment echoed in Europe in countries like the UK, Germany, the Netherlands, Norway, Finland, Denmark, Sweden and France.

Working with several retailers, including Safeway and Jewel in the US and Australia, Peapod soon accounted for 20 percent of their business, with revenues growing daily and exponentially. It then went one step further, providing its service nationwide, using its own warehouses and couriers to do the deliveries. Tim De Mello, founder of Streamline, had offered his idea to several retailers initially, but was rejected out of hand. The reply from retailers was: 'We have a great store, where we can display our merchandise and influence purchase behavior. Customers who come in for some things usually buy other things on impulse.' But as far as De Mello was concerned: *'In an ideal world, a new box of cornflakes would magically appear when the old box is empty. Why can't we achieve this for customers?'*

De Mello finally resolved to do himself what others weren't doing, or refused to do or, given their algorithm, couldn't 'see' a reason to do. A Streamline representative comes to a home and gets information on household preferences and buying habits. This, plus a scanning of products throughout the home, builds a personal shopping list. A 'service cupboard' is installed in the customer's home and refilled when necessary, getting the kind of customer lock-on to the organization that other companies would find difficult to dislodge.

GIVING
DIRECT LINE
ITS DUE

Similarly, it was entrepreneur Peter Wood of Direct Line (he has now moved on), backed by the Royal Bank of Scotland, who revolutionized the insurance industry in the UK with the innovative use of telephone technology. 'How many people like buying insurance?' he asked himself, and set out to improve that number. Direct Line was the first to offer a *new way of handling motor insurance* over the phone, and changed an industry that had not altered how it dealt with customers in decades. Direct Line has become the standard for the industry.

Direct Line then stretched into general household policies, providing instant quotes and cover 24 hours a day, and now over half of all domestic insurance is sold over the phone in the UK. One by one, the insurance companies have copied its direct technology, adding telephone insurance and a host of telebrokers to their selling systems, providing instant quotes. Brokers have responded in the usual way – reducing premiums, handling claims better and extending cover – all long overdue. Lack of innovation has drawn in plenty of outsiders to the industry, who are now hot on the trail and are breaking out beyond what has, until now, been similar to the original Direct Line concept.

And in the news arena, we see Microsoft shifting from just software – its core item – to form a multifaceted network known as MSN. Fast and furiously it has become a gateway Internet site for both the household and business markets. This is an opportunity to lock on customers that was missed by Netscape, which invented the browser but, by its own admission, was initially just thinking about the core item. Said one Netscape executive, '*I thought we were a software company – we build software and put it in boxes and we sell it. Oops. Wrong.*'

MICROSOFT'S NEWS TRAVELS FAST

Microsoft has transformed the way customers receive news, having joined up with NBC, an American TV channel, to form MSNBC, so creating a joint television, information and chat network. NBC had the content and video, and Microsoft's network knew how to make the content interactive, so customers get dialogue on the Web as opposed to monologue. They now get what they want, instead of having to accept what they are given.

But here is the interesting point: Microsoft is not trying to replace or even improve newspapers, i.e. the core item. An existing newspaper online is just a new rendition of what already exists, like an existing supermarket that home-delivers what it has in stock. Ultimately, both end in diminishing returns. Instead, Gates is trying to lead the way to create a standard for *new ways of providing global news*. He expects 25 percent of Microsoft's revenues to come from media holdings within a short while.

Thus we get to the second principle of customer capitalism: **leaders get increasing returns from becoming the standards for new ways of doing things for and with customers**. They don't just replicate what's already being done or improve existing products and services (see Table 3). These new ways of doing things bring customers the results they are after, which the old way never could and never will be able to do.

	TRADITIONAL CAPITALISM PRINCIPLES	CUSTOMER CAPITALISM PRINCIPLES
1 **AIM**	Maintaining the status quo	Fundamentally transforming
2 **LEADERS**	Replicating and improving products and/or services	Finding new ways of doing things for and with customers

Table 3 Principles of traditional and customer capitalism

This leaves us with the obvious point that the core items matter little on their own. What matters is finding new ways of doing things and becoming the standard. 'Seeing' and actualizing these new ways of doing things, to create new markets before others do, is equally important.

But even this means nothing unless corporations can get customers to lock on to them, bringing them back, again and again, to get their deeper, broader, more diverse and longer commitment and spend. That's what engenders the momentum, which creates the cumulating advantage and potential for increasing returns.

Let's go on...

PART TWO

THE TIME VALUE OF CUSTOMERS

CHAPTER 5
LEARNING TO CUSTOMER ORIGINATE

LONDON-BASED REUTERS HAS BEEN THE LARGEST AND MOST powerful global market data provider and news agency information owner for 150 years. Having begun as a foreign information service to UK newspapers, it developed screen-based information systems that dominated the desks of traders worldwide. But it persisted with the distribution of information (the core item) with little real innovation for users until the Bloomberg terminal came along. Started by Mike Bloomberg, a former US Salomon Brothers bond dealer, this changed forever the way traders and the growing number of independent advisers and fund managers worked. Bloomberg made his firm the new established standard for financial trading, benefiting in the process from the new market and economic dynamics of increasing returns.

We have already asked the question: Why is it that traditional players resist the natural logic of new customer needs, declaring them niches and newcomers niche players? If Mondex does indeed become either the new form of world payment or one of the platforms for an even bigger concept, banks will have to restructure dramatically. In the past, their most significant role has been looking after the physical distribution of physical money – this will then be defunct. This is no niche phenomenon. By the same token, by the time Reuters and Dow Jones woke up to what Bloomberg was doing, so many customers had become used to its new way of dealing that it had become a serious full-scale competitor, not a niche player. Like with Amazon, Auto-by-Tel, Direct Line or Peapod, the customer base locked on to the corporation. As one banker using the Bloomberg terminal put it: *'Look, Reuters is a fine system. But if my boss decided to pull the plug on my Reuters machine, would I mind? No.'*

Product vs customer origination

Bloomberg knew that financial professionals wanted more than just the latest news and data delivered in the normal, discrete way. So, instead of churning out more and better discrete bits of information, he made it easy for customers to process and use it according to their own specific needs, creating a new market and ground-swell advantage. His goal was to make the sleek Bloomberg terminal an indispensable analytic tool for anyone in the business of debt or equity. Unlike Reuters in Europe or Dow Jones in the US, he concentrated on originating for customers rather than originating for technology. He says:

> *Even though ... it wasn't obvious that the customers would appreciate what we were attempting from the beginning, I was convinced we were doing something nobody else could do. Nor was anyone trying. Our product would be the first in the investment business where normal people without specialized training could sit down, hit a key, and get an answer to financial questions, some of which they didn't even know they should ask.*

Bloomberg gave clients the ability to select investments, do 'what-if' scenario analyses on their securities portfolios and communicate over a private, secure e-mail system with their customers, suppliers and associates. This occurred quickly, accurately and easily, without customers having to enter the complex, detailed variables, delimiters, limits, constraints and so on that most computer systems required. Customers were also able to study markets and securities in absolute terms and relative to alternative investments, and could, for the first time, research companies, buy and sell stocks and bonds, even create new financial instruments via the terminal.

Additionally, on the Bloomberg terminal they could calculate the exact cost of a mortgage based on existing interest rates and then obtain one from a broker in real time. They could do this while simultaneously watching the latest world and national television news, purchasing brownies, flowers, teddy bears, jewelry or clothing online, selecting a flight for their next visit overseas, checking their favorite company's latest quarterly report, or listening to the head of a central bank prognosticate on interest rates (even though he or she had actually done this days earlier, in another language and on the other side of the world) – all on the same screen.

What Bloomberg and so many of the other new leaders demonstrate is that **compounding returns and durable advantage can only come from customer origination, not just inventing technology**. This is the next principle to add to the list (see Table 4). And since, ironically, this often emanates from outside an existing industry structure, benchmarking with companies already in there can be more of a hindrance than a help.

With customer capitalism, leaders are not necessarily those who invent or own a new technology. They are those who 'see' the market opportunity and make it happen. IBM pioneered technology from which others, like Microsoft in operating software, Oracle in relational databases and Sun Microsystems in chip architecture, made fortunes. Xerox invented the PC and the icons used on it, but never changed the world with it. The CD, video camera and fax were invented by the Dutch and the Americans, but are now Japanese domains. Microsoft didn't write the original DOS program: it was purchased for $75,000 from a small, start-up company, just as Microsoft licensed software from Spyglass,

FINDERS
KEEPERS?

	TRADITIONAL CAPITALISM PRINCIPLES	CUSTOMER CAPITALISM PRINCIPLES
1 AIM	Maintaining the status quo	Fundamentally transforming
2 LEADERS	Replicating and improving products and/or services	Finding new ways of doing things for and with customers
3 INNOVATION	Inventing new technologies	Originating for and with customers

Table 4 Principles of traditional and customer capitalism

Inc. when Gates realized that he had been slow to get into the Internet avalanche that Netscape started.

Tim Jones and Graham Higgins, Mondex originators, didn't invent the new technology. They combined different pieces that already existed. Mondex is neither money nor a smartcard – it puts together all of these with symmetric cryptography, which allows unrestricted and safe value exchange (you know the money is there) between spenders and receivers.

Amazon, selling to customers in over 160 countries, didn't invent anything either. Bezos didn't know much about books or information technology, just about the power of e-commerce and how to translate that into a new market. In fact, the wholesalers from which Amazon gets some of its stock could easily have done what Amazon did. But they didn't, because they didn't 'see' the new opportunity.

The point is:

➡ With **traditional capitalism**, new technology was assumed to be the core of corporate innovation and wealth-creating ability.

➡ With **customer capitalism**, new wealth only comes from the insight and ability to use technology in a unique and customer-relevant way.

This happens at the level of countries as well as companies. The quartz watch movement was not invented by the Asians, yet they took the lead in the worldwide watch market in the early 1980s with brands like Seiko and Casio. The Swiss invented the mechanism, but they were too busy keeping watches perfect and expensive to 'see' the new opportunity. It was only when Nicholas Hayek was appointed chairman of SMH, Switzerland's largest watch company, that Swatch, a low-cost, high-quality fashion watch ('an accessory that happens to tell the time') came about, recreating Swiss leadership in that industry. And Hayek transferred his dream from watches to cars, a dream he has now realized.

Increasingly, customers are drawn into the planning stage of customer originations. For example, when Amazon went into music (it is now the largest online CD vendor), it got customers, artists, music industry professionals and music lovers to help build 'the music store of their dreams'. Most of the site's most popular features are the result of those suggestions, according to David Risher, VP of product development. Some of the questions visitors to the site answered included: 'Tell us about your dream music store: how does it help you find music you like? How does it help you avoid music you won't? What makes it unique?' Customers were also asked to publish their opinions – both positive and negative – by reviewing and rating CDs; other potential customers could read these as they made their buying decisions. In appreciation of these suggestions, Amazon entered all visitors who offered input into a draw

INVOLVING
CUSTOMERS IN
ORIGINATIONS

for a $1000 gift certificate redeemable online for music, books or both.

The result was that more than 125,000 CDs are offered, 10 times the selection of the average music store, at discounts of up to 40 percent. Similar to the book-searching facilities, music fans search by CD title, artist, song title or label, and also can listen to more than 225,000 songs over the Web. Expert and customer reviews, interviews with artists, essential lists, news and an updated index of the hottest CDs are also included, all according to customer design. By popular customer request, the site was expanded to include 42,000 classical and opera CDs. Amazon customers didn't merely want a wide selection, they also wanted information about the various recordings of the same classical work, since these are very different from popular music songs that tend to have one version only.

Based on demand and feedback from customers, Amazon.com Kids features a catalogue of more than 100,000 books for children, teens and their parents. This mini site also has in-depth articles, reviews, interviews and targeted search and recommendation services.

Building in obsolescence

With customer capitalism, leaders push frontiers to set the standards for *new ways of dealing with customers*. They also often seek allies, despite having little or no data to substantiate what feels like the correct move to find markets. Bear in mind that these markets do not yet exist and there is no real proof of their potential. Shifting to this sort of mindset is not easy for the generations of established enterprises that have been used to the traditional capitalism model of successive slight modifications or product/ service improvements, which made what they did before better but could be copied very easily.

On top of that, customer capitalism requires origination, which often involves the complex challenge of having to build obsolescence into one's own offering before someone else does. New leaders need to be able, as Tom Peters puts it, to simultaneously build up and tear down, in the process of making real what Joseph Schumpeter calls the whole process of creative destruction. This takes a particular temperament and understanding of how the new market and economic dynamics work. OUT (BEFORE OTHERS GET IN)

For example, Richard Branson, in announcing his new range of Internet shopping services, said: '*We plan to be in the forefront of Internet ... if anyone is going to damage our existing business, **we want it to be us**.*' His Megastore On-Line now enables people who have the right recording equipment to download music recordings on to their PCs instead of buying them.

Microsoft, even though it pioneered the widespread use of the MS-DOS operating system and effectively cornered the market, spent a fortune to replace it with Windows 3.X, quickly followed by Windows 95, Windows NT and Windows 98, in the interests of enhancing the performance of its systems for customers before competitors could.

Andy Grove, too, keeps building obsolescence into his Intel offerings instead of waiting for others to do it for him. Having sensed in the 1980s that mainframes – the product for which Intel had been created – had to be replaced by microprocessor chips for the emerging PC market ('*big machines don't need to think for computers, small chips can do the job for customers*'), he created not just his own mega-empire but exponential growth in the whole computing sector. This happened even though, as one of Grove's managers put it, the experience of Grove getting out of mainframes was '*like Ford getting out of cars*'. INTEL JUMPING THE GUN

Grove's next step is to build obsolescence into computing as the only way to originate for the interactive information that customers want. His point is that there shouldn't be a battle between PCs and TVs (that's an old product argument). Instead, he is concerned with anything and everything that is needed to bring interactive information into the customer's living room – screens, a central box and loads of access points.

Winning at the new book battle will mean going for innovations that could make obsolete the online buying and selling of reading material that metamorphosed the industry. In its place is fast coming direct, online receipt and delivery of books, information and documents downloaded on demand from the Internet on to a PC or delivered to a digital reader – a pocket-sized reading instrument. Amazon, Barnes & Noble and Bertelsmann are all investing heavily in this. And, once the technology is ready, Amazon, with the largest Internet database of film and TV shows, will no doubt be doing the same with these, enabling customer subscribers to download them directly on to their screens.

MCDONALD'S GETS OBSOLETED

Contrast this to McDonald's which, despite quite obvious consumer changes in taste towards alternative food, home delivery and pre-cooked meals, limited itself to its old hamburger image. It kept the same menu and cooking techniques, and a tightly controlled, highly industrialized workforce churning out millions of standardized products a day, right up to the last few years of the century, when it was already getting into trouble. As a *Time* observer remarked: McDonald's *'got obsoleted on their [own] food.'* America wanted the taste that McDonald's could no longer give them.

It is true to say that corporations need to have budget in order to build in obsolescence. As important, however, is time (time bought from boards who are often still pressured only to produce the short-term results that push share prices up, despite what the new theories and theorists may advocate).

MONSANTO'S QUANTUM MODE

Bob Shapiro, CEO of Monsanto, the global agricultural and chemical life sciences corporation, had that challenge. So unconventional in attitude and appearance was Shapiro that his first meeting with the crop group is still remembered by his colleagues from the agricultural division. In fact, he looked so unusual that someone actually asked him to leave: *'We have an important meeting in the room with the new CEO,'* Shapiro was told.

One executive recalled:

> *The meeting finally began. Shapiro ignored the conventional presentation, and business plans, and SWOT analyses prepared by the team, designed to show where they were, and where they were going to be if they continued to go the way they were going. He didn't want to see trends, or what was going to be done better. He wanted to know what could be done differently for and with the customer to make the real money of the future.*

Up until then, like other manufacturers of its type, Monsanto had replicated strategies year by year, constantly improving its technically driven range of products, making better, cheaper versions of seeds and herbicides in order to thwart the competition – with inevitable diminishing returns. But there was one exception, its quantum investment in biotechnology (not without its share of controversy), which today enables the company to produce more relevant products for segments like bread makers which get better nutrition for end users, or feed manufacturers which make digestion easier for animals. There are also chemically and biologically engineered products which can build the information into molecules, thereby rendering them more durable and recyclable. Conventional practice can then be replaced by more effective applications. Having said all this, these are still just products. Are they enough, we have to ask ourselves, to get the customer lock-on that keeps competitors out?

Monsanto doesn't think so.

Like other enterprises, Monsanto understands that customer capitalism does not aim to dominate the market with the core items that are all too easy to copy. It does not try to monopolize through technical standards (though it may possess these standards). And it doesn't try to make customers captive when they have no good and sufficient reason to stay.

These corporations go beyond technology and technical standards of core items working with old notions of product lock-in. Instead, they originate for customers and become the standard for doing things differently and more effectively for and with customers. Then they make themselves indispensable to these customers, getting them to lock on to their organizations by delivering measurable and cost-effective value over time, leveraging from the new compounding dynamics of the six positive reinforcing loops of customer capitalism.

And that's how they get increasing returns.

CHAPTER 6
CUSTOMERS AS LIFELONG INVESTMENTS

JEFF COX, HEAD OF ONE OF MONSANTO'S 'GROWTH TEAMS', KNEW that there was only one way to make Monsanto's customers lifelong investments rather than transactional purchasers of seed and herbicide products: try to change the way farmers farmed. There was also only one way to get out of the diminishing returns syndrome that had plagued strategies in the past. Monsanto needed to redefine its role from being product supplier to being provider of lifelong customer value. In a long-term and ambitious growth project, model farms were set up to build the knowledge base that would make Monsanto the expert on farming productivity for the new millennium. Variables like crop rotation, disease prevention, microclimatic conditions and different soil types were simulated in an attempt to predict expected outcomes for customers so that the output of their farms over time could be maximized.

To get this optimal agricultural and financial result for customers meant working closely with a highly complex set of conditions and variables. Typically, farmers lived in mega-uncertainty – they were unable to foresee how the political situation could change, what output they were likely to get in a given year, what the prices of yields would be, or how these factors would affect their cash flow. Cox decided that what farmers needed was to remove as much of this uncertainty as possible from farming, once and for all. Selling seeds and herbicides was one thing, but if Monsanto truly wanted to grow market opportunities and

MONSANTO'S
SUPER-SEEDING
STRATEGY

its own criticality in a new playing field, customers had to be provided with this risk assurance.

The need for this was becoming ever more urgent in regions of Europe like France, Germany and the UK. A growing number of farmers were reaching retirement age and large amounts of productive land would become available in the EU at the beginning of the new century for succession, acquisition or consolidation. It is likely that these would be run by professionals, even more concerned with managed financial success, or by better-educated younger farmers, more willing to adopt new technologies and manage the business side of farming. This was combined with the fact that in emerging and developing areas like China or Poland, reduced government spending meant that individual farmers were increasingly having to pay their own way.

Nothing like this had ever been done before in the industry. Relationships were essentially transaction based. Growth strategies relied on the familiar 4Ps marketing formula of improved products, price cuts, expanded distribution (place) and promotion push and selling through linear chains. Though it was making money year by year, distanced as it was from the marketplace, Monsanto increasingly found itself lacking the intimacy of dialogue or the long-term bonding with end users needed to both give and extract value on a lifelong basis. If it couldn't do this, it couldn't generate the growth that would take it headlong into the new millennium. Said Cox:

> *In the past we had not challenged the farmers or ourselves. We said: here is a seed to grow wheat, here is the herbicide to kill the weed – we sold seeds and weed killer. But that wasn't the real issue or the big market opportunity – growth meant developing ways to get the maximum yield to farmers. Which was not only an exciting opportunity for Monsanto, but would grow the entire market for everyone.*

The system based on traditional capitalism had been
straightforward. Farmers bought products – cheap and in
bulk, based on specification and price. These were
demanded from a distributor's salespeople 'just in time'
(JIT), as the farmers wanted to incur as few costs as possible
up front. For example, 'Take All' is a deadly and unpredictable disease, which, without warning, attacks the roots
of wheat, the main cereal grown in France, Germany and
the UK. However, given their algorithm, many farmers
would rather risk the disease than pay to treat a disaster that
may never happen – though, when it does, their whole crop
can be wiped out.

To get the full benefits that Monsanto planned, farmers
would have to change their way of thinking and more
actively manage their crop methods to avoid the disease.
Farmers would have to work with an integrated and long-
term vision and concept. The problem was that both they
and suppliers had always viewed seed, seed treatment and
other products and services as separate. This was despite
the fact that they are part of the same system which sought
to maximize the agricultural and financial outcomes of a
farm over its life. Monsanto was determined to make this
integrated view understood and accepted as *the* standard
for *new ways of farming*.

Achieving a maximum yield per farm rather than just
selling bags of seeds or cases of herbicide down the line
would include all sorts of services never before provided:
disease prevention; helping farmers take better decisions on
what to grow; based on how, when, how often and where;
and merging all of this with their cash flow (always a major
problem in farming). This combined approach was essential
if customers were to get the results they were after and
Monsanto was to gain from their consequent value as lifelong investments.

Building lifelong customer value

TWO
RECIPROCAL
COMPONENTS
In whatever industry we choose to look, a company's on-going relationships with the people or organizations to whom it sells is essential. A dual, inseparable and reciprocal goal is core and central to the generative behavior that brings about increasing returns from these customer relationships, and the gains characteristic of customer capitalism, namely:

The lifelong value of the corporation to the customer
and
The lifelong value of the customer to the corporation.

The new enterprise knows how to do both. One without the other and it is back to traditional capitalism and diminishing returns. The problem was that companies just didn't think of cumulative or lifelong customer value in the years when making and moving core items supposedly brought wealth. Take a simple example – insurance underwriting. The fact that a person may have had half a dozen life policies with a single firm didn't have the slightest impact on the price of their seventh policy. Each policy was a discrete purchase in an industry dominated by minimizing its own risk, rather than maximizing the return for customers. Insurers sought only to maximize the profitability of single sales, rather than the long-term value of the customer.

Contrast that to what companies such as Rand Merchant Bank Holdings in South Africa or Aegon in the Netherlands are doing today, moving from insurance to 'outsurance'. In the interests of locking customers on, Rand Merchant Bank pays customers for not claiming and doesn't hike their premiums if they do. Aegon rewards customers if they keep fit and stay healthy to a certain age.

BANKING ON
VIRGIN
Today we see enterprises explicitly moving in a different direction, with the dual goal of giving and getting value to

and from customers over time. Look at Virgin's move into banking. Clever indeed, because what most customers want is help with financial planning to ensure liquidity, security and prosperity *over their lifetime*, not to have to face a bank manager if and when they are in crisis. Instead of being badgered to 'pay back or else', customers who need extended credit to deal with the various activities and events over their lives – predictable and unpredictable – now deal with one company. They pay for all their financial transactions, including their mortgage scheme, in such a way that they have enough cash available until retirement, at which point they will have paid off what they owe and be able to get a fixed amount on their savings on which to live (more later).

The new Virgin Banking approach is original by modern standards because it combines a strong brand with innovative new ways of doing things for and with customers, rather than just patching together cheaper/better versions of traditional products or services. As opposed to selling customers discrete units from time to time, it offers them an integrated, cash management result which gets them to lock on, with consequent cumulative time value advantages and disproportionate gains to the corporation.

CHAPTER 7
GIVING MARGINS A BREAK

WITH CUSTOMER LOCK-ON CENTRAL TO STRATEGY, THE NEW enterprise switches to leveraging from the time value of customers, instead of trying to maximize margins on each unit of product or service made and sold.

It was the fixation on margins that lost the US its lead in compact cars. Although Volkswagen had demonstrated the need for a low-cost, small, fuel-efficient car for decades, US manufacturers were initially not interested in compacts because margins on each unit were too low. The Japanese took the lead, and from there moved upmarket into the luxury car segment, taking their customers with them.

LESSONS FROM SATURN

All that is changing. In the US and Japan, General Motor's Saturn division, for instance, targets students and others starting out in adult life with its low-cost compact car with the express purpose of holding on to these individuals, upgrading them as they progress and advance. Although the company is losing money per car, it does not intend to create wealth from the margin of each vehicle sold. Instead, it intends to make itself the dominant or sole customer choice, extracting value over time from a lifelong relationship. Saturn has calculated that if, for instance, it gets customers at 18 and holds on to them until they are 65, the value is half a million dollars: what is lost initially on margins is more than made up in the long term. (Many banks have of course done this with students for years. However, because they don't make money from them in their youth years, they typically cut down on service, missing the point and losing out on gaining a cumulative and compounding advantage with them.)

In the used car market – on the way up – strategies are being revitalized by entrepreneurs like Wayne Huizenga. He has shaken up an entire US industry, building a multi-brand, nationwide network of new and old car outlets and warehouses at no small cost. What Huizenga does is to combine superb service, haggle-free pricing, money-back guarantees and direct access over the Internet. The strategy is not to get instant high margins, but rather to extract value as customers lock on to his brand as they move from new to used vehicles and one used vehicle to another.

The ultimate value of customers

Fixating on managing margins can (and does) seriously twist logic. It prevents corporations from making the time, energy and money investments that lead to customer lock-on and expanding and exponential rewards. Customer capitalism tells a different tale. Durable competitiveness cannot be achieved by making money on margins per unit transacted. It can only be achieved by **maximizing the time value of the customer**, the next principle of customer capitalism (see Table 5).

This is achieved in several ways. Baxter Europe's Renal division, part of the worldwide healthcare company, is one example. The UK had several options when Peter Leyland, corporate entrepreneur, was appointed as the business unit director early in 1997. Despite its still close to 80 percent market share in the UK peritoneal dialysis (PD) market – equal to about 20,000 dialysis bags sold a day to patients with kidney ailments – events had marked what could have been an irreversible downturn for the company. Most significantly, a number of important accounts had been lost to the competitor which had had the other 20 percent of the PD market. Moreover, a new competitor had entered the scene, invited in by hospitals because of its lower-priced bags.

BAXTER RENAL'S TURNING POINT

	TRADITIONAL CAPITALISM PRINCIPLES	CUSTOMER CAPITALISM PRINCIPLES
1 AIM	Maintaining the status quo	Fundamentally transforming
2 LEADERS	Replicating and improving products and/or services	Finding new ways of doing things for and with customers
3 INNOVATION	Inventing new technologies	Originating for and with customers
4 OBJECT	Optimizing margins on unit transactions	Maximizing the time value of customers

Table 5 Principles of traditional and customer capitalism

The whole trauma began with a shift in decision making from the clinicians to the economic buyers and business managers in hospital trusts, something that Baxter had not foreseen. In common with other countries in the world, the cost of healthcare in the UK had been steadily rising over the previous few decades, while government budgets remained flat. The new economic buyers' main goal was to balance the budget and lower hospital costs, whereas in the past, the clinicians and nurses who had made the decisions had been more concerned with patient care. Leyland had at least three options:

➡ Discount the bag, which was what the economic buyers wanted, and lose the profit.
➡ Keep prices as they were and hope to show the added value that Baxter could bring through superior products and services.

➡ Create a whole new way of working for and with the various customer stakeholders, given that some had conflicting objectives.

Let's get into a little more detail here, because this case demonstrates some significant points. First, renal patients with serious kidney problems need to undergo two treatments, namely periodialysis (PD) at home, or hemodialysis (HD), which requires spending three days a week at hospital, for four hours at a time, followed by short stays back at hospital for monitoring. Usually, customers begin their treatment with PD and then move on to HD, but this depends on numerous factors, including how quickly the disease is diagnosed and treated – the worse off they are when they are initially diagnosed, the more suitable is HD, the competing treatment to Baxter's.

Secondly, the bags contain a liquid solution used to extract and dialysize the toxins from the patient's blood stream. PD's share of the overall market had gone down when Leyland arrived: whereas in 1992 PD accounted for just over 50 percent of all dialysis treatments, by the end of 1996 it accounted for about 42 percent. The main reason for this, according to the Baxter Renal team, was that on a fluid bag-for-bag basis, HD (competitor) was cheaper than PD (Baxter), which was driving the economic buyers' decisions.

What did Leyland do? He decided to cut the margin on the bags, in order to retain its market presence. However, typical of customer capitalism, instead of rationalizing service, thereby reducing value and market growth, he moved in exactly the opposite direction. The reasoning was this: instead of cutting its costs (and thus quality) to make up for the loss of margin on the core item, which conventional logic would have dictated, Baxter would introduce whatever was needed to extend the time value of the various customers involved and therefore focus on superior value for

DID BAXTER
HAVE AN
OPTION?

the end-user patient. This was done by innovating in several ways, for example:

➡ With its new (expensive) extraneal solution fluid agent, which acts as a sieve through which more toxins could be drawn into the bag, the deterioration of a patient's membrane could be significantly slowed down. With the patient's membrane functioning more efficiently for a much longer period, they could remain on the PD treatment longer, gaining in both lifestyle and longevity.

➡ Baxter also developed a machine which treated patients overnight – this was less uncomfortable, increased lifestyle prospects, and gave them more productive time during the day.

➡ Baxter offered value-add services: consulting and software to doctors; better information through interactive computer programs and audiovisual material to patients so they could make informed choices; it also monitored blood toxin levels by placing nurses in hospitals, crucial for customer efficacy and longer life, all at Baxter's expense.

➡ In addition, a 'one price per bag' policy was employed, irrespective of the solutions inside the bag, thereby enabling practitioners to prescribe whatever produced the best and longest outcome for individual patients without price getting in the way.

➡ In the largest single investment, Baxter created and managed patient training centers. The aim was to train PD patients in those hospitals that were understaffed. In 1997, close to 500 patients were trained in London, a figure expected to rise given the ageing population combined with the large ethnic communities in the city who were especially susceptible to the disease. The cost to Baxter of this training was £1000 per patient, but those patients who underwent the training stayed on PD therapy longer than others.

The theory goes into practice

Although specifics may differ depending on whether a country is privately or publically funding a therapy, the Baxter Renal example demonstrates quite dramatically how, in a conventional industry, the principles of customer capitalism are being converted into business practices, getting customer lock-on with consequent cumulative advantage and increasing returns. The proviso, however, is that everyone gains over time.

The lifelong value of the company to customers is obvious in this case – the patient gains because Baxter's strategy has shifted from selling dialysis bags to providing patients with results – more survival time with prospects for a better lifestyle and more productivity. The hospitals gain because budgets are met and costs go down as hospital resources are freed up. The authorities gain, as do clinicians and doctors, by virtue of better patient care, enhanced resource utilization, and improved management of the population's health.

The lifelong value of the customer to the corporation is equally obvious – Baxter gains by retaining its market dominance and impact. It gets value from the accumulated knowhow and benefits from buyer lock-on, including longer-term commitments, reduced costs of doing business together and accelerated market acceptance of new ideas and offerings. Additionally, networking effects go into motion as its infrastructure grows, and as more players and developers are attracted, this adds to the life extension and wellbeing of patients, keeping Baxter constantly ahead.

And more bags are sold. Specifically, the break-even point for the loss in margin, plus the cost of training of £1000 per patient, was initially calculated at three months' longer life per patient. The extension of customer life and lifestyle continues to be surpassed well beyond this point, through various ongoing innovations, and could, in the future, extend to 10 years or more.

PART THREE

FROM MARKET SHARE
TO MARKET SPACES

CHAPTER 8
ONE MORE TIME: WHAT'S WRONG WITH MARKET SHARE?

THE REVOLUTION AND QUEST FOR MARKET GROWTH AND sustained competitiveness in the book, journal or news business aren't actually about books, journals or news (the core items) at all. They are about creating standards for *new ways for customers to manage their discovery of information and knowledge*. Similarly, the revolution in the auto business is not just about the quality, cost, price or technology of a vehicle, or about making and distributing cars – *'a dying science'* is how one executive described it. It isn't even about retention or loyalty to specific car brands. It's about changing ideas about how customers move around.

So rather than compete for premium on quality or simply haggle on price, auto manufacturers and dealers worldwide, in every market echelon, are seriously having to rethink their businesses:

AUTOS GET
INTO GEAR

- ➡ How do they create a new market?
- ➡ How do they get customer lock-on?
- ➡ What are the relative roles of the different players in giving value to customers to get this lock-on?
- ➡ How will an industry steeped in tradition be able to rid itself of old, restrictive ways of doing business?

What's the real problem? The linear channel and franchise system built to make and move cars are as outmoded for competing in our modern economy as Ford's 'anything as long as it's black' was for the post-industrial era.

Manufacturers, chiefly after market share, have piled dealers up with stock. Dealers have responded by selling stock, rather than helping customers buy the correct vehicles.

So what do we find? In an industry that made price the dominant motivator, it is estimated that about 25 percent of the people who want cars in the US and parts of Europe are prepared to pay an intermediary not to have to go through the vehicle-buying drama. Customers are not only saying they are prepared to pay for this intermediary service but, they declare, a single car or brand won't do for the diversity of their lives and certainly not for the longevity of their lives. (This is why car manufacturers are scrambling to broaden their offerings through merger-based acquisitions.)

AUTO-BY-TEL
ON THE SCENE
On to the scene (and screen) in the mid-1990s comes an outsider, Auto-by-Tel, to offer an alternative way of doing things for and with customers, creating enough shockwaves in the industry to force it to recreate itself. Dealing electronically, directly with customers, Auto-by-Tel gives the service without the hassles, and products are cheaper because costs are dramatically lowered. Operating in the US, Canada, the UK and Scandinavia, it also has plans to go into France, Germany, Japan and Brazil – all markets that combine Internet growth and high vehicle sales per head of the population. Auto-by-Tel gives clients access to the entire range of vehicles on the market – old or new – and finds them the closest dealer with the best price. It arranges to have the car delivered to the customer's house for a test drive, orders the vehicle for them, does the paperwork, the financing, insurance and post-servicing etc.

This is more than a makeover. With customer capitalism, the relationship between the customer and the firm is based on prospects for a long-term association. Auto-by-Tel's customers are asked to indicate whether or not they are immediate buyers or likely only to buy in the near future so as not to waste dealer time. The dealer states its best sell or lease price up front, without using the discount routine as a bait – that's part of the 'no hassle no haggle' arrangement.

In addition, Auto-by-Tel does not collect fees for delivering buyers, which it fears would push dealers, with whom it works in regional communities, to push units. Instead, it charges a monthly subscription fee to them for representation on its Web site, tiered for area and potential traffic. Within the first two years Auto-by-Tel sold to a million people, and in its first trading years was responsible for more car sales in the US in a single month than the largest traditional mega-dealer makes in an entire year. In addition, revenue continues to mount exponentially as the reinforcing looping mechanism takes effect.

The problems with market share

One of the main reasons that the established manufacturers and dealers allowed Auto-by-Tel and others to get access to their customers was that, in true traditional capitalism fashion, they clung to market share as *the* key driver (so to speak) for their business decisions. The assumption that market share was the prime determinant of profits has paralyzed management thinking for decades, and has been one of the underlying forces perpetuating diminishing returns.

From the 1970s through to the 1980s, several works like PIMS (Profit Impact of Market Share) quantified the link that market share equaled profitability, making the already strongly held tenet still stronger. Through its popular strategy matrix, the Boston Consulting Group (BCG) encouraged corporations to go for the products and business units that had these high relative market shares, which it called the 'stars'. But as it turned out, many of these products and units were not the ones from which the new wealth and growth opportunities sprung. Companies unable to attain high market shares, given up by investors as 'dogs', often achieved great success over time, because they were small enough to concentrate on long-term customer relationships and agile enough to quickly take up the necessary innovations.

The belief that market share leads to long-term competitiveness is inaccurate. Far worse, it was (and still is) seriously dangerous, because it hides rather than exposes the real opportunities and competitors. In the 1980s and early 1990s, Xerox's market share in copiers (the core item) looked good. But while Xerox was telling its customers to 'make one and photocopy the rest', Hewlett-Packard (HP) was saying 'forget copiers – make as many as you want with our printers'.

Ask IBM today who are its greatest competitors for the vital customer relationships and it will tell you that it is Andersen Consulting or the software houses. These organizations provide services to customers during critical parts of their decision making and long before machines are specified, tenders go out or the core items are bought. Or IBM will mention a company like Cisco, a corporation growing at 80 percent a year since 1990, which heavily involves customers in devising their strategies to offer end-to-end solutions, connecting networks of computers across companies and industries globally over the Internet. So it's worth reiterating one more time:

➡ market share invariably costs money
➡ firms may be getting an increasing share of a shrinking pie
➡ it is a lag statistic and says nothing about the durability of the customer relationship
➡ it gives no clue as to how many customers are unhappy or switchable
➡ or how many customers the corporation lost and had to replace
➡ or the cost of that
➡ or whether they have the correct customers

➡ or how a firm is doing relative to those it will compete with in the future

➡ it doesn't tell a firm about customer usage (compare having a card with actually using it)

➡ or whether the corporation has the 'correct' customers (would you have gone out of your way to get Microsoft or Virgin as a customer 10 years ago?).

Essentially, what market share did was help traditional capitalism present a view of competitiveness within static product/service categories. It produced economies on the supply side of the business, but it never produced ideas for getting results to customers, or exposed new markets or propeled corporate growth. In fact, rather than broaden managerial perspectives of opportunities and threats, it made competitive perspectives incredibly short-sighted and narrow.

Reframing the playing field

Market spaces, on the other hand, frame the wider competitive arena, and become the new competitive playing fields. Unlike the product/service categories of traditional capitalism, market spaces take the customer's perspective: they become the articulation of the results that customers are after, the new corporate 'activity arenas'. NEW 'ACTIVITY ARENAS'

So characteristically, market spaces:

➡ encapsulate in a few words the desired, totally integrated experience or results that customers want

➡ cross company, country, division or unit product/service-specific boundaries

➡ span whatever may be legally, technically or organizationally separate, defying traditional categorizations of an industry.

The benefits of customer capitalism and its reinforcing looping characteristic, which bring about increasing returns,
come to the enterprise that gets itself away from the notion
of having to have the largest market share in a static
product/service category. Instead, **the company concen-
trates on dominating activities that provide superior
value for customers in the ever-expanding vistas
opened up in these market spaces**. This next principle to
add to the list then is shown in Table 6.

	TRADITIONAL CAPITALISM PRINCIPLES	CUSTOMER CAPITALISM PRINCIPLES
1 AIM	Maintaining the status quo	Fundamentally transforming
2 LEADERS	Replicating and improving products and/or services	Finding new ways of doing things for and with customers
3 INNOVATION	Inventing new technologies	Originating for and with customers
4 OBJECT	Optimizing margins on unit transactions	Maximizing the time value of customers
5 MEANS	Increasing market share in product/service categories	Dominating activities in market spaces

Table 6 Principles of traditional and customer capitalism

The best way of describing these market spaces is to look
at some examples of well-known companies (see Table 7).
The table compares the core items in the left-hand column

TRADITIONAL CAPITALISM Product/market categories, core items	CUSTOMER CAPITALISM market spaces (and sub-market spaces)
Amazon: Books	Managing information and knowledge discovery
Amazon: CDs, videos, gifts	Leisure activities supply management
AMEX Travel: air tickets (corporate)	Total corporate travel management
Baxter Health Care: medical products and diagnostic equipment	Total wellbeing and life extension
Baxter Renal: dialysis bags	Renal sufficiency
Citibank: loans	Global financial management
Fedex: overnight delivery	Total logistics management
Financial Times: newspapers	Global financial and business information management
IBM: mainframes, PCs	Global electronic networking capability
LEGO: building construction toys	Total family edutainment
Lotus Notes: software	Electronic collaborative group support
Mercedes: cars	Short-haul mobility
Monsanto: seeds	Farming risk assurance
Streamline: groceries	Cupboard management
Peapod: groceries and chores	Household supply management
Virgin Banking: mortgages	Lifelong event cash management
Xerox: copiers	Document management

Table 7 Examples of market spaces

with the results that customers want, or market spaces, in the right-hand column.

Articulating the market space(s) is the first step to getting the lock-on that customer capitalism seeks. And the new enterprise wants this lock-on from increasing numbers of customers because otherwise it risks locking itself out. Ask yourself this: had the telephone companies of yesteryear thought in terms of *mobile communications, virtual office management,* or any other relevant name they had chosen to give to the market space that was clearly emerging as the *new way for people to communicate,* would they have allowed Nokia, the then obscure paper-processing mill and rubber plant nestled on the Nokia river in Finland, to take a hold on their market and become the number one choice of 50 million-odd customers in Europe for cellular mobile phone technology?

And a decade later, had these telephone companies articulated the new playing field as, say, the *electronic information management networking* market space, where people interact, meet and talk, exchange and adapt information and visuals virtually in real time, would they, despite their several millions in investment, have allowed a company like Qwest, built by an ex-AT&T employee, to have more bandwidth than AT&T, Sprint, MCI and WorldCom put together, and to be the number one carrier, to the tune of a predicted 80 percent of the Net's customer traffic in the new millennium?

No way.

CHAPTER 9
MARKET SPACES AND CUSTOMER CAPITALISM

IT BEGAN IN THE 1970S WITH THE FAST TRANSPORT OF PACKAGES from one destination to another, thereby inventing a new industry. But anyone could copy a company that was moving goods from point *A* to point *B*. So in the 1980s, Frederick W. Smith, realizing that information about these packages was as important as the overnight delivery he promised, began investing in the infrastructural information technology that would keep Federal Express (Fedex) ahead and magnify opportunities for it, and everyone else associated with it, in the decades to come.

Having become equally at home with moving packages or information, Smith grew convinced that in the 1990s the future was about virtual warehousing – supplying stock only on demand. He exposed a new market space, *total logistics management*. Fedex's purpose was to become critical in the cost-effective inventory and delivery business of its corporate manufacturing customers, orchestrating the high-speed flow of goods and information between them, retailers and suppliers.

Fedex's vision is to be 'the official airline of the Internet' in this *total logistics management* market space. This is to be achieved by merging operations in cyberspace and physical space to get the millions of bits and pieces sorted, collected and delivered around the world, enabling its customers to compete more effectively. In the process, Fedex has become something of an increasing returns legend, leveraging exponentially off its massive investments in technology and the lock-on that it has forged and reforged with customers over the years.

Expanding heads and horizons

OPENING UP
THE
STRATEGIC
VISTA The point about all of this is that once the market space is articulated, then (and only then) can the new enterprise open up the strategic panorama and decide where, how and with whom it wants to play to get increasing returns. Only when Xerox went from copiers to the market space it called *document management* was its top management able to recast the company and begin to truly transform the business. The same can be said of IBM, now good and solid in the thick of the *global electronic networking capability* market space, driven by e-commerce and Louis Gerstner's vision of 'Net-centric' solutions based on an open, integrated environment.

So here is yet another distinction that one can observe between old and customer capitalism:

➡ With **traditional capitalism**, growth and market opportunities are described by core items, i.e. new products or services.
➡ With **customer capitalism**, growth and market opportunities are described by market spaces.

Let's get into more detail.

Market spaces change corporate direction

Once the market space has been articulated, it changes an enterprise's thinking forever. It moves away from gaining more share of core items and eventually getting diminishing returns, which is what occurred with the traditional model. It becomes a corporate purpose that directs resources, energy and priorities into producing results for customers who then lock on to the organization, with potential for increased revenues through depth, breadth, diversity and longevity of spend and decreased costs, major levers for positive disproportionate gains.

Take the automobile industry. Manufacturers and dealers have been seeking to extricate themselves from the demise of their 15-year diminishing spiral. There is also talk of legislation aimed at limiting the number of cars on Europe's urban roads, plus new entrants in the industry like Auto-by-Tel. All of this has shifted attention and resources from 'motoring' to 'mobility' in the market space now known as *personal mobility*. Mercedes calls it *short-haul mobility*, and its intention is to dominate activities in that market space through several innovative products and services stretching way beyond traditional vehicle manufacturing and distributorship.

Others, too, are getting into this market space. The Royal Automobile Club (RAC) was started as a traditional breakdown company at the beginning of the twentieth century to assist British motorists in the UK and Europe. Having made a loss of £12.4 million in 1995, CEO Neil Johnson and his top team returned it to profitability in just a year by going from an almost exclusive focus on their core breakdown service business to finding ways to multiply their share of customer mind and pocket in the sub-market space (a micro-territory within a market space) that they term *journey management*.

RAC'S RACE INTO JOURNEY MANAGEMENT

Today, advanced vehicle technologies can alert motorists to impending engine or other mechanical failures, so reducing the overall car breakdown rate. With the cost of chips and other technologies already plummeting, this is becoming likely for even the less expensive vehicles.

This technology has one obvious effect, and that is that it reduces the number of breakdowns so that the breakdown service business declines. Added to this is the fact that some projections suggest that the car itself could become a less significant part of modern life due to teleworking, videoconferencing, use of IT and sales by phone and the Internet.

There is also increased public and legislative concern about urban traffic congestion and related pollution, all of which prompted Johnson of the RAC to take his unprecedented decision: focus strategy, resources and investment on *journey management*, i.e. get member customers to and from destinations with the least aggravation and cost in the shortest time – whether by car, motorbike, bicycle, bus, train or foot. The RAC became the first company to offer live, interactive traffic and travel information on the Internet. It could immediately tell customers what their best route was, how to avoid traffic congestion and also give weather details and advisory warnings.

Market spaces are dynamic and expansive

EXISTING, EMERGING AND IMAGINED

Within market spaces, possibilities don't just add up, they multiply as new trajectories begin to change habits and aspirations, and make possible opportunities for giving and getting customer value never before envisaged.

These market spaces can be divided into three categories: the existing, the emerging and the imagined – those yet to come. Using the health arena to illustrate: if we were to shift from a product definition, say drugs, to a market space definition, the three categories would look something like this:

➡ **Existing** market space: disease management (diagnose and cure).
➡ **Emerging** market space: managed healthcare (predict, reverse and prevent).
➡ **Imagined** market space: total wellbeing and life extension management (preserve and prolong).

Quite obviously, whether a market space is existing, emerging or imagined very much depends on the economy, country and market. That is not to say that some of the emergent and developed countries will not leapfrog or at least have a strong contingent of customers who follow global patterns. For example, since there is no set way of operating competitively in China, Monsanto finds that it is easier than one might imagine to introduce new ideas on farming to the various institutional and individual players there. It is the same in Poland, where as Jeff Cox puts it, *'They are starting with a clean slate.'* In under one generation, black South Africans have gone from low or semi-literacy, and in some instances even a tribal lifestyle, to running small businesses, taking advantage of the most sophisticated high technology that money can buy. In Turkey, rather than go on to a weak cable system, customers have gone straight for mobile communications. This tallies with many emerging and lower-income economies, which are registering double the growth rate of richer nations in new wireless and cellular services.

In an interview with the *Financial Times*, Nicholas Negroponte of the Media Laboratory, an academic research institute run by the Massachusetts Institute of Technology (MIT), says: *'Five years down the line the most commonly spoken language on the Net will be Chinese, not English.'* Negroponte is the author of *Being Digital* and the man who predicted the growth and impact of the Internet when most of us didn't even know it existed.

So market spaces are dynamic and expansive, in the sense that what is an imagined market space today will be an emerging market space tomorrow and an existing market space thereafter. Already in some countries and markets, *managed healthcare* is mainstream and *wellbeing and extended life management* are on the horizon. Other countries and markets are still in *disease management*, moving to *managed healthcare* and so on, or the market space is different depending on what segments we are talking about. The new enterprise knows the difference. The trick is to be able to work in all three simultaneously, dominating the existing while creating and preparing for the emerging and imagined, bringing them into being through foresight, stretch and commitment.

Market spaces link customer benefits

DEMAND
DRIVING
INNOVATION

Market spaces encapsulate the linked benefits that bring about the looping reinforcing behavior of customer capitalism, for the simple reason that to produce these linked benefits requires all of the six loops to be operative.

Most experts talk about 'evidence-based medicine' (choice of drugs based on more facts) being the future, but this is still a product approach. It is probably truer to say that the future is about integrated medicine. In this scenario players will share their ideas, information and knowledge and compete together to produce an ongoing superior individual customer experience at low delivered cost, with developers continually innovating. All will be connected by one huge networked infrastructure in the *wellbeing and extended life management* market space.

The emphasis cunningly shifts, of course, from the diagnosing and curing era of making more and more core items, to the predicting and preventing of disease, to preserving and prolonging life and wellbeing over a patient's lifetime. The relationship starts from the reproductive process, and goes through lifelong lifestyle and health management, including reversal and regenerative processes if and when clinical trouble appears. (Can traditional players survive this shift? What opportunities does it represent for newcomers?)

THE
'UNPATIENT'
MARKET

What makes this a huge growth market and the opportunities cumulative and compounding is the new chunk of customers known as the 'unpatients'. Unpatients are those people who are not ill and who will pay for products and services that will prolong that fact. As the unpatients are drawn into the markets and bring others with them, this increases demand driven by innovation, making boundless the prospects for keeping an increasing number of people well and wanting to stay well rather than becoming sick and requiring a cure.

Facilitating integrated medicine – or integrated care as it is sometimes referred to – is advanced technology, such as that developed by the Department of Biological and Medical Systems at Imperial College, University of London. Traditionally in the US and Europe, not much information has passed from doctor to doctor, or from general practitioners to hospitals, and, even within hospitals, care has been based on a serial-type system, where the patient has to go from one doctor and one clinic to another. Today, from Imperial's 'electronic patient-records software system', any doctor can see the entire file of a patient they are attending and multiple clinicians, anywhere in the world, can simultanously discuss an individual case. Multimedia images can be accessed and moved around the world within seconds simply by turning on a computer screen. And instead of the data acquisition, diagnosis and treatment being physically bound by one geography – usually a local hospital – it can be done anyplace, anywhere in the world, wherever it's relevant and most cost effective.

Seeing a market space first

Entrepreneurs and new corporate leaders are able to articulate and communicate market spaces first, not because they can prove that they exist, but because they can feel and anticipate what is to come. In fact, lots of data they can only get afterwards. They know how to spot the true new opportunities, not from a single statistic drawn out of past figures or new extrapolations, but from a deep conviction that something new and unusual is happening which, if catalyzed and pushed, will take off. When the idea for Lotus Notes was first conceived there was no sensible way to make a business case. PCs had barely taken off, LANs were just starting and it didn't seem that important. Though e-mail was being used, it was not yet considered a signifi-cant internal communication tool. But founder Mitch Kapor 'saw' the discontinuity, made sense of it in market terms, articulated it, and took the risks and steps needed to turn a technological innovation into the *electronic collaborative group support* market space that the firm (today part of the IBM contingent) now dominates.

These individuals can sense and articulate market spaces first because they have a really good gut understanding of how things connect. They think of markets as living systems, moving any which way, not just linear extensions of the past. They ask: How do things interact? What's happening that could influence what? Where can that lead? They see the dynamics of behavior and how people influence people, and events influence markets, to create new opportunities. They feel like customers. ('*Why,*' as one executive interviewed asked, '*is it that when we are at home or out, we know what it's like to be a customer and what we want but, the moment we get back to the office, we forget?*') In short, they are able to detect future changes before they happen, and understand them when they do, making sense of them in a way that others cannot see at first. Then, through imagination, courage and stamina – often despite resistance – they make them happen.

Though competitors thought he was crazy at the time, John Reed was determined in the 1980s to give customers an ongoing global banking experience, from Munich to New York or Tokyo, whether they were in a branch, in their car, on the high streets, at home or in the office. Before, for Citibank and for many others, being global had meant being big and being in several countries. However, cus-tomers had to scramble to manage and coordinate their financial affairs across borders. As Reed noted:

We made an important discovery that drove everything we did later ... people's attitudes about their finances are a function of how they are raised, their education, and their values, not just their nationalities. What works for our market in New York also works in Brussels, Hong Kong and Tokyo.

As he saw it, there were emerging global financial market spaces in which upper-income, mobile customers would demand integrated and consistent services wherever, whenever, whatever. From day one, Reed sought to build a business independent of geography. This may sound obvious now, but at the time that was far from the case.

CHAPTER 10
CONVERGING INDUSTRIES AND
NEW MARKET SPACES

NEW TOYS LIKE BARNEY – THE 16 INCH ELECTRONIC INTERACTIVE dinosaur from Microsoft – were only a warning signal to Lego in the mid-1990s that kids were going high-tech. Barney had a vocabulary of 2000 words and was endowed with a variety of other software that moved its arms and legs, sung songs, played games and interacted with TV episodes.

Then there were electronic cyberpets or *tamagotchi* (lovable eggs), invented by the Japanese company Bandai as a substitute pet for children. These caused an equal stir in an industry that had had little innovation for decades but lots of copy-cat competition. They had cross-cultural and cross-age appeal. A tamagotchi lived in an egg and, by pressing buttons, it could be fed, cleaned and disciplined; it called out when it needed help, and died if it didn't get it. Following on closely from tamagotchi was artificial life technology, combining artificial intelligence with three-dimensional graphics, promising virtual toys that could *feel* hungry, tired, afraid and even bored.

MORE THAN A TRIVIAL PURSUIT For sure, the way kids played had changed irrevocably. Children were spending more and more of their spare time with computers, video games and TV rather than with conventional toys. This in turn was changing the whole notion of what was, and what was not, a toy, and in the process altering the face of the entire industry. So while Lego had been gaining market share from its legendary brick construction toys, construction toys were losing their grip on the real new market. Up until then, the family-owned firm headquartered in Billund, Denmark, which had evolved from a small woodworking shop in the 1930s to becoming the world's fifth largest toymaker operating in 138 countries, could sell everything it made. *'We had to control demand of our business,'* in the words of one executive.

In 1995, Lego had a world market share in building construction toys of 72 percent, in Europe just on 90 percent. Clearly, there was much more at stake for Lego than producing another high-tech toy, or trying to use conventional marketing means to increase market share. Lego would need to dominate activities in new market spaces and help invent those still to come if it was to retain criticality in the way that families with kids spent their spare time. This was the dilemma that faced Kjeld Kristiansen – grandson of the founder of the Danish toy manufacturer – as he designed the strategy he hoped would take the firm into the twenty-first century and make the Lego brand the customer's first, and enduring, choice over a lifetime.

From trends to convergences

From Lego and others we learn that trends within products, companies or industries cannot produce market spaces, either existing, emerging or imagined. These come from the convergence of industries, lifestyles and technologies. For instance, the convergence of telephony, consumer electronics, computer technology, data interchange and communications has rendered differences in time or geography irrelevant, and made mobile communications *the* significant market space, and growth opportunity, in telecommunications.

One just has to stroll in the spring sunshine in one of the Italian ski resorts to be reminded that for fun, we could add fashion to this convergence. The huge growth rate of mobile phones in Italy as the latest designer accessory complete with different colors and styles for the fashion-conscious

Milanese taking their Easter or weekend break is testament to the growing convergence of mobility, fashion and communications. More importantly, it illustrates the blurring of the notion of work and play. Having abandoned their offices for the alpine *pistes* (restaurants, boutiques and bars), these customers stay in contact with families, colleagues and clients (selectively, of course).

NEW LEGO
MARKET SPACE

One way to describe Lego's market space, made up of the convergence of toys, education, interactive technology, entertainment, computers and consumer electronics, is *total family edutainment* (see Figure 2). A Lego executive expands:

> *Just having the interactive technology without the learning is no good for parents. Learning without the entertainment and fun, kids will resist. Toys that don't use interactive technology are no good because the computer has become the greatest learning tool for kids and they love it. Interactive technology without the ability to be creative and enjoy yourself will turn kids off. And virtual without a more physical form of entertainment will bore them. Our business is now about how to merge all of this together in our offerings for our customers...*

To capture increasing shares of spare time from kids and their families in this *total family edutainment* market space, Lego has stretched its brand beyond children and toys into Lego parks. One is being opened every three years around the world and by the year 2050 the plan is that most of the planet's population will be within half a day's drive of a LegoWorld theme park. Packed with rides and giant detailed models, the object is to make the Lego brand more prevalent in world markets for adults and their children throughout their life stages. To attract customers at as early a stage as possible, the company even includes gentle rides to attract three- to five-year-olds, who, it says, are too young for many of Disney's attractions.

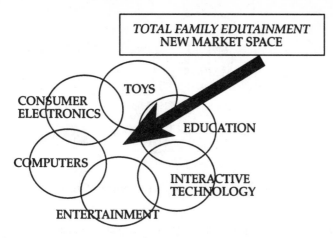

Figure 2 Lego – convergence map for total family edutainment market space

Another part of Lego's strategy has been to create and dominate activities in the newly created *home learning* sub-market space, a micro-territory of *total family edutainment* (see Figure 3). This sub-market space merges learning and playing in the home, largely possible because children who enjoy Lego also like computing and programming. Says CEO Kristiansen:

HOME LEARNING SUB-MARKET SPACE

> *It's the same way of thinking – constructing and creating. Parents want to stimulate their children instead of just having them sit at the TV or play games. And children can have fun but learn how to do something specific and, if it doesn't work, they can keep figuring it out until it does work. It teaches them to think, program and problem solve while they're having fun in their spare time.*

Lego has been customer originating on a number of innovative fronts in order to try to dominate activities in this new *home learning* sub-market space. Through work with MIT's Media Laboratory spanning a decade or more, it has brought together the virtual and physical world for kids with its intelligent brick, combined with interactive software.

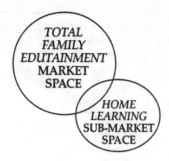

Figure 3 Lego home learning sub-market space

Kids (including the hitherto unserved females, to whom this also appeals) build their models and program them to act in a certain way. If the model does not behave as they want it to, they reprogram it until it does. They thus learn how to build programs and how to go through a series of tasks to find solutions, while still having fun.

A model could, for example, get players in an ice hockey game to find the pockets that will take the correct color ball – accept it if it does, or reject it if the color doesn't match. Or the children can program a car to stop when it gets to the edge of a table, or build a bird feeder that takes pictures of certain birds. It is also perfectly possible for a young person to be in, say, Paris and control an Internet penpal's Mars Rover model in Boston, over the Internet.

Families and schools bring children to several 'Learning Centers' around the world, where they learn to build and program their own robots. Special chat pages on the Internet enable these young customers from all over the globe to share their experiences. The intention is to have a virtual community of Lego alumni, thereby getting young customers to lock on to the Lego brand to get the exponential and cumulative benefits of making them customers for life.

HEALTHY
CONVERGENCES   There are of course many other examples of convergences in industry, technology and lifestyle where energy, time, money and effort are going into strategies to create

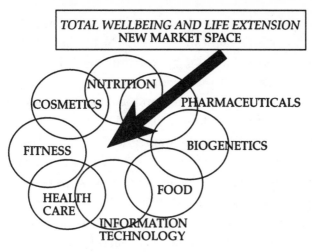

Figure 4 Convergences map for total wellbeing and life extension management market space

new market spaces and dominate activities within them, specifically with a view to leveraging from new wealth dynamics. For instance, the *total wellbeing and life extension* market space comes from the convergence of a variety of industries, lifestyles, technologies and demographics (see Figuₗe 4).

Several new industries have sprung up due to two or more mergings in this map, such as cosmeceuticals (cosmetics and pharmaceuticals); nutriceuticals (nutrition and pharmaceuticals); genetic diagnostics (biogenetics and information technology); functional foods (organic food, nutrition and biogenetics); telemedicine (self-diagnostic products and services for such things as HIV identification); bioinformatics (the processing and presentation of vast quantities of medical data on an individual), and so the list goes on...

Companies are taking advantage of this merging which, together with baby-boomer demographics, is producing infinite opportunities to sell products and services that focus on the personal happiness and wellbeing of the individual, not just illness. They range from what was previously frowned on – banishing fat, improving sexuality, making hair grow and lifting flab – to products that stop age-related degeneration, by growing new blood vessels, restoring joints and preserving (and growing?) organs, in order to keep people looking and feeling fit and well into the decades that used to be called old age.

Corporations will make money from these products in the short term. But they are still just the core items, vulnerable to better/cheaper core items when these come along. It is more ambitious and competitively durable to become *the* standard for *new ways of keeping people looking and feeling healthy* over their lives, in the *total wellbeing and life extension management* market space, and then getting customers to lock on. Once lock-on is established, it makes it difficult for others, no matter how compelling their offer, to compete.

This takes more.

PART FOUR

GETTING IN SOONER, STAYING IN LONGER

CHAPTER 11
OPPORTUNITY MANAGING IN THE CUSTOMER ACTIVITY CYCLE

THERE ARE MANY EXPLANATIONS FOR WHY AND HOW IBM LOST its market power in the late 1980s and early 1990s. Here is mine. Andersen Consulting spent months with a corporate customer, participating in and analyzing its strategy. Software houses like Microsoft and EDS had been working on a customer's systems for weeks, getting to know its business processes and users. By this time, the best IBM could hope for was to get orders based on price and specification for its core items.

Maintenance and repair, though earning millions through technical service warranties, was still considered a mundane and dull place to be; one executive described it as the *'dungarees and spanner brigade'*. It was all about reactively *'waiting for a problem to be solved, rather than proactively making things happen'*. It has become routine and reactive, indifferent to customers, and this allowed third-party newcomers – lean, keen and mean – to get into vital activities in the 'customer's space', offering services like installation, training and online recovery.

Put differently, IBM lost out because instead of customers getting increased value from its increasing size, they got less value – diseconomies and complacency had set in. With relationships wearing down over the years, it became increasingly difficult for the corporation to hold on to its existing customers or attract any new ones. So, inevitably, the spiral of diminishing returns set in.

For a corporation to get the positive reinforcing loops that produce the increasing returns of customer capitalism depends on its ability to link benefits and deliver a totally integrated experience to its customers over time. This is the next principle to note (see Table 8).

The strategies of the new enterprise increasingly reflect this. For example, Virgin's venture into banking (also with the Royal Bank of Scotland) is an attempt to give people who are 'in the red' lifelong event cash-managing facilities over the various stages of their lives. It aims to save them time, energy and money on a variety of fronts. The 24-hour telephone banking operation covers several products and services, all of which were previously bought from different sorts of vendors, all doing their own thing. Not only did customers suffer all the inconveniences, inconsistencies and irritations of having to deal in this way, but, according to Virgin, customers with significant borrowings and savings rarely got the best financial deal.

A loan from Virgin is designed around a mortgage but, unlike standard product home schemes, Virgin allows customers to pay for all their financial transactions over their lifetime. This is not just mortgage repayments but includes the payment of bills, credit card accounts, standing orders, direct debits, salary transfers and deposit account savings.

This saves stress, time, effort and money, because a single variable rate is calculated daily and charged monthly. There is no tax to pay while the customer is in net debit, because they are borrowing rather than saving. Virgin executives say that over 25 years, a customer with an income of £50,000 and a mortgage of £100,000 could gain £125,000.

The customer activity cycle tool

The customer activity cycle is a methodological tool that gives structure to the process of deciding on the value adds needed to link benefits. In so doing, it seeks to provide

	TRADITIONAL CAPITALISM PRINCIPLES	CUSTOMER CAPITALISM PRINCIPLES
1 AIM	Maintaining the status quo	Fundamentally transforming
2 LEADERS	Replicating and improving products and/or services	Finding new ways of doing things for and with customers
3 INNOVATION	Inventing new technologies	Originating for and with customers
4 OBJECT	Optimizing margins on unit transactions	Maximizing the time value of customers
5 MEANS	Increasing market share in product/service categories	Dominating activities in market spaces
6 VALUE	Making and moving more core items	Linking benefits in an ongoing integrated experience

Table 8 Principles of traditional and customer capitalism

customers with one integrated experience, vital for achieving customer lock-on. The methodology involves looking at the various activities that customers go through, or could/should go through, to get the results that they want in a market space or sub-market space. (We could, if we wanted to, regard a market space as an aggregation of all the customer activity cycles in a particular segment.)

These critical activities that customers go through to get the result in a defined market space or sub-market space fit a well-researched, generic model that consists of three stages:

➡ **Pre** the experience, when the customer is deciding *what to do* to get the result.
➡ **During** the experience, when the customer is *doing it.*
➡ **Post** the experience, when the customer is *maintaining the result or keeping it going – reviewing, extending, upgrading and updating.*

In a customer activity cycle exercise, these questions should be addressed:

A CUSTOMER ACTIVITY CYCLE EXERCISE

1. What are the critical activities customers go through, 'pre', 'during' and 'post' experience, to get the results they want in this market space?
2. What are the opportunities for adding value at each critical point: 'pre', 'during' and 'post' experience?

The following example demonstrates an IBM banking client's activity cycle, in the *global electronic networking capabilities* market space (see Figure 5). It depicts the critical value points that these banking customers go through to get the networking result that they are after.

Eliminating value gaps

The significant point is that any interruptions in the flow or integrated experience create 'value gaps'. These open up access to innovative newcomers who get into the customer's activity cycle at critical points (see Figure 6). Here they establish vital links and relationships, build reputation and trust, and open up new opportunities for doing more and new business with customers. This is the last thing that any company (or industry) which wants customer lock-on needs, but it is what happened to IBM in the 1980s and it

Question (1): What are the critical activities customers go through, 'pre', 'during' and 'post' experience to get the results they want in this market space?

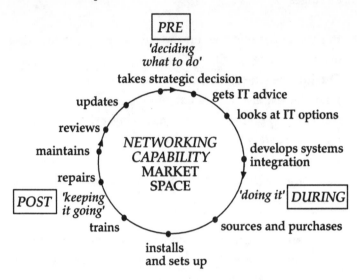

Figure 5 Customer activity cycle for IBM customer in the global electronic networking capability market space

continues to plague corporations (and industries) trapped in the old capitalism model.

So, for example, we have seen Virgin moving into these value gaps in airlines, banking etc., or supermarkets offering withdrawal services at a place or time when or where customers need cash, and even broadening their services to taking deposits at checkout tills, as South Africa's Pick & Pay does, offering above current interest earning rates plus allowing customers to pay their utility bills at checkout tills.

Avoiding value gaps and getting customers to lock on over a lifetime is why Lego, which in the past had access to kids up to the age of 14 but then lost them until they had their own children, has now moved into the full range of activities in the *family edutainment* market space, ranging from parks to games, CDs and music to books.

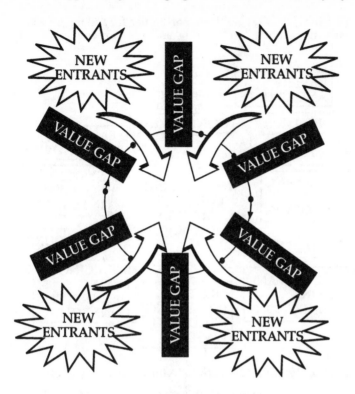

Figure 6 Value gaps in the customer activity cycle and opportunities for new entrants

This is why the super small 'Smart Car' for urbanites that Mercedes and Swatch have launched, mostly for singles who want trendy, runabout appeal rather than traditional passenger vehicles, is now being sold as a totally integrated transport system (way in advance of any government, although it is also not without its problems). Called the micro-compact car (MCC), it offers customers a plane or train ticket when needed for long-hauling between cities. It also includes a 'mobility box', complete with mobile phone, navigation systems and time schedules for trains and other forms of public transport. Additionally, airports have dedicated 'Smart' parking places, smaller and cheaper than conventional slots – all in the interests of avoiding value gaps and locking competitors out.

SMART MOVES
BY 'SMART CAR'

Question (2): What are the opportunities for adding value at each critical point, 'pre', 'during' and 'post' experience?

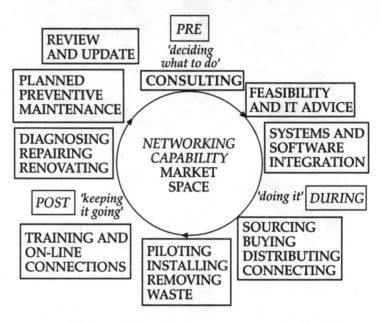

Figure 7 Value adds in the customer activity cycle for IBM customers in the global electronic networking capability market space

A NEW BLUE   The same reasoning is behind Louis Gerstner and his team's creation of a 'New Blue', fiercely attacking new challenges by innovating to produce added value at each critical point on the customer's activity cycle. It thereby ensures that customers get the results that they are after – not just the core items that anyone else can supply (see Figure 7) – and IBM gets customers to lock on.

Looking clockwise at Figure 7, from the top of the customer activity cycle, a bank approaching IBM starts by trying to figure out where it is going strategically and the various capabilities it needs. Given new technology, the object is to get networking power to employees and machines in the bank, or to customers direct, so as to deliver superior value in both content and contact terms.

For this, IBM offers consulting advice, followed by software and data-management services with specific features. These are designed to enable people and machines to interact as one system, integrated and inter- and intra-networked to give end users service and support across the world. The bank then looks for and purchases the actual hardware, for which IBM offers sourcing, buying, connecting and installation services, plus training (a huge proportion of downtime is still caused by the business system and people, rather than the equipment itself).

IBM has invested in making its old product-maintenance unit a proactive leader in planned, preventive and remote repair and maintenance in the 'post' stage of the customer activity cycle. This is because ongoing use of the network is essential, and huge opportunity costs can arise from an interruption. IBM offers instant recovery services when and where failure does occur, so that customers do not have to go to different parts of the IBM organization or hop from one supplier to another.

Customers need constantly to review, scale up, expand, develop and update, given advances in strategy, technology and applications. All this must be done without losing on previous investments. IBM's involvement here ensures the smooth transition of the relationship from one cycle to the next.

Getting rid of value gaps by adding value at each critical point on the customer activity cycle produces new ways of doing things for and with customers and engenders the positive feedback loop that reinforces relationships and keeps killer entrants out (Figure 8 sketches this conceptually). It is this that enables the new enterprise potentially to get the far-reaching and exponential effects of customer capitalism.

If we look at Richard Branson, he has taken advantage of the value gaps in the customer experiences in several industries to win them over and lock them on. In travel management, Virgin is challenging the diminishing returns, capacity-managing algorithm of taking people from *A* to *B*.

VIRGIN
TRAVELING
HIGH

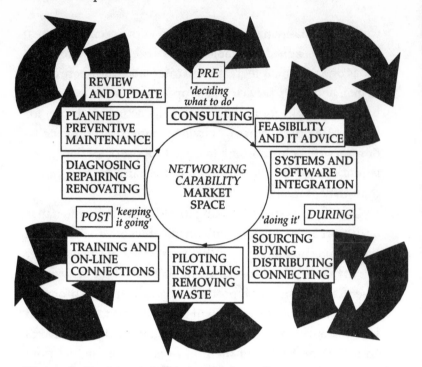

*Figure 8 Positive reinforcing lock-on from an
integrated IBM customer experience*

It is doing this with innovations and a continuous attempt to
provide customers with services that integrate their transcon-
tinental business and personal travel experience. It began
with limobikes that sought to get customers to and from
Heathrow Airport more quickly. Then more services were
added on board, including the airline's high-profile in-flight
tailoring for passengers traveling to Hong Kong. These passengers stayed three days on average – not long enough to
have a suit made – but passenger measurements are taken
during the flight and the information faxed to tailors in Hong
Kong, fittings are arranged while the customer is there, and
the finished product is delivered to the return flight.

Virgin is now in trains in the UK, trying to overcome the
problems that have beset the UK rail system so as to rival
the crowded motorways with more and faster trains. In airports like London's Heathrow, Boston's Logan, New York's

JFK and Newark and Washington's Dulles International, in concert with limo companies, Virgin takes business-class passengers to the airport free of charge, checks them in and issues an invitation to the Club House lounge en route. At a drive-in check-in specially designed for Virgin, a porter asks security questions, collects the luggage and issues customers with boarding passes. At the Clubhouse, passengers can take a shower to freshen up, have a free manicure and pedicure, facial and haircut, or take a hydrotherapy bath. The Lounge Games Rooms are equipped with bars, 'virtual' skiing devices, communications centers, libraries, music rooms with jukeboxes, roof-top conservatories and Clubhouse cuisine. Recent in-flight innovations include jacuzzis, showers, ship-style sleeper cabins, live TV and Internet-surfing possibilities to take the tedium out of long-haul journeys. The idea is to convert an aircraft into a flying hotel and restaurant in the future by making part of the cargo hold into sleeping, leisure, eating and exercise areas. What Virgin is aiming for is to reduce the personal space that business-class passengers have during the take-off and landing part of their travel experience, and to use the extra space to give them new services, like restaurants and lounges so they can walk around and enjoy themselves during the flight.

Branson gets much of the funding for the extra airport services from the leverage he generates from offering these extra services in the first place, because the looping mechanism feeds off itself. Virgin now has the highest customer-retention rate, the highest employee productivity level and one of the lowest costs per employee in the industry, though it attracts high-caliber staff. It pulls full economy and even first-class customers from other airlines to its business class. In addition, its brand has gained such broad prevalence that it has enabled the explosive growth of Virgin group activities across industries at very low customer-acquisition costs. (The group now has hundreds of companies with a combined turnover of billions of dollars.)

This is not the traditional capitalism conglomerate model of a corporation with some sidelines. Virgin's primary market is the same group of customers. What Branson is trying to do is to foster increasing returns, giving customers a high-quality total experiences and leverage off the depth of their spend over time. Revenues per customer are still rising, as are profits, and Branson continues to stretch the brand to get maximum breadth and diversity from customers' overall spend. In theory, this can succeed for as long as people keep getting the results that they are after from the Virgin brand.

CHAPTER 12
ON HIGHER GROUND

By 1998, THE ROYAL AUTOMOBILE CLUB (RAC) ALREADY HAD tens of thousands of people who were not members regularly accessing its traffic information on the Internet. Though in traditional terms those accessing its information may not have been members of the breakdown services club, they were touching the RAC brand. For the RAC this was an ideal way to make it into a subscriber community with lifelong prospects.

Its reasoning was that, with today's youth inclined to Internet browse, greater numbers of young people will be touching its brand electronically before they actually become vehicle buyers or drivers. This is how the RAC intended to capture this future market, way before they become eligible motorists. Whenever the customer encounters the RAC via its Web site, a bonding takes place which can create customer lock-on if cemented through high-quality content and contact. The enterprise can leverage from this, selling these individuals the various services they will need over their lifetimes in their journey-managing experiences.

TAKING A RISK EARLY ON

This is what motivated CEO Neil Johnson's decision to buy the British School of Motoring (BSM) – the largest in the UK and the RAC's first acquisition in 100 years. The object was specifically to make the driving school the beginning of a lifelong experience with the RAC for the young, making them part of the installed customer base and growing their value over their lifetime. About 700,000 learners pass their tests at the BSM every year out of an annual UK total of 1.6 million applicants. Also offered are virtual simulators with which learner drivers can be introduced to skills before they even have a license.

This is an intriguing twist. In the past, conventional insuring standards considered the young to be too high a risk for the RAC. 'Better to deal with them when they turned 25 or so and were more stable and drove better-quality cars' was the standard industry refrain. The result was that the front, middle and back end of the customer's driving experiences were totally out of sync. This contrasted with Neil Johnson's objective – to bring the lifetime customer activities together in one integrated experience, getting the RAC squarely into the customer activity cycle sooner and staying in longer. He remarks:

> We say 'no' to the old logic – and get them younger, train them better and provide them with 'mobility life skills', adapting these skills to their lives as the technology changes as they move from the ages of 17–70. This includes accessing for them that information they need to enhance that part of their lives to do with journey management so they can get where they need to go depending on their circumstance cheaper, better and quicker. And offer whatever services are needed over their life-span to be and stay mobile cheaply and painlessly.

Getting in earlier, staying in longer

Much of the value-add opportunities for high-ground interaction, premium services and customer lock-on now come from the 'pre' and 'post' rather than from the 'during' stage of the customer activity cycle. This has made IBM, for example, number one in computer and high-tech services and a leader in e-commerce today. It sells more solution packages on how to get cost-effective results from computers or Notes, for instance, than the core hardware or software items themselves.

The following hold for the modern enterprise in almost every field:

➡ The ever-common, never-to-be-stopped commoditization of the core items, be they products or services.
➡ Difficulties in differentiating by traditional marketing means (i.e. product, price, distribution (place) and promotion).
➡ Customers increasingly demanding results.

These facts are shifting the action swiftly up to the 'pre' stages and through to the 'post' stages of the customer activity cycle. A value shifting is occurring both for enterprises and for customers.

Therefore, getting into the customer activity cycle sooner and staying in longer, as the RAC is trying to do, is fundamental to the long-term horizons and exponential goals of customer lock-on and increasing returns. Look at what Microsoft is doing in toys, or what Amazon is doing with Amazon.com Kids. In Microsoft's case it is a deliberate strategy to get kids accustomed to PCs and software (and Microsoft's software in particular) early on in their learning cycle. Microsoft is determined to do this itself, rather than let someone else do it and have it end up as the commodity software supplier. Amazon is also trying to get to know and lock on young customers as early as possible and benefit from the exponential effects of their lifelong value.

However, to get in earlier and stay in longer, the new enterprise needs to be constantly on the move and follow customers also on the move (literally and figuratively speaking). For example, PressPoint, another new start-up company working with Xerox, plans to deliver copies of titles like *El Mundo* of Spain, *Der Standard* of Austria and *The Times* of London to hotels in major cities of the world on demand, thereby following its customers on their global travels. The aim is give them their local news from home, rather than just a global publication. The stapled documents will be printed by Xerox's worldwide document management service according to each newspaper's layout and editorial pages.

The new enterprise also has to adapt its offerings constantly as customers develop and change or, in the case of business-to-business dealings, undergo major transformation or expansion. Only with this capability can the positive disproportionate gains from new opportunities for increased revenue and decreased costs be reaped, which can further multiply as trust and relationships are strengthened over time. Information and expertise provided sooner rather than later more often than not give the customer a superior result, saving them money in the long run, further reinforcing positive looping.

PREDICT, PRESERVE AND PROLONG
Some of the value shift has to do with the predict, preserve and prolong theme pervading many market spaces as customers want ongoing results without having to forfeit the cost of initial investments. Even in cars, manufacturers are talking about updating increasing portions of the vehicle, particularly the intelligent bits, rather than customers having to get rid of their vehicles altogether. In medicine, predict, preserve and prolong form the major thrust today, with R&D going into the preservation of cells rather than just the cure for a diagnosed disease.

For Baxter Renal this shifting of value and therefore time, money and effort was a very different approach from just selling more bags (see Figure 9 for a conceptual sketch). And its experience reflects other fields in medicine and hosts of other industries. Certainly it has been a major factor for the escalating success that Baxter Renal is enjoying. From its research, the company knows that quicker referrals lead to better outcomes for customers and less cost for hospitals. The longer the patient waits for treatment, the more acute they become and the more expensive per day. So hospitals can save by avoiding the horrendous costs associated

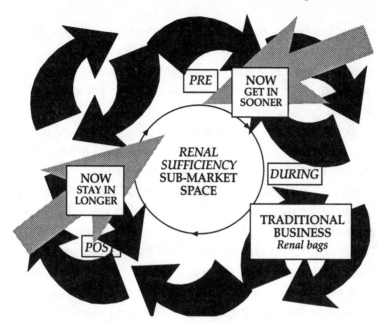

Figure 9 Getting in sooner, staying in longer, to get positive reinforcing lock-on for Baxter Renal

with the final stages of the disease if it is caught too late. Plus the faster the patient is diagnosed and referred as a 'planned' rather than a 'chronic' case, the better the chances of slowing down the disease, avoiding complications or the likelihood of picking up some other disease, and the higher the success rate with an eventual transplant. Additionally, if more people are diagnosed and referred to a managed treatment plan earlier, health authorities can get a lot more patients through the system on their strict fixed budgets.

However, research in Scandinavia (thought to be reasonably representative for Europe) shows that 50 percent of the patients that come through the system do so as emergencies and have to be treated as 'acute chronic', because they have not been spotted early enough. One reason is that they often go to a GP for whom renal disease is not a high-incident problem and it is therefore easy to misdiagnose or miss. Once they are 'acute chronic', patients have no option but to go on to HD, the competing dialysis bag, with treatment carried out at hospital. In contrast, of the other 50 percent of patients caught in time and treated as 'planned chronic,' at least 70 percent will prefer the PD (Baxter) home treatment.

For Baxter, 'pre' services – getting in sooner and intervening earlier – involved raising GP awareness levels, helping with early referral and diagnosis, training patients on treatment use and advice on lifestyle modification. Staying in longer at the 'post' stages has included home care and management of supplies (more on this later) and monitoring progress on a regular basis. This includes nurses taking blood tests and urine samples in the patient's home and doctors changing prescriptions remotely, machines in the customer's home having been programmed to facilitate this. Additionally, Baxter provides travel coordination including holidays (for which it has a holiday club) and reviewing patient cases in order to collect data, decide what it means, and build a knowledge base from which the whole renal community can gain.

TRAVEL IN A NEW MARKET SPACE   Advanced technology enables the new enterprise much more readily to gain access to customers, 'pre' and 'post' in their activity cycle, which is partly what is driving the value shift. Look at the travel industry. Worldwide figures point to more and more revenue coming from the 'pre' stages, when customers are looking for information, rather than from the traditional, highly commoditized booking business. Airlines that previously paid significant commissions to travel agents are now paying half to Internet counterparts like Microsoft's Expedia, now one of the top travel agencies in the US, and customers get a better integrated service.

To break out of their commodity mode some travel agents, like American Express (AMEX) Travel, are moving into these 'pre' and 'post' stages in a big way, especially for corporate customers (60 percent of world travel business). They manage the entire experience rather than just handling reservations.

They assist with total budget planning, negotiate the fare structure, buy tickets in bulk and pass on the ensuing discounts, handle car-rental contracts, monitor employee compliance with company travel policies, and manage total travel expense accounting, offering one expense report instead of a series of bills which, for many of their customers, represents substantial savings in time, money and effort.

Getting on to higher ground

Getting in sooner doesn't just mean an earlier intervention in the customer activity cycle by salespeople or more distribution or promotion to fight trivial battles, with traditional competitors ultimately reverting everyone to the *status quo*. It is a whole new way of pushing forward, looking at the role of the enterprise, what it offers, when, how and with whom. It involves deliberately creating discontinuities early on so that a standard for a new way of doing things is brought about in the interests of getting a superior result at low delivered cost to customers. These individuals then lock on to a corporation, which is able to extract the exponential gains from opportunities, presence and influence throughout the customer activity cycle over time – the dramatic lesson learnt by, and from, IBM.

Let's go back to the *renal sufficiency* sub-market space. Pushing still further into the 'pre' stage to get customers diagnosed earlier and more swiftly could mean investments in new ways to identify symptoms. This could include early genetic testing, self-diagnostic kits, the creation of clinics specializing in renal diagnosis (which could be done in any visible high street area or venue such as the allergy-testing service done in Safeway stores with Unichem chemists) and generally making patients aware of early warning signals, through training at school or on the Web. Waits between diagnosis and treatment, caused by supply and demand

PREVENTION IS BETTER THAN CURE

restrictions at hospitals, could be overcome by the introduction of new mobile units in which doctors could perform the needed functions at any time or in any place. The point is that either Baxter drives or provides these innovations or someone else will, which would relegate Baxter to the diminishing returns model of selling the cheapest bags.

Getting on to the 'pre' and 'post' high ground is part of the new business model's challenge, without which customer lock-on is almost impossible. To accomplish this, corporations need a new and constantly innovative approach, able very quickly to build, buy or partner into the expertise needed. Of course, they not only have to learn to do different things but must also acquire influence in ways and with people with whom they may never before have had to deal. How to gain access to the correct people becomes a key part of the challenge. Having made their contacts and invested in capabilities at the 'during' stage of the activity cycle (mostly about selling and supplying the core items), firms often find that they know the wrong people in the customer organization; or, rather, they are not able directly to influence those taking the decisions early on. Getting on to the high ground invariably involves matching their employees with counterpart employees in customer organizations and senior executives with customer senior executive counterparts. This is difficult to accomplish unless heads and hearts are in sync with new customer capitalism horizons.

CHAPTER 13
THE NEW ELECTRONIC GO-BETWEEN SERVICE PROVIDER

DESPITE PREDICTIONS THAT THE INTERNET WOULD MEAN THE END of the middleman, disintermediation being the obvious path, the World Wide Web has made possible the meteoric rise of a new global 'middle role' – the powerful and potent electronic go-between service provider. This can fill important value gaps in the customer activity cycle and create others where no access points or contact ever existed before. By undermining traditional forms of competition, these enterprises have opened up opportunities hitherto unseen or unattainable, reshaping industries and turning the tables on several traditional players and their play.

The magic of networks

One reason that these enterprises have been able to grow and thrive is that they, like many other organizations today, leverage from network effects, or network externalities as they are sometimes referred to. The value of a network depends on how many people or machines (collaborating around a particular technology) are connected to it. Think of it this way: when two phones are connected there is only one possible connection between parties; when three phones are connected that one connection jumps to three.

The tendency for a network to explode in value has come to be known as Metcalfe's Law (after Bob Metcalfe, the engineer who invented the Ethernet, the precursor to the

Internet). Mathematicians have actually proved it: the sum of a network increases as the square of the number of its members.

Customer capitalism doesn't just take advantage of the arithmetic; it also states that networks, i.e. people and machines connected, should produce linked benefits for customers, for it is then (and only then) that the true value explodes exponentially. Each customer gains from an infrastructure gaining in value. And each player connected to this infrastructure is able to extract more of the overall value pool.

INTERNALIZING
NETWORKING
EXTERNALITIES

The go-between service provider relies on this networking phenomenon. It works like this: the service provider wants to get as many active customers as possible online and locked on to its organization, which means that it needs as many relevant machines and people as possible in its infrastructure. This makes possible the connections which produce the superior customer value, which attracts more customers, which keeps enlarging and enhancing the network, which produces superior customer value and so on and so forth...

The *Wall Street Journal* is working with other news providers on the Net and directing customers with specific interests to these sites to gain more in-depth knowledge. Amazon has a referral system whereby it takes customers to and from other specialized Web sites that is now at the 200,000 mark for participants and growing daily. The object is that customers should be able to find exactly what they want irrespective of where it may be found on the Web, and that they should be able to access these sites constantly and seamlessly in pursuit of their specific interests. Starchefs is an example. Part of Amazon's giant network, it is intended to save the gourmet customer time, energy and money when looking for cookbooks.

Positive reinforcing loops at work

So here is the theory – the more the Amazon network expands, the more access customers get to books they may or may not know they want. Amazon then accumulates more information about them, so that access and offering improve, attracting more customers and more spend. This means that more nodes are added to the network, which improves and strengthens what is offered further, so more customers lock on – with upward increasing return potential.

But of course, it is not just the networking effects that get results for customers and increasing returns for go-between service providers. It is all of the loops interconnected and working together in one cohesive strategy. Let's examine this in more detail.

➡ The **relationships loop** is operative because of extensive and ongoing contact, which produces a high-quality personalized offering, locking customers on to the corporation, so increasing the depth, breadth, longevity and diversity value of their business.

➡ The **networks loop** goes into action because the more nodes drawn into the interactive online infrastructure, the more the infrastructure can offer, so the more value customers get, so the more they lock on, so the more valuable the infrastructure and each part of it becomes.

➡ The **intangibles loop** is triggered because the ideas, knowledge and information going to and fro enable more proactive and precise offerings and closer links with customers, so customers lock on, which encourages still more sharing of information, and spend.

➡ The **players loop** is reinforced because customers get products and services that link benefits through various parties working together, which increases customer spend, attracting in more players.

➡ The **developers loop** goes into gear as, seeing market acceptance, developers innovate, thereby providing increased innovation to customers, encouraging more market take-on, which attracts still more innovation.

➡ The **costs loop** functions because of low overheads and the new economics of the Internet, with almost zero marginal cost per extra customer (more on this later). In addition, the prolific use and reuse of intangibles lowers costs of production (again, more later) which, together with superior personalized value, strengthens the relationship with customers, so pulling down the cost of doing business together, which brings customers back for more, which reduces costs still further.

Abandoning the linear system

A NEW MIDDLE   The go-between service provider turns the tables on traditional capitalism modeled on linear chains. It demonstrates quite dramatically that corporations don't have to function in linear chains or be organized vertically in a single industry any more. It also demonstrates that a corporation doesn't have to own anything to make money. It used to be that 'ownership' passing hands down the linear chain was how corporations produced wealth. A 'middleman', or even several 'middlemen', sat between the company and the end user and passed this ownership of the core items, margins (and costs) down the line from one party to another, serial fashion.

The go-between service providers lodge themselves at the center of two sets of people – those who want something and those who have it. Amazon, for instance, connects people looking for reading material with those who have it. (Today it's the publisher and the wholesaler, tomorrow it will be the self-publishing authors and independent musicians.) Auto-by-Tel connects people looking for a trouble-free driving experience with a set of people who can supply this.

More than 'infomediaries', who collect and sell information electronically and about which a great deal has been written, these new enterprises use the power and potential of advanced interactive technology to integrate and deliver the total experience to customers.

To deliver the totally integrated experience, these go-between service providers deal with several different players. In Amazon's case it is publishers, wholesalers, retailers, transport companies, post offices, Internet media companies and so on. But like other go-between service providers, Amazon makes sure that the customer is bonded to the Amazon experience and comes back to it again and again.

The thinking of the go-between service provider is completely different from the thinking that moved the core items down sequential chains. Importantly, anyone situated anywhere on the present chain can do. As we have said, the wholesalers, or the retailers, or for that matter the publishers, could have done what Amazon did.

Interestingly as well, some manufacturers, for instance Toyota and GE, are using this same model internally. They have abandoned their traditional linear distribution and logistics system and now match any dealer and any retailer with end users. For example, to obviate a customer going to a dealer who does not have the car they want in stock, which results in the loss of a sale and, perhaps more seriously, the customer for life, Toyota has created a virtual centralized stock pool from which dealers can draw, behaving as though it has everything in its backyard. (The same principle could apply to anything branded, like clothing or cosmetics.)

INTERNAL GO-BETWEEN SERVICE PROVIDERS

Similarly, GE Connect, having got rid of the belief that 'dealers loaded are dealers loyal', has introduced a virtual inventory system, which allows stores to behave as though a full inventory complement is sitting in their back room. Costs are saved all round: GE saves on time and money on order enquiries, marketing and distribution costs, and gets valuable information on what customers are actually buying, instead of what retailers are stocking. Dealers don't have to hold stock or lose a customer. Also gone are the bulk discounts that led to holding costs, and the pressure that customers faced, often having to buy what the salesperson wanted to sell rather than what they needed. Goods are delivered by GE straight to end users within 24 hours, locking the customer on to its brand.

Key success drivers

Go-between service providers combine all the trajectories of our modern age to establish an accumulating advantage with customers. Rather than focus on making short-term profit, they set out to build market momentum, which, once achieved, results in volume sales and disproportionate gains due to the six loops of customer capitalism.

Importantly they:

Link benefits
Bezos, Amazon's CEO, originally defined Amazon's role as being an information broker in the *new way of buying and selling books* that he invented; but let's not oversimplify. The whole point about the go-between provider is not that it just acts as a broker for core items. To be successful, it needs to use its expertise to link benefits at each critical stage in the customer activity cycle, pulling together all the bits and pieces needed to get a superior integrated result to the customer at low delivered cost. This entails linking players and networks so that the customer can't tell when one part of their experience begins and the other ends. Auto-by-Tel doesn't just sell cars: it orders the vehicle, arranges to have the car delivered to the customer's house, does the financing and insurance and so on. If the customer opts to buy, the desired vehicle is found at the best price. If the customer hesitates, Auto-by-Tel helps them to make the right decision. *'Information is gathered and given,'* says Karl Nord of the

Scandinavian operation, *'until a customer's needs are assessed, a set of options can be generated, and the best choice can be made.'*

Have access

Amazon's literary library means that it holds 10 times as many more books on its screen, which are immediately available to customers, than even the biggest standard bookshop. Customers are no longer confined by what's 'in stock' or 'on the floor'. Amazon keeps the bestsellers itself and the rest are in a nearby wholesaler's warehouse. This is why Bezos moved to Seattle in the first place (it is the largest location of one of the largest book warehouses, Ingrams – a company which Barnes & Noble plans to buy). Having such access not only means that Amazon can quickly get its hands on 2.5 million books, but also that they can be shipped out in record time.

Take non-value out

Characteristically, electronic go-between service providers are less expensive than traditional business models because they benefit from the inverted costs of the Internet (more on this later). Their goal is not simply to cut costs; instead, they look to eliminate the non-value-add activities that they, others or customers engage in that increase price and may even detract from the overall customer experience. Having few overheads, even with shipping costs included, Amazon's success partly depends on whether it is able to match the largest discounts being counter-offered by others, by taking non-value out of its system. As a constant reminder that it shouldn't spend anything unless it leads to customer value, all desks at the company are made of old doors!

At first this goal was achieved by being virtual. A physical bookstore of Amazon's size would have needed a vast sales staff, distribution network and stock clerks. Teams of employees would have spent time, effort and money looking for prime sites, decorating them, promoting them

BEING
VIRTUAL
IS NOT ENOUGH

and doing various other interior and administrative chores which, Amazon reckoned, didn't really add value to the growing chunk of customers who wanted a completely different shopping experience. Now, with most stores having gone online, Amazon is constantly on the lookout to take non-value add out of the system, prompting the opening of distribution centers on the East Coast of the US and in the UK and Germany, to cut down delivery time as well as transportation and mailing costs. The next move in the battle of the books will be to get rid of those costs altogether, getting printed material directly into customers' homes and offices through the Web site in hard or electronic form. All in the interests of eradicating wasted time, money and effort, and giving the customer an improved result.

Offer competitive products

Go-between service providers offer the full range of product and service brands that customers may need. Take that away and they become direct marketing tools or sales outlets for corporations; which is what many franchises may be for manufacturers, but is not what these service companies are about. The whole point with them is that they work by the new model of customer capitalism: they give customers the range, the choice, the information, the multiple brands. They help them choose, if that's what they want, or they get the products and services they want to them when and how they want them. This is partly what drives their success, but they are also seen as impartial and credible, able to get to the customers not just their goods – in Amazon's case books, or the books it has in stock – but any book the customer may want or need.

Concentrate on value-add service and services

DIRECT SELLING OR AUTOMATION IS NOT ENOUGH

These go-between providers, who seek to add superior customer value through services and service to get customers to lock on, should not be confused with Web sites designed for direct sales or automated delivery. Neither should Web sites discounting core items be confused with these service concepts, where the object is to offer high value at low delivered cost to give customers good and sufficient reason to come back again and again.

Amazon got its lead because it found a way to add value to customers by taking the hassle out of buying books, i.e. getting to the store; looking for a book; waiting to be served; standing in queues to pay; lack of follow-up when books were not in stock; and when they were, having to go through the whole procedure again.

It also sold books more efficiently: it turns its inventory 150 times a year, compared with the three or four times of the traditional bookstores. Additionally, it helped customers search for a specific title, topic or author, or browse their way through a catalogue, or fill up their virtual shopping basket and pay by entering in their credit card information quickly. In addition, orders were immediately processed and mailed the same day. It quickly added new services such as information about when a book is due as well as advice and recommendations – a community of book critics from several media, including the *New York Times*, review books and interview authors. Amazon also has capsule descriptions of books and customer comments and reviews, as well as excerpts from other books by authors in which that particular buyer is interested.

As much time, money and energy are spent on service and building relationships with individuals as are spent on selling. In fact, according to Amazon managers, they go to greater lengths to exceed expected standards when a customer needs help on, say, a query title, a mistaken address and so on. *'Then the humans take over from the machines in full force'* – 20 percent of its staff do nothing but answer queries from its e-mail center.

THE HUMAN ELECTRONIC INTERFACE

Ideally, the electronic go-between service provider works to enhance not just content but also contact between itself and its customers. In the past, the only contact newspapers had with their readers was through a corner news-stand or letters to the editor. With strategies becoming increasingly electronically focused, the whole relationship structure that these firms have with customers has altered. Beyond having a Web site, the London-based *Financial Times* (FT), part of the Pearson Group, offers the complete range of information that its installed base of customers may need, instead of just what it prints. In the *global business and financial information* market space it has taken a go-between, electronic lead, consolidating its stature as provider of broad coverage, analysis and commentary for key business and financial decision makers. Customers are now able to be in contact with editors and journalists on a one-to-one basis, and through electronic debate forums on relevant issues they can also be in constant contact with each other.

Stretching the brand

Amazon is getting deeper and deeper into the *global information and knowledge discovery market space*. To this end, Bezos is stretching Amazon's lists almost endlessly. Authors can check to see how their new book is doing daily from a globally assembled listing, plus students are using the Amazon lists as reference sites (as one student involved with a project put it, *'It's so much easier than going to the library!'*).

Amazon is also stretching its brand into other market spaces. Using its all-encompassing customer formula, it offers CDs, videos, computer games and gifts, and is pushing even further into areas such as healthcare. And Amazon continues to invest in search companies, which provide the engine needed to find almost anything on the Net.

If the firm continues to work with the principles of customer capitalism, the more people will come and buy, and the more suppliers, authors and publishers will be attracted, which will attract even more customers and thus suppliers, authors and publishers. And the more customers buy, and the more information Amazon tracks and uses about an individual's tastes and interests, so the better (and cheaper) it will potentially become at building preferences into offerings, anticipating, adapting, extending and stretching its brand to reap cumulative and multiple benefits.

Through its Internet network (MSN), Microsoft is also stretching its brand into a number of new electronic services like broadcasting and news, travel, investing and banking, providing content and contact to individuals at critical access points in the customer activity cycle. The object? To become a go-between service provider and leverage from the reinforcing looping mechanism which brings about increasing returns.

For example, with Expedia Microsoft is in the forefront of travel in a market that is expected to grow multifold with Internet penetration and the arrival of new entrepreneurs who know how to turn the technology into an exciting new market. In the US and Europe alone, the value of online travel services is expected to increase from millions to billions, with customers able to get information on travel, make the correct decisions and the necessary arrangements more easily and more quickly.

EXPEDIA TRAVELING UP IN THE WORLD

Microsoft decided that it would provide travelers with the full range of information that they could either not get or not get quickly by telephoning their traditional travel agent. It launched Expedia in the US in 1996 and in the UK, Germany and France in the following two years. The service provides all the information needed to enable people to travel for business or pleasure, 24 hours a day, with data updated every half hour. It includes information from regional weather reports to arrival times, from illustrated guide books to the best ways to get to a particular business or holiday location. It includes different (and exact) prices and an insider's guide to the lowest published fares. On many flights, customers can pick the seats they want, find out if rental cars are available at any airport in the world and reserve them. Customers can pay any way they like – online or over the phone with a credit card – and tickets are delivered overnight.

Yet again, the lead has come from a new entrant rather than an established industry player. Though making quantities of difficult information easy for customers to get and use for travel decisions, 'pre', 'during' and 'post' traveling activities, was always the prime role for travel agents (anyone can sell tickets), the traditional players simply didn't come up with one integrated and global vision. So they have lost a potential lead. In 1998, for instance, independent travel agents in the US handled only 52 percent of airline reservations, compared to 80 percent in 1996.

Expedia had the vision. Travelers can get advice or make their own decisions. Because of its dynamic mapping technology, clicking on a part of a city within a price range produces a description of the hotels available in that price area and a room can be reserved. Not only do customers see comments made by the hotel on the Web site, but also comments made by guests. They can zoom in to focus on bulletin boards and get information ranging from local bus services to sales tax rates. By clicking on to Citiscape, Expedia's online, worldwide entertainment magazine, they can see what is on in each city in terms of sports, art, food, culture and so on as well as self-booking where relevant. Says Expedia:

> We will keep track of your past and future travel plans so you can review them at any time. For your future trips, we won't forget whether you prefer an aisle or window seat, a vegetarian or kosher meal. We'll also make a note of which airport you prefer to travel from. We'll keep a record of your frequent flyer numbers so you have them available whenever you need them. Expedia will be your personal travel assistant, remembering all your vital information so you don't have to.

PART FIVE

CUSTOMERS AS COMPETITIVE BARRIERS

CHAPTER 14
MAKING INTENTION THE LEVER

MICROSOFT'S
REAL
GAME ANYONE WHO IS NOT THINKING ABOUT MICROSOFT'S STRATEGY more broadly is missing the point. Expedia is another case where Microsoft is trying to become the standard for new ways of doing things – this time in global travel. The object is to use the reinforcing looping mechanism to get customers to lock on, offering them value at each critical point in their activity cycle, benefiting from the ensuing positive disproportionate gains over time. This is a quite different approach from product lock-in, which creates a monopoly through technical standards of discrete core items. Customers have no choice and are therefore captive, at least until the next new technology comes along.

This distinction is vital to the mind and spirit of customer capitalism, because with customer capitalism the only barrier to competitive entry is the customers themselves who want to do business with a corporation – now and in the future.

Like many others, Microsoft's relationship with customers used to be that people bought the core item – a box – took it home, used it, and then a few years later got another box. This worked in the past, but what Microsoft is now after is for customers to join the Microsoft network (MSN) and lock on to it, becoming part of an installed base. This enables the company to stretch its brand into many market spaces, creating prospects for both giving and getting value over time and ensuring exponential and sustainable competitiveness.

If Amazon retains its lead it will not be because of discounts or the services it is offering; these can and are being
copied. Retained lead will come from the new market and
economic dynamics of customer capitalism. Amazon is constantly able to produce a fully integrated and superior personalized experience for customers at low delivered cost. In
addition, the rapidly growing base of installed customers
that it has accumulated has consequently locked on to the
company and its brand. These customers stay longer with
Amazon and the offering becomes better, leading potentially to lifetime relationships.

Counting on an installed customer base

Customers in an installed base do not have to be electronically linked as in the Microsoft or Amazon case. Rather,
these customers – the installed customer base – **are those
people who want the firm or institution as their dominant or sole choice on an ongoing basis**. And they display
some specific behaviors to prove it, including:

➡ asking for advice (not necessarily related to your product
   or service)
➡ sharing confidential information
➡ inviting you to be involved in important meetings
➡ asking you to solve problems
➡ accepting your ideas and advice
➡ giving feedback, good or bad
➡ giving information on competitive offerings available
➡ discussing their future plans
➡ discussing options rather than discounts
➡ relying on expert contacts referred by you
➡ involving you early on in decision making
➡ allowing you to take decisions for them
➡ wanting you to succeed.

The reason for the last point is that if customers are part of an installed base and lock on to an organization, it is very important to them that the enterprise with which they deal stays in business and does well. This is part of the attraction, their intentions being long term rather than a series of one-offs.

Customer capitalism sets out continually to make more and more individuals part of this installed base, rather than transactional purchasers who come and go. This constitutes the next principle (see Table 9), making this installed customer base ever increasing, ever lucrative, turning advantage into greater advantage, success into more success.

DISSATISFACTION WITH CUSTOMER SATISFACTION

Whether we want to admit it or not, with traditional capitalism and marketing tools we were not very good at achieving an installed customer base. In fact, driven to achieve immediate bottom-line objectives, we often didn't understand, or care about, the difference between long- and short-term customer intentions, or know how to measure them in the way that market share was measured.

Customer satisfaction, we now realize, is a lag measure about something that is already past. It is no real indicator of a customer's intention to continue to do business with a company or institution and therefore is not indicative of a corporation's ability to compete sustainably. Research shows, for instance, that 60–80 percent of American customers who changed brands of automobile had, less than six months earlier, said that they were satisfied. Customers were often satisfied with what they were getting, compared to what others in that industry were offering, but it was what they were not getting that meant that they could be seduced by newcomers venturing outside traditional norms. So customer satisfaction is a passive state – a willingness on the part of a person to stay on until something else and better comes along. It is, therefore, no barrier to competition. It may make a corporation feel comfortable, but it can also make it incredibly vulnerable.

	TRADITIONAL CAPITALISM PRINCIPLES	CUSTOMER CAPITALISM PRINCIPLES
1 **AIM**	Maintaining the status quo	Fundamentally transforming
2 **LEADERS**	Replicating and improving products and/or services	Finding new ways of doing things for and with customers
3 **INNOVATION**	Inventing new technologies	Originating for and with customers
4 **OBJECT**	Optimizing margins on unit transactions	Maximizing the time value of customers
5 **MEANS**	Increasing market share in product/service categories	Dominating activities in market spaces
6 **VALUE**	Making and moving more core items	Linking benefits in an ongoing integrated experience
7 **TARGET**	For markets and average customer	For individual customers in an ever-increasing, ever-lucrative installed base

Table 9 Principles of traditional and customer capitalism

For some time now we have accepted the cause-and-effect connection between customer retention and financial metrics. Frederick Reichheld is an authority on the subject of retention and through his research has shown that existing customers are more profitable than new ones. He confirms that the average company still loses half its customers every five years because of poor service

RETENTION VS LIFELONG CUSTOMER VALUE

rather than poor products. He also shows that even a 5 percent reduction in the loss of customers can increase profits from 25 percent to 85 percent, depending on the industry. This figure applies to software makers and others in fast-growing industries, not just those in saturated markets.

The commonly accepted view of retention or loyalty can differ from the notion of giving and getting lifelong customer value, through customer lock-on, in some subtle but significant ways. If customer retention or loyalty is based on bringing customers back for repeat, discrete transactions of the same core items to augment market share in product/market categories to meet sales quotas, it is traditional capitalism and will ultimately lead to diminishing returns. In other words, it's a tool simply to get transactional costs down and avoid the replacement expenses of acquiring and cultivating new customers to make up for those that are lost.

If, on the other hand, retention is based on getting ongoing results throughout the customer activity cycle in market spaces, and aims to adapt, augment and update offerings as customer needs and technology evolve, it is customer capitalism. In addition, if it makes central the simultaneous goal of lifelong value for the customer from the corporation and for the corporation from the customer, then it is the new model and will get the customer lock-on that leads to increasing returns and longlasting success.

What matters to the firm are thus the prospects for obtaining exponential rewards by virtue of benefits that multiply as relationships get stronger. Offerings become superior through the sharing of ideas, information and knowhow, more developers innovate, players create linked benefits and networks get larger. In turn, the costs of doing business with customers are pushed down. As a cohesive strategy, this brings about difficult-to-imitate advantages and converts transactions into relational assets, which is what raises barriers to competitive entry and increases a corporation's worth.

In this context, most customer retention, and management's interpretation of it so far, has essentially been product driven, transaction based and just another version of traditional capitalism. Nigel Piercy describes it in his book *Market Led Strategic Change* as '*a mad dash back to the dark ages of marketing*'. This mad dash has produced plastic loyalty cards, club cards, frequent flier programs, promotion and payment methods, all easy to imitate and attack.

Even loyalty cards are not producing strongly loyal customers. In fact, some of the research on loyalty programs says that for repeat purchases they can actually have diminishing returns – the costs of retaining customers at some point outweighing the benefits. This is the case if all that corporations are doing, and customers are getting, is what they did and got before, reminiscent of the sales era in which, in the words of one Bain executive, corporations were '*simply bribing people to come back again*' – creating, as Piercy terms it, '*hostages*' rather than customers.

Therein lies a distinction too important to miss:

➡ With **traditional capitalism**, the object was to get customers back for repeat purchases of core items, making them captive or loyal to reduce the costs of transactions.

➡ With **customer capitalism**, the object is to make the enterprise the individual's dominant or sole choice, maximizing the growth and value extracted from customers by increasing the depth, breadth, longevity and diversity of their spend.

Changing the contours of marketing

Marketing's traditional role shifts dramatically with this distinction. Increasingly, it has become acknowledged that:

➡ **Products** in and of themselves cannot only be copied but are more valuable when they are connected or connectable to other products and services in order to provide customers with *linked benefits* than they are on their own.

➡ **Price** of core products and services matters of course, but it is not a competitive weapon. In any case, as customers get more and more information, price differences tend towards *zero*.

➡ **Place** (distribution) is more about how we get to customers and give them immediate *access* to us than where we place our goods for them to find and collect. New technologies enable customers to get access to products and services more efficiently, and more cost effectively, without losing intimacy.

➡ **Promotion** has largely moved from media monologue and broadcasting to *interactive dialogue* in which everyone can speak, listen and contribute. With this interaction, offerings can become more customer precise and proactive.

INFLUENCE WITH INTEGRITY
Retention or loyalty programs based on customers coming back for the same repetitive thing or cross-selling initiatives or mergers may increase corporate profits and performance in the short term. However, if these programs are launched without the express intention of linking benefits in a cohesive, integrated experience, they will not make customers the barrier to competitive entry. The programs will also fail to provide the enterprise with the long-term leverage that comes from turning relationships into the kind of relational assets that bring about increasing returns.

They will also not get the influence that comes from access to, and contact at, critical points in the customer activity cycle – be they face to face or electronic. This influence can only come about from the integrity that happens when customers who know more, want more, have more informed choice and participate more, get the results they want and expect to go on doing so. In other words, customer lock-on, and the resultant time value to corporations, rests not solely on building and managing the outward brand image, but on building and managing the total experience that customers get from the brand.

Customers are more powerful and informed than ever before because, for the first time, technology allows them to talk to each other. As more customers go online and chat, the firm becomes more transparent and less able to control its image or influence by traditional marketing means. Individuals can discuss what they feel and what they have experienced with other customers, regardless of geography. They may even have some common objectives and take on a power of their own. Stan Davis and Christopher Meyer in their book *Blur*, which considers issues of new technology, state that a day may come when customers charge for information about themselves, or do so on an organized basis as groups.

ENCOURAGING CUSTOMERS TO CHAT

With new networked technology, customers can influence each other. This influence can be positive, based on their experiences (or perceptions of their experiences), and customers are even forming 'fan clubs' that attract still more customers. However, this can of course work in the opposite direction. As Bezos of Amazon says: *'If you make customers unhappy in the physical world they might each tell six friends. If you make customers unhappy on the Internet they can each tell 6000 friends with one message to a news group.'* Being online is the same, he adds, as *'a restaurant which has to treat every diner who comes through the door like a potential reviewer for the Michelin guide.'*

Mirror, mirror on the wall

Making this transparency valuable is a real challenge. Though in principle the new enterprise is interested in *its* relationships with customers, it cannot rely solely on this. Relationships need to be built *between* customers, who

CUSTOMER COMMUNITIES OF VALUE

become virtual electronic communities, interacting and exchanging information and experiences. The new enterprise is not afraid of this. From business-to-business sales to fast-moving consumer goods, connecting customers and turning virtual communities to its compounding advantage has become part of customer capitalism's marketing weaponry. Citibank provides customers with chat rooms on its Web site so that they can share experiences and information, drawing themselves closer together and to the bank. Virgin does the same for its cola drinkers on a site it calls the 'Gas Room'!

Beyond a marketing ploy, the object is to get customers to form a cohesive group and create true communities of value, setting in motion the positive looping mechanism of customer capitalism. In Baxter's strategy, for instance, renal patients can learn from each other instead of relying on leaflets. Baxter acknowledges this, and has made this spreading of ideas, knowledge and information, which enhances value and pulls costs down, a formal part of its management systems. Through the Internet, doctors and hospitals are also linked into the Baxter Renal network, sharing experiences, information and patient data with integrative and exponential benefits all round (more on this later).

A LEGO STOCK EXCHANGE? Lego's customers plan and build models together and share experiences, which has the distinct advantage of making them feel 'part of the club'. (The fact that kids might begin to use the Internet to share or swap the actual products in the future is an interesting thought. If they do so, how will Lego deal with this secondhand market?) Amazon has become a rapidly growing virtual gathering spot for book, music, video and gift buyers. Members post up their views, are invited and encouraged to rate what they experience, give advice and supply other forms of content on the network, which gives the community a value and integrity of its own.

Customers in online or virtual communities also give voluntary individual or group feedback to corporations, which is new to most traditional organizations. However, the ability of firms to get a true reflection of themselves, and act on this, is an essential part of building the installed customer base that will take them into a durable future. Says Esther Dyson in an interview in *Harvard Business Review*:

> *[Now] the world can see organizations for what they are, not for what they pretend to be ... like seeing themselves in a mirror, it may at first be uncomfortable, but it is inevitable – and it might even prove useful. Those companies and business leaders who will succeed in the years ahead will learn to respond to feedback rather than crush it, and they will become adept at influencing what they can no longer control.*

CHAPTER 15
GETTING PERSONAL

THE LOGIC OF PERSONALIZING OFFERINGS SEEMS TOO OBVIOUS
even to mention, so fundamental is it that the new enterprise caters to individuals to get customers to lock on. This
means providing value for customers with individual preferences on a one-to-one basis, so as to bring a particular person back again and again.

What personalization is (and isn't)

BEYOND
SEGMENTATION

Not to confuse old definitions with new, let's for a moment
discuss the meaning of personalization.

Personalization is not just choice

Personalization is not choice in the sense that the corporation simply offers a larger number of products or services or
optional features from which the customer can choose. An
automobile company once tried to offer 87 different types of
steering wheels, hoping that everyone would find at least
one that they liked and would be happy with. However, the
last thing customers wanted to do was wade through a list
of 87 steering wheels!

One of the reasons that choice is not enough is that customer preferences are not always predictable; in any event
they change with different circumstances and evolve over
time. This makes it important that whatever the organization offers, it seeks to create flexibility, so that content and
contact can be adapted *in situ* and in real time.

Technology certainly helps to make this possible. For instance, UK retailing and electronic industries are joining forces to remove the frustration of clothes shopping due to the frequent mismatch between customers' bodies and the clothes they try on in the shops, or order by mail order or on the Net. Body scanners, able to capture the size and shape of individual shoppers, will be installed in stores nationwide. Customers can see themselves in 'virtual clothes' on a computer screen at the shop or at home before trying on or ordering anything. The scanning process takes less than 10 seconds and, once done, the customer can be fitted with virtual clothes, animated on the screen to see how they look or how the fabric changes shape as they move.

Personalization is about giving individual customers exactly what they need to suit their unique requirements

With breathtaking speed, online news providers, like the *Financial Times*, the *Herald Tribune*, *The Times*, the *Wall Street Journal* and *The Economist*, to name but a few, are increasing their global reach at minimum cost, enticing new customers by providing each day's newspaper story in an expanded form on the Web, with photos and graphics that customers can access at will. They also offer video and audio clippings that bring news to life for audiences and they include breaking news events. Stories are dissected for readers and are told from different points of view, in whatever medium that customer is comfortable with, and they can see color photos, get radio clips or special features if they want them.

On-demand TV services will increasingly enable customers to build their own 'personal channels' against monthly budgets and specific interests and preferences. And these services will be able to be updated by the server as it learns about viewers' reactions to selections made.

The *Financial Times* (FT) personalizes its Web pages to suit individual customer and country needs. News articles can be found in their original languages, searches can be done by sector, company, industry publication and region or according to specific requirements like competitive analysis for a marketing manager. Searching can be done by customers themselves, or by *FT*'s Business Research Centre, which boasts an extensive team of people who provide information on international business issues, encompassing everything from basic enquiries to in-depth research projects.

Multiple linking

The customer and newspaper company had only one link in the past – the news-stand on the street. Now there can be multiple links. Readers can interact with editorial staff, add their own experience, get exactly what they want to know in the format they choose, and be connected to special reporters or key figures behind a story.

The name of the new game is not just automation of the same old core items. It is interactivity, for which an entirely new approach is required.

Bill Gates elaborates:

> *One of the things you quickly learn on the Internet is that those stories that you just take from the newspaper and put up (electronically), people aren't very interested in. Stories where you get interaction and you say OK, under this tax proposal enter what your income is and see how it affects you, or type in your zip code and we'll show you they are giving out a lot of traffic tickets in your area. Things that are interactive and draw on what that person cares about, are great.*

Mercedes customizes interior and exterior bodies and engines all the time. But now its sports car also adapts its shifting speeds to suit an individual's specific and unique driving habits. It also accepts that no one car (or brand?) can cater to the diverse needs of all individuals, so in a 'variation' pool leasing scheme with Porsche, it allows a customer to drive any car they want, when and where they want it, to suit the occasion or climate. For example, a person may drive a Mercedes sedan during the week, use something more sporty for weekends, and hire a jeep for holidays.

In Singapore, Mercedes is working with condominium developers, selling them a range of cars to make available to individual dwellers as and when needed as part of the services of those premises. The cars are kept at the owners' location and are serviced by the manufacturer. Other dealers, like Daihatsu in the UK, allow customers to switch cars for weekends or special occasions, an initiative it has orchestrated via a joint venture with Avis.

The new Swatch/Mercedes super-small 'Smart Car', bought by customers for its size, can paradoxically have a distinct size disadvantage at certain times, for example on a touring holiday. Owners can get a larger car free of charge at a time they specify when buying the car, as part of the total deal. Alternatively, in another tie-up with Avis, they can get special discount deals on renting a larger car if and when they need it. And the manufacturer promises to change the color when customers tire of it, by the easy use of interchangeable panels!

Personalization is not just about the customization or mass customization of a product or service at a moment in time

Personalization is not just about the customization or mass customization of the core items transacted. Global Music Network (GMN) or Virgin Music let their customers mix and match what they want, as distinct from having a CD with set music on it. Customers can also talk to artists and play an instrument with them in their own 'jam' session.

A PERSONAL NOTE

Personalization is about giving individuals the content and contact they seek at each critical point in the activity cycle. Mercedes, pushing still further into personalizing offerings in the *short-haul mobility* market space, is looking to offer a set of products and services that will cover an individual's entire journey across the globe by land or air. For example, an air trip would include driving to the airport, parking, baggage handling and the connecting services at destination – all of which Mercedes would provide or ensure under this scheme. Offering a 'mobility guarantee' instead of an 'automobile guarantee', in 23 countries it provides 24-hour assistance in case of breakdown, including paying for hotels, repairs, taxis, rental cars or sending a customer in trouble to wherever they have got to go by alternative means.

In a sub-space of the same market space, the RAC is intending to build the biggest road traffic information system in the world. The object is to dominate the information side of traveler activities. Its Intelligent Transport System, which includes IT and computer-applied mapping, navigation and telematic systems, allows the best route to be designed for drivers trying to get from *A* to *B*, be they a Mercedes chauffeur or private customer. The RAC's information system is designed to offer advice on all travel planning and execution. The information is fed to and from customers in a highly personalized fashion, which includes personal advisers to individual customers through various access points, plus a body of 500 people on the phone handling routine questions, 24 hours a day. These employees can tell whether the caller is a member or not as they ring in, and adjust the amount of information or price charged accordingly.

HOMING IN
ON HOME CARE

Baxter Renal has, through its pricing policy, encouraged the personalization of prescriptions for solutions that go into the renal bag so that cost does not become a barrier to providing unique treatment to customers. Its state-of-art equipment in the customer's home allows doctors to change the solution remotely, depending on the state of the patient. All training and other services are highly personalized as well. However, it still considers its home care service to be its most important link to the customer, where the object is to establish individual relationships with individual people.

The patient is called once a week or more, depending on their needs, by the same person whom they first got to know. The driver – the person they see most often – 'becomes their best friend', someone on whom they can learn to rely, which is what a renal patient requires most of all – i.e. to know that their dialysis bags will arrive when they need them. To this end, promises made by Baxter employees are upheld with paranoiac attention, taking the needs of each person into account. Customer's keys are kept in a special safe so that drivers can enter a patient's home without disturbing them or requiring them to be home to receive a delivery. The driver sets up the machines, prepares the solutions, and does the carrying, storing, stacking and disposing of packaging, as well as helping with uncomplicated problems and installations. Stock is separated and rotated to avoid wastage for the hospital and placed in the home wherever it is most convenient for the patient. Says CEO Peter Leyland:

> *We go for one patient at a time. If we do the best for this patient today, we'll get another and then another, and if we treat each individual patient we are responsible for with love, and care, and attention, all the other things we are measured against come quite naturally.*

Personalization is not about averages, it's about handling different customers differently

The new enterprise handles customers and adapts its offerings depending on individual preferences (which are allowed to change) instead of expecting people to adjust to them. Direct Line thrives on this as a matter of policy.

TAKING OFF THE PRESSURE

Determined to move away from the stereotypical high-pressure selling of insurance, and to avoid making the customer feel captive or the subject of a sales pitch, its emphasis is on giving individuals enough information so that they can make their own choice. After the first call customers are sent a pack, phoned to make sure it has arrived and encouraged to ask questions if they have any, instead of having to study the fine print on the document. From one executive comes this remark:

> *If [that particular] customer at that point does not want any contact, then that is literally all they will ever get from us, other than their six monthly statements or annual review if they went through our advice service. We won't write to them or phone them unless they ask to be kept informed of other products, which incidentally most of our customers do.*

Acting on intelligence

REMEMBERING CUSTOMERS

With customer capitalism, personalization is not just about accumulating intelligence on individual customers (or selling it so others can sell yet more core items to them), but acting on it so that accumulated value is accrued. This can be passed to the customer, but ultimately it reverts to the corporation. Total knowledge of a person – getting to know them better and better – is what gives the new enterprise the edge.

Amazon made knowing who was buying its books a priority. In this way, it took advantage of the fact that no one – neither publisher or bookstore – in the traditional linear chain knew anything about end users. Says Bezos:

> *We know 2 percent today of what we will know 10 years from now, and most of that learning is going to revolve around personalization – the notion of making a (cyber)*

store ideal for a particular customer, not for a mythic aver-
age customer.

With a vast database of customer preferences and buying
patterns from its e-mail and postal address system, Amazon
can leverage from the ability to 'remember' people and treat
them as individuals. Returning customers are greeted by
name and offered a list of recommended titles based on the
books they have already bought. A search agent, called
'Eyes', e-mails a customer if a favorite author comes out with
a new book, or when something new appears on their topic
of interest.

Such personalization involves constant adaption and
extension of offerings. This requires an environment – face to
face, electronic or both – in which dialog and contact flow
freely, and there is constant innovation to make offerings relevant as customers (or the technology) change or develop.
With Amazon, customers can click in and add or change their
profile at any time, and their files are updated daily, to see
what they buy, for whom, and what else they have become
interested in.

This involves anticipating what the customer may want.
Bezos and his team are now working on building systems that
can help individual and unique customers who do not know
exactly what they want to find the book that may *'change the
world for them'*.

In the billion-dollar battle for biotech crops (controversy   FIELDS
aside), Monsanto aims to get cost-effective results for indi-   WITHIN
vidual farmers, individual farms and the individual fields   FARMS
within farms. You may remember that its object is to reduce
the risk of uncertainty in crop management. Everything
from the number and types of seeds and how and when
they grow to the personal needs of the farmer is taken into
account. What do they want to grow? Does such and such a
farmer want to do this even though it may produce a better
crop? Then Monsanto tries to maximize the outcome for a

particular farmer in a specific climatic and agronomic circumstance. Increasingly, as biotechnology develops, it takes this challenge all the way down to programming individual seeds to behave in a specific way.

No two farms are alike, so Monsanto continuously assesses the risk for disease for each farm, field and farmer as microclimatic conditions change. This entails simulating individual farms and fields within farms, exploring and validating predictions and the impact on each field, and as well the effects on each individual farm's income level. Building a model from quantitative research on soil maps and meteorological data, a detailed picture for each country can be simulated to explore and validate predictions instead of working with averages. Coupled with full financial analysis, net income levels are maximized for each farm, each field and each farmer in each country.

The Internet as a one-on-one medium

The new enterprise gets customer lock-on because it interacts with customers with the express purpose of learning about them and converting this learning into superior offerings on an ongoing basis.

THE GREAT INTERNET PARADOX

Internet technology makes this an increasingly easy feat to accomplish because, ironically, the global computer network of the Internet is not a mass medium but a one-to-one medium. It is as much a relationship revolution as an information revolution. It is a powerful tool for customer personalization because it enables the new enterprise to manage interactively part or all of an individual's online experience. The paradox – much to the increasing returns advantage of the enterprise which uses the principles of customer capitalism – is that while the Internet makes one-on-one relationship management possible, this can be done with millions of customers simultaneously.

Through an ongoing memory bank of information and dialog, Streamline knows customer orders, comments, preferences and changes in taste and circumstance. It endeavors to get feedback at the end of each shopping session and this is used to make daily changes. Deliverers are also expected to come back with information about customers' preferences and habits, or any piece of information that can help enhance the customer's reasons for staying with the company. CEO De Mello regards this behavior as essential to building the customer lock-on from which the time, money and effort put into establishing rapport and dialogue can leverage lifelong rewards.

Each individual feedback enables his people to give each single customer exactly what they want: '*We learn that they like starch in their shirts and that they want them on hangers. We learn that they like their bananas green. We learn that their children like to watch Disney videos.*' This information is used to continuously build better offerings. As Streamline gets smarter about customers' needs, shopping lists are updated, and knowledge about those customers is used to help it become more proactive and precise about individuals, thereby increasing its share of mind and spend in the *cupboard management* market space.

The Peapod global concept is an even more spectacular example of the use of technology to personalize offerings. The Parkinson brothers were determined to give a highly personalized experience to busy people who didn't have the time or desire to go to necessity-based stores. It is not just automating the buying of groceries, as many others are doing through home-shopping schemes; instead, its 'cyber shoppers' can have a virtual supermarket on their screen, reorganized by any category they want. This virtual supermarket can be organized by aisle, much as they would have in their regular store or according to their own arrangement, merchandised to accommodate what they like and are interested in. Alternatively, their cyber supermarket can be arranged by specific product category or brand, alphabetically by brand, by price or specials and promotions. Customers can shop by nutritional requirements, how much fat, calories, sodium or cholesterol there is in products, with shopping baskets automatically tallying up the customer's set quota.

SURROGATE SHOPPERS   Expert surrogate shoppers act in the stores for the customers, with specific directions on what to look for, choose and buy in the case of perishables such as vegetables, cuts of meat and so on. Comments such as preferences can be added to orders, for instance 'I only like ripe tomatoes', or substitutes in case an item is out of stock. Individuals receive menu-planning assistance and, when a recipe is selected, all the ingredients are automatically placed in their virtual shopping carts unless otherwise directed. Goods are delivered to them around the clock, at a time convenient to them, with coupons accepted by drivers on delivery.

CHAPTER 16
MOVING TO THE POINT OF ACCELERATION

TRANSACTIONAL THINKING, WHICH LED TO THE SELLING OF MORE of the core items that happened to be popular (or profitable) at a particular moment in time, resulted in the kind of volatility in banking that produced the diminishing consequences that we have seen in some banks in the last few decades. The good years were really good, but the bad years were terrible because no real customer lock-on was accomplished. Without this, corporations could not get into new revenue streams so they lost the market, and their good people, which led to the loss of even more market, and more good people, in a never-ending negative spiral.

Following Reed's global vision to have Citibank become the *'lead international financial institution in the world'*, serving the growing group of mobile customers, Ed Holmes, managing director of Citibank's corporate banking division, dedicated his team to cultivating lifelong relationships with customers. With an instinct for new ways of doing things and an eye for detail, Holmes not only set about making lifelong relationships the cornerstone of Citibank's business in Europe, but also tried to fathom the intricacies of what it would take to make it work.

GLOBAL
'CITIBANKING'

Holmes believes that each relationship must reach a certain point before the exponential benefits of increasing returns set in. The linear assumption on which traditional capitalism hinged was that you added a bit and you got something back. However, the case was that what you got back diminished over time until it became negative. With customer capitalism, once a certain point is reached – which I call the 'point of acceleration' – the enterprise gets customer lock-on and a cataclysmic or exponential effect.

Up to this point, the firm or institution must be content with diminishing returns. That is, for a while it will get out proportionately less than it puts in. However, once the critical momentum is gathered, revenues grow with remarkable rapidity, costs decline and returns arch upward. And because of new market and economic dynamics, the new corporation gets disproportionate gains on resources employed. The time this takes, and details of how to achieve it, depend on the nature of the business. Consultative banking is one specific example, but the principle is the important point here.

Reversing old logic

Customer capitalism is entirely opposite to the traditional model, where the classic 'S' or 'product lifecycle' curve assumed that return invested in a customer would be maximized up front (see Figure 10). It was reckoned that money should be made as early on in the relationship as possible because, when competition came in – as it invariably would – margins would go down, and there would be less and less payoff – diminishing returns having firmly settled in.

FLIPPING   Corporations were intent on maximizing the point on the
THE CURVE   curve rather than the sum of what was under the curve, namely the time value of the customer, the factor for which customer capitalism strives so diligently. The consequences were inevitable: salespeople moved on to the next customer quickly, and customers moved, just as quickly, on to the next supplier.

If we look at increasing returns, the curve (and the logic) flip. At the beginning of a relationship, there are minimal or even diminishing returns (see Figure 11). Thereafter returns increase disproportionately, with outputs (money) exceeding inputs (time and resources) at an exponential rate.

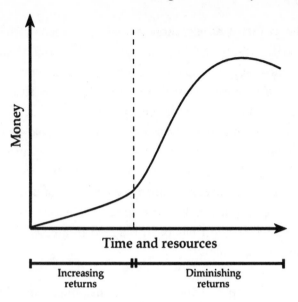

*Figure 10 Classic S-curve or lifecycle curve –
traditional capitalism*

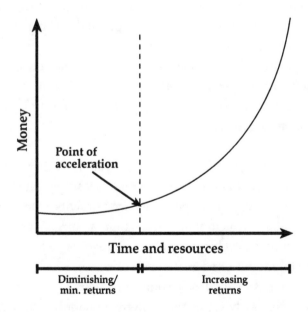

*Figure 11 Relationship investment curve –
customer capitalism*

The point of acceleration is reached because, through familiarity, trust, sharing and knowledge, the customer experiences superior value. As dealings become more complex there is more involvement, which the new enterprise, like Citibank, works consciously and conscientiously to achieve. The breadth and diversity of services sold increase, particularly the value-add services pre-, during and post-experience, which are knowhow and information intensive – for example, in a deal structuring or a merger or acquisition.

GAINS PAST
THE POINT OF
ACCELERATION

The disproportionate gains one can expect once the point of acceleration has been reached in a customer relationship are as follows:

➡ a greater depth of spend (selling customers more)
➡ more high-ground opportunities (higher value-add services and influence in the customer's activity cycle)
➡ more diversity of spend (cross-selling related to linking benefits in the customer's total experience)
➡ brand extension and stretch potential (selling to customers in several market spaces)
➡ opportunities for extensions, upgrades and new innovations (as customers and the technology develop)
➡ joint ventures and risk taking (commitment to new initiatives together).

Clearly, getting to the point of acceleration, which is when the new market and economic dynamics set in, takes time and money. Payoff on customer investments won't show immediately, which may mean that a special customer research and development (R&D) budget is required with time bought out of normal operations.

PROOF OF
CONCEPT

In the past, Citibank account managers were impatient to get sales early on in the customer relationship, judged as they were on units sold. Now, account managers typically spend a good deal of time with prospective customers, assessing new trends, giving them proposals and ideas and establishing 'proof of concept', before they try to sign up any deal. And the account managers are evaluated accordingly, based on such factors as:

➡ presence and upward mobility in the client organization
➡ involvement and evolution of significant relationships
➡ reinvitation, increased attention, time and customer interest in doing business with the bank
➡ fostering the customer commitment behaviors that we talked about in the previous chapter.

Crossing a threshold

All of this is like crossing a threshold, which is where Citibank aims its customer contact managing. When this is achieved, barriers to entry fall and access to relevant people goes up, as do relationships with customers. This is the ideal situation, which Citibank works to achieve in a systematic way. The object is to be present, get exposure, influence and contribute so that the point of acceleration is reached, at which time the enterprise becomes the customer's dominant or sole choice. (One interesting side issue to consider is that whereas in the past it was difficult to become the dominant or sole-choice bank, because most firms wanted to deal with several institutions to spread their risk, it can now be seen that as firms globalize, they look increasingly to a single financial institution to integrate the set of services they need across the world.)

CUSTOMER CONTACT MANAGING

Not only is this point of acceleration obtainable, but it is also predictable, says Holmes, because there are certain milestones and time horizons. The object is to move the prospective customer through these milestones to the breakthrough, then the relationship becomes largely self-sustaining. However, moving through these stages requires different degrees of effort; sometimes, once it has been reached, de-resourcing is feasible and can further reduce costs.

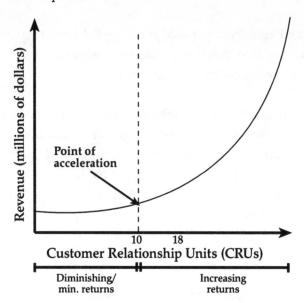

*Figure 12 The Citibank relationship investment curve
– customer capitalism*

The new enterprise is constantly aware of the time it takes to get to the point of acceleration, while also being aware of the signals that show, first, that it is happening, and, second, when it has arrived. While the object is to reach this point as quickly as possible, this isn't always realistic when dealing in intricate, face-to-face, high-ground services that take time, trust and a level of funding. Some enterprises, like IBM product support services division, deliberately concentrate on customers who have the highest propensity to build such long-term relationships. IBM consultants focus their time, money and effort on undertaking an ongoing series of engagements with these customers to achieve this end, managing the contact, and they are rewarded accordingly.

THE
TWO-YEAR
TUNNEL

According to Holmes, in banking this can take two years, what he calls the '*two-year tunnel*'. '*With a traditional capitalism mindset this two-year period may feel like a loss, but really it's a win.*' To quantify its relationship intensity with customers, Citibank has created a measure it calls Customer

Relationship Units (CRUs) which is currently a product/geography index: the more products the customer is taking in the more countries or regions, the higher the CRUs. Citibank measures the impact of CRUs on its global revenues in millions of dollars (see Figure 12).

For Citibank the first point of acceleration is around 10 CRUs. The next is 18 CRUs, though there are several other points where there is a quantum jump in relationship intensity. The lesson to be learnt, says Holmes, is this:

> *It needs sustained commitment, no short-term thinking will do. This includes selling the loans, which are basically commodities and on which no money is really made. But these service products are an investment in a customer growth factor, rather than an end in themselves. The customer expects this – it's what develops the relationships and the trust which builds the integration of minds and businesses that create the opportunities to get the long-term revenues and profits.*

PART SIX

NEW COMPETITIVE WHOLES

CHAPTER 17
THE ART OF CONNECTIVITY

READ ANY NEWSPAPER OR JOURNAL, SIT IN ON ANY board or management meeting, and it is possible to see that false boundaries still dominate conversation and reporting: false because they go against the natural progression of customer activities and needs.

Even in the relatively new, sophisticated high-technology industries like telecommunications, fixed and mobile have been kept separate. So, for a variety of reasons, top management in these industries have found their corporations' assets out of kilter with the new wealth opportunities coming from the merging mobile world of work and home. It is exactly what happened when Steve Jobs tried to make false separations between people's education and home lives.

FALSE BOUNDARIES PERSIST

Take the present set-up with air travel in Europe. Each player encountered by customers – travel agents, airlines, car hire, baggage handlers, airports, hotels, taxis etc. – still does its own thing, irrespective of the negative impact on customers' overall experience and the diminishing return consequences. As a result, airlines, despite now being as full as they have ever been, will be increasingly vulnerable to Euro-trains and teleconferencing in the future. This is not because of some major regulatory, economic, legal or technological threat 'out there in the system', or some business cycle downer they can't control, but because too little has been done to get rid of the incredible congestion, inconsistencies and value gaps that most customers endure in an airline travel experience.

And what about the world of medicine, where professionals are probably more dedicated than in any other sphere on earth? Each party – insurance, pharmaceuticals, doctors, specialists, hospitals, health authorities – does its own bit to its own highest standard to suit its own objectives. Each still operates as a separate entity, fighting its own battles and celebrating its own victories. Unless this is consciously altered, with corporations learning to connect with others to produce integrated results for customers, diminishing returns will live on. The question is: will they?

Getting rid of industry silos

But like airtight structures holding grain or missiles, industrial and corporate silos were built as closed systems. This old model still permeates management thinking, or it certainly seems that way. With traditional capitalism, units, divisions and countries were kept separate to ensure that a problem in one didn't contaminate the rest. Each could then be individually accountable and accounted. Separate profit and loss (P&L) accounts for different products, services, units or divisions within one firm aggravated the situation still more, causing rivalry within a single company for the same customer. This meant that firms lacked the coordinated effort and investment needed to bring about an integrated offering and customer lock-on.

BREAKING DOWN THE BARRIERS   The same artificial separation persisted between channel members organized vertically in single industries using traditional capitalism logic. Though parties in the channel shared a common end-user customer base that sought one integrated result, corporations saw themselves as distinct and they transacted serial fashion among themselves, instead of working together as one, customer value-delivering process. The next person in the linear chain was regarded as the customer; even then, parties often adversarially engaged to maximize their own welfare, haggling about price and bringing about overcapacity and discount wars, instead of together seeking to bring about the real value that end users were looking for.

The grand irony was that everyone lost. For instance even today, despite the dramatic rise in sales from electronic sites, car sales as a whole are still lagging in the US. Why? Because, according to research, while customers turn to the Net to avoid hassles and save time, when they go to the showroom they find the old problems: *'Dealers still shove them through the same process they use with people who come in off the street.'*

With traditional capitalism, companies from autos to air travel, books to banking compared themselves to others in the same industry silo, fighting to gain incrementally over those others on best practice, rather than breaking with convention and give the customer the experience they were after. That's how new, innovative entrants like Auto-by-Tel, Expedia, Amazon and Virgin Banking got in to reshape the ground and took customers from under the traditionalists' feet. For, as previous chapters have tried to show:

➡ Customers respond holistically – they don't care how corporations are organized, to whom they legally belong, how they are divided up, into which industry they fit, or to whom they report.
➡ Many of the new great breakthroughs for market creation and growth come from convergences between industries, rather than from an extension of a single industry.
➡ The only way to get customer lock-on is to provide integrated results within market spaces or sub-market spaces, which cut across units, divisions, companies, countries and industries.
➡ The biggest threat for corporations – that others will gain access to their customers and new opportunities – comes increasingly from outside traditionally defined boundaries and from new entrants.

LETTING
GO OF
INDUSTRY
DEFINITIONS Let's face it, industries are no longer a useful way to describe a unit of competitiveness. Neither do they help organizations make the mental leap from old to new ways of creating wealth. While old distinctions may have technical and even regulatory significance for corporations and governments, they are product representations and quite irrelevant for lifelong customer relationships and competitiveness. In his masterful work *The Death of Competition*, James Moore puts it this way:

> *The notion of 'industry' is really an artefact of the slowly paced business evolution during the middle of this century. The presumption that there are distinct, immutable businesses within which players scramble for supremacy is a tired idea whose time is past. It has little to do with what is shaping the world. The designation itself is simplistic, describing certain players better than others. But, in truth, the label is not much more than a crude grid used to compare and contrast businesses, a fiction conjured up by policy makers and regulators, investment analysts, and even academic students of business strategy.*

Working as one enterprise space

NO ONE CAN
WIN ALONE

The new enterprise working with the principles of customer capitalism acknowledges that no one can win alone because no one can single-handedly provide the linked benefits for customers throughout their activity cycles. The interaction of others is not only significant but crucial to success in a modern setting. Because of this, the new enterprise actively looks for participating players (what Andy Grove of Intel calls *'fellow travelers'*) with whom to connect. When all are closely integrated into one (open) system, these players become a single enterprise space, the new competitive delivering entity for our modern age.

Just as at a simple level an automobile manufacturer becomes stronger when superior services are offered by its dealers, so it is with these players. Connected together, they provide superior customer value in the enterprise space and all players within it get cumulative and compounding gains. Examples of players connecting are Amazon, with publishers, wholesalers, transport companies, couriers, other Web sites, portals and post offices; and Auto-by-Tel, with dealers, bankers, insurance companies and technical service operators; and Virgin Atlantic, with limos, limobikes, limoboats, travel agents, baggage handlers, lounges and so on.

The *Financial Times*, with its authoritative journals, news wires, trade journals, company information, industry reports, country analyses and market research companies, forms yet another enterprise space. And, by the completion of a single form on the Web, US-based Insweb, the largest and most comprehensive Internet-based insurance company, brings together various players to form an enterprise space so that customers can apply for auto, homeowner/renter, life, annuity, individual medical, short-term disability, motorcycle insurance and other coverage in one seamless customer experience. Additionally, it works with research centers to offer insurers data and assessment tools so that they can manage and prevent risks. For example, cell phone users can get a specific analysis of how their call activities and conversations affect their driving patterns, and what they can do to avoid hazards.

Enterprises – across company, country and industry – form the new economic wholes enabling the creation and acceleration of new markets and whole new industries, never before imagined, at a pace never before accomplished. In this one collaborating and synergistic framework, the ongoing design, delivery and support needed at each critical point in the customer activity cycle become the locus around which all decisions on mergers, acquisitions, diversification and working arrangements hinge. Participating players may be large, multifaceted corporations, or small businesses with highly specialized skills. They may be in

SHARING THE VALUE POOL

direct contact with customers on the activity cycle, or they may be supplying products and services to others who are. They may previously have been in related businesses, or come from industries or firms totally unrelated. They may be units, divisions or countries within a single company, or virtual teams who coalesce for only a specific activity when and where needed.

Either way, with customer capitalism, the object is to jointly produce customer value from which everyone gains. And due to the sharing of resources, infrastructure and knowledge and the reductions in waste – duplications of activities having been eradicated – costs are pulled down. So rewards grow exponentially, though the exact proportion clearly differs from one circumstance to another.

Any modern enterprise needs to ask these questions:

ASK THESE
QUESTIONS

➡ To what enterprise space does my corporation belong?
➡ What is its role in getting end users results in the market space in which we are jointly dealing?
➡ What is the total value pool to be shared by players in the enterprise space?
➡ How much of that can my company or institution extract?

Operating as one enterprise space, rather than working in bits and pieces, is one of the most important ingredients in a strategy based on customer capitalism to get customer lock-on, including having to choose the correct partner with which to achieve this and setting common standards of performance.

THE
DIRECT LINE
ACCIDENT

Direct Line, for example, wants people in its installed base to call it when they have an accident, for reasons other than just to make a claim. In this way, Direct Line becomes indispensable to customers when and where those customers need it. It makes itself present and visible to handle all the problems, and opportunities, arising.

This is what has moved Direct Line around the customer activity cycle into new services to offer accident repair in the *personal mobility* market space. Its repair center consists of 140 shops, and it basically has a set of independent players integrated under the Direct Line brand into one enterprise space. The customer calls Direct Line when they have a problem, the car is picked up, fixed, returned and automatically charged through their bank or card. Claims are made to the insurer by phone. Direct Line, as the lead company, has set standards to ensure that the enterprise space works as one. There are common, consistent and acceptable service levels, such as provision of a 24-hour recovery service; 24-hour collection and delivery to and from the customer's home; contacting the customer within 30 minutes of a call for help; and recovering the stranded vehicle within an hour.

The connectivity needed to give the customer an integrated experience is still foreign thinking to companies working with traditional capitalism. In contrast, it becomes quite obvious once the new enterprise embraces the principles of customer capitalism, though it acknowledges that there are well-recognized skills to be learnt and nurtured. The new enterprise must live beyond the corporation's own product/market categories; pushing for more new venturing and other reciprocal investments; forging formal and informal links and participating more in electronic and face-to-face networks. There must be more information, knowledge and value sharing along with conscious elimination of duplicated and non-value-add activities. They must master business–community relationships and design, setting and sharing common service standards and dealing with the ever-present contradictions of simultaneously competing and collaborating.

CHAPTER 18
LEADING TO WIN–WIN

CUSTOMER CAPITALISM, UNLIKE TRADITIONAL CAPITALISM, MEANS that a corporation's success is not based on the failure of others. The expertise and cumulative advantage developed by the lead company do not belong to it exclusively, because the new market and economic looping dynamics turn increasing returns into an opportunity for all participants. This is because it is only in combination that their behavior produces the value and cost advantages for customers that lead to positive and self-reinforcing rewards all round.

With customer capitalism, the enterprise forgets the adversarial, linear, single-industry relationships of the classic business model, recognizing that **a cumulative advantage with compounding benefits can only happen when several players from several companies and industries in one enterprise space are interdependent on each other to provide customers with results.** This results in a win–win for all contributing players, the next principle of customer capitalism to add to the list (see Table 10).

Interestingly, new genetics considers win–win to be the only way to succeed. Darwin's traditional evolutionary theory stated that the strongest species are those that dominate and destroy the others. New genetics says that the best genes – and therefore the ones that have the strongest chance of survival – are those that know how to work together.

WHEN AMERICAN EXPRESS FAILED   In fact, any attempt by one party to innovate and create the standard for new ways of doing things will fail unless everyone who contributes to achieving an ongoing customer experience is involved and stands to gain. American

	TRADITIONAL CAPITALISM PRINCIPLES	CUSTOMER CAPITALISM PRINCIPLES
1 AIM	Maintaining the status quo	Fundamentally transforming
2 LEADERS	Replicating and improving products and/or services	Finding new ways of doing things for and with customers
3 INNOVATION	Inventing new technologies	Originating for and with customers
4 OBJECT	Optimizing margins on unit transactions	Maximizing the time value of customers
5 MEANS	Increasing market share in product/service categories	Dominating activities in market spaces
6 VALUE	Making and moving more core items	Linking benefits in an ongoing integrated experience
7 TARGET	For markets and average customer	For individual customers in an ever-increasing, ever-lucrative installed base
8 UNIT OF COMPETITION	By units/companies/ countries/industries	With win–win for all contributing players in new enterprise spaces

Table 10 Principles of traditional and customer capitalism

Express (AMEX) did a superb branding job on its credit card in the 1960s, 1970s and 1980s (*'never leave home without it,'* said its advertising, and we didn't dare), but it suffered all the effects of diminishing returns because it failed to see what was obvious with hindsight. A single organization, no matter what its size or effort, cannot stand alone and exclude key players in the customer activity cycle, and still hope to provide the kind of long-term associations that bring about durable success.

In the AMEX case, merchants (other than in some select industries), complaining of higher fees and administrative hassles, didn't support the card so fewer customers were able to use it, so fewer merchants supported the card, so fewer customers wanted it and so on. This cost AMEX its lead (AMEX is the single largest issuer of credit cards world-wide but the Mastercard and Visa association of banks has much higher usership) and started it on a downward spiral from which it is only now beginning to recover.

The power to lead

WINNING THROUGH WIN–WIN   The lesson to be learnt here is that once the new enterprise space becomes the unit of competition in the modern economy and the object becomes a win–win for all contributing players, the notion of power switches:

- ➡ With **traditional capitalism**, power came from the control of others in the linear supply chain, or control (vertical integration) of the whole chain.
- ➡ With **customer capitalism**, power comes from pulling together and coordinating players into an enterprise space so as to provide a continuous, integrated experience to end users.

Had AMEX had this more interconnected customer vision, it may have taken on a completely different role and structure than the one it chose for itself. And the card industry might have followed a very different innovation path, an AMEX path, which would have fed on itself and prospered – instead of the competitive alternative.

Visa took the cooperative route and now has the single biggest installed base of customer spending power in the world. In new, exponential form, each player benefits from the joining of the next, which entices in still more players and so on. Visa decided only to be a skeletal organization, linking the operations of its collaborating members into one large, flat, cohesive delivery system. The brand was strengthened by the positive, generative behavior of customers drawn to Visa because of ease of use thanks to global-wide acceptance, the worldwide relationships fostered between members and card holders and constant innovation. (Founding chief executive Dee Hock says that because power is shared and distributed, new ideas can continually and speedily evolve, and be turned quickly to customer advantage.) Added to this were the networking externalities produced from the ever-expanding infrastructure. Characteristically, as more customers locked on, so more members came aboard in an ever-compounding upward spiral.

VISA'S COOPERATIVE ROUTE

As we already observed, IBM allowed the Microsofts, Ciscos and Andersen Consultings of this world to get into positions of power with customers, which is why these companies have been able to magnify their growth. IBM neither shaped the new enterprise space that would deliver the linked customer benefits in the fast-emerging market space, nor gave it life in the late 1980s and early 1990s. It saw the disaggregation of its collection of businesses as the vehicle for making money, while customers, deeply confused with the increasing sophistication of technology, wanted more integration, not less. Customers didn't care in the least how firms structured themselves, so long as they got the benefits they wanted. Once Gerstner articulated *global electronic networking capability* as IBM's market space, the various disparate internal and external organizational strands began to be pulled together and IBM's potential as a leading, global company was reinstated.

The power of one corporation does not exclude the power and prosperity of others in the new customer capitalism business model. In fact, quite the opposite is true and that's another reason that the meaning of monopoly has changed. As Kevin Kelly says in *New Rules for the New Economy*, the difference between the dangers of monopolists in the old world and the new is *'monovation'*, i.e. when there is only one source of innovation. This is definitely not the case with customer capitalism where no one can win or gain alone.

The role of the lead company

With customer capitalism, leadership may come from established players or from a newcomer, from new intermediaries who find gaps and lead where traditionals fail to jump or from established corporations engaged in a major turnaround. It may also come from one player or two. Individually or collectively, they become thought leaders and they see themselves as fulfilling a leading and indispensable role in the formation of ideas and in the formation and performance of the enterprise space.

Consciously they lodge themselves at the 'center', ensuring:

➡ a compelling vision as an anchor to parties who see (or are made to see) the dramatic value they can give and get in the market space and their respective roles
➡ that customers have no good reason to go looking for other products, services or corporations outside the delivering enterprise space
➡ wide membership of players (each exceling in their own microterritories) to achieve both size and richness, and

to make players feel reluctant to join another rival enterprise space

➡ that players know that in addition to being in the thick of existing business opportunities, they will also be part of the future because the leader is robust, can stay strong and is able to keep new entrants at bay by the continued enlargement and entrenchment of customers and contributors

➡ ongoing feedback and communication of ideas, innovation and plans – a feat that has become easier on a nationwide, pan-European or global basis through electronic networks

➡ the ongoing expansion and furthering of additional capabilities by players in the enterprise space to produce continuous, high-value and relevant offerings.

Another role of the lead company is to ensure that profits are reinvested in innovative ideas. These will manifest themselves in extensions, updates and future generations of offers that will bring customers back again and again and set the whole enterprise space ahead in a way that will make it difficult for others to catch up.

How LEADERS PAY

The leader often reinforces this role by making innovative contributions to the enterprise space itself. Part of the reason that Andy Grove keeps building in obsolescence is to keep everyone else on the move. But, additionally, hundreds of millions of dollars in the Intel Architecture Laboratory feed players across traditional boundaries, driving the creation of products, services and infrastructure to strengthen the enterprise space as a whole. And in the process, several hundred billion dollars have gone into the joint value pool that is expanding exponentially at record speed.

CHAPTER 19
PRACTICING COMPLEMENTARITY

'GET A GOOD THING AND BUILD A FENCE AROUND IT IS AN IDEA *rooted in basic human instinct but is now out of date,'* says John Crewe, American Express (AMEX) president of international marketing and product development based in London. AMEX adopted a more open-minded approach in the late 1990s. It opened up its network to a larger number and broader range of establishments with which its customers had contact and reduced merchant charges. The establishments included supermarkets and small businesses. Partnerships were developed allowing banks like Britain's NatWest, France's Crédit Lyonnais, Turkey's Akbank, Spain's La Caixa and Banco Comercial Portugues in Portugal to use its brand and system and to co-issue cards. '*Co-existence is not a problem,'* says Crewe. '*Everyone has expanded as a result.'*

AMEX also started co-branding in other market spaces in order to connect with players with which it needed to be working to provide integrated results from the customer's point of view. For example, it created a Delta SkyMiles card with Delta Airlines in the market space of *total travel management*. It also worked with Accor, the Paris-based hotel chain consisting of Novotel, Sofitel, Ibis, Motel 6 and Formula 1, each with their own distinct installed base, offering services at all stages of the customer activity cycle. These services varied from travel agencies to car hire and accommodation to restaurants, including diners on auto routes. AMEX is co-branding, allowing travelers using Accor's services to pay with one single card but still earn AMEX travel points.

The great lesson to be learnt from AMEX and others is that corporations can no longer keep themselves, or their technologies, proprietary without incurring the diminishing returns penalties of traditional capitalism. Nature has long since proved this. Arie de Geus used a blue tit experiment in his book *The Living Company*, to demonstrate the point. Food for birds was hidden under an aluminum wrapping. One of the blue tits pierced the cover and got to the food but, instead of guarding this discovery (classic Darwinian behavior), the bird shared its knowledge with the other members of its flock and the flock survived and thrived. This contrasted with other species in the experiment, like the robin, who died because such sharing did not take place.

And apparently the more brutal the natural environment, the more this applies. Author Stephen Jay Gould, the well-known Harvard paleontologist, uses an observation by the Russian scientist Kropotkin to explain this in his book *Bully for Brontosaurus*. In Siberia, because of the poor conditions, the animal species with the greatest chance of survival are those that cooperate most closely. The selfish survival of the fittest behavior as described by Darwin is more valid in the relatively calm, predictable, non-threatening environment of the Galapagos Islands, which is where the famous evolutionist did his work.

Piggy-backing is OK

In business, research continues to show that corporations that connect, collaborate and share for the right reasons – i.e. to provide a superior, total customer experience in a market space – outperform those using old competitive techniques. The acid test is this: Do we have a common customer base for whom benefits need to be linked, and if so can we jointly gain? If the answers are 'yes', there is every reason to collaborate, even with corporations which would

WHAT
NATURE
TEACHES US

previously have been regarded as rivals in the traditional business model's definition.

Many say that the feud between Microsoft and Netscape probably should not have happened. If the two companies had worked together from the start, customers would have got a better Internet experience more quickly and more easily by having the benefits of both the technologies in one non-proprietary system. As it is, they have to choose between two boxes – the core items. This has stoked the corporate battle and perpetuated outdated legislative product-based arguments on monopoly.

Let's translate all of this into a consideration of how traditional capitalism and customer capitalism differ:

➡ With **traditional capitalism**, the corporation maximized its own competitive position by keeping what it knew, and had, secret and proprietary.
➡ With **customer capitalism**, technology is shared in the interests of a integrated experience that is continuously improved for shared customers, with gains more than proportionate for all.

The reason that gains are more than proportionate for all is that the loops of customer capitalism go into motion. The more benefits are linked for customers by collaborating players in the enterprise space, the greater the value the customers get, attracting a deeper, broader, more diverse and longer share of spend at decreasing costs. This draws increasing numbers of customers into the installed base fold, which enlarges the total value pool for players. This in turn pulls in more players, more developers, more customers and so on.

This of course means that, invariably, dependent players are allowed to piggy-back on the innovation of lead players, which goes somewhat against the grain of traditionalists but is par for the increasing returns course. For example,

American NewsWork has transformed its powerful local franchises to become part of the new world of interactive media, and is thus increasing traffic to its site. It has gone beyond being an online newspaper consortium and built itself into a multiple-source reporting network, complementing the print-based offerings of the players with which it collaborates. The aggregated news site combines multimedia news and stories, and shares advertising revenue with the international media, metropolitan and local papers.

Among the 5000 news sources on which the *Financial Times* draws in its capacity as a go-between provider, which go back at least 10 years (some even to 1980) and are updated six times a day, are competitors such as the *Wall Street Journal*, the *Daily Telegraph*, *Die Welt* (Germany) and *Il Sole 24 Ore* (Italy).

Bankers Trust, a leader in mutual trusts in Australia, is another example. It invited its competitors to join forces in pooling information about customers' investment portfolios in an electronic service it called Investment Link. This was designed to give 6000 financial advisers the consolidated information they needed to make better decisions for their common client base. Similarly, Insweb has 300,000 people visit its site a month, and integrates the total customer experience by helping them look at options, compare prices, make decisions, and cover and manage the entire range of risks, continuously evaluated and updated. It uses more than 6000 competing insurance carriers to help carry out its services.

As customers become more informed about the virtue of these kinds of centralized, integrated services, made up of seeming competitors, and see the decreased costs and hassles that these services bring, plus better long-term results, these systems will grow in dominance, increasing demand (the number of customers) and supply (the number of insurers, service players, hardware and software developers), fueling potential increasing returns for everyone.

At war and peace

The difference between complementors and competitors becomes very blurred with customer capitalism, as we can see from the above examples. In their book *Co-opetition*, Barry Nalebuff and Adam Brandenburger, respectively Harvard and Yale business school professors, try to distinguish between them:

➡ When customers value your product more because they have it in conjunction with another player's product, then that other player is your **complementor**. Complementarity makes your product more valuable.

➡ When customers value your product less because they have the other player's product, rather than your product alone, then the other player is your **competitor**. Competition makes your product less valuable.

If we move from a product into a customer frame, it is possible to see that:

➡ Products and services that achieve a linked benefit for a common group of customers in a market space are **complementary**. They are not only complementary but necessary for each other, if everyone is to compete effectively.

➡ Products and services that result in that same linked benefit for that same group of customers in that same market space are **competitive**.

COMPETITION
AS
COMPLEMENTARY

Once the principles of customer capitalism are uppermost, what was competition can suddenly become complementary to an enterprise. For example, it is not enough for the various players in the air traveler's experience – travel agents, airlines, car hire, baggage handlers, airports, taxis – to join forces in a new enterprise space. If they are to offset the threats of alternate means of communication and transport, they have to connect with former arch rivals. This can be seen in Virgin's move (albeit a painful one) into trains. The trend will accelerate with innovations like the German magnetic levitation trains, described as the biggest scientific breakthrough for travel since the airplane (though they were invented by the Americans 30 years ago). The talk is that by 2005 these magnetic levitation trains, traveling at 450–500 kilometers per hour, could carry 40,000 passengers a day between, say, Hamburg and Berlin in less than an hour. They could easily become the backbone for *new ways of traveling across Europe*. In addition, since there is no contact made with the rails, wear and tear is minimal and the train can easily pass over snow and other obstacles. Moreover, it uses less energy than cars or airplanes and cuts down on noise pollution.

Baxter Renal is another example of making what was previously competition complementary in the interest of a linked customer benefit and consequent customer lock-on. In 1998, UK management took a strategic decision to go into HD, previously regarded as competitive. However, from a customer's total lifetime therapy perspective, HD is actually complementary, because customers have to go through it eventually to maximize their survival time and wellbeing.

CANNIBALIZING THE FEAR

HD competitors had kept out of the customer's home for fear of cannibalization and stuck to hospitals where they perfected their technical expertise, but Peter Leyland and his team decided to give increasing, not decreasing, emphasis to being with customers in their homes. Once there, Baxter established its criticality, making home care the standard for *new ways of doing things for renal sufferers*. Then Baxter Renal stretched its brand into HD products, so rather than patients being on PD in their homes and then having to go to the hospital for HD, they can now get both treatments at home as part of one total, integrated care experience. And under the company's Unicare Direct delivery

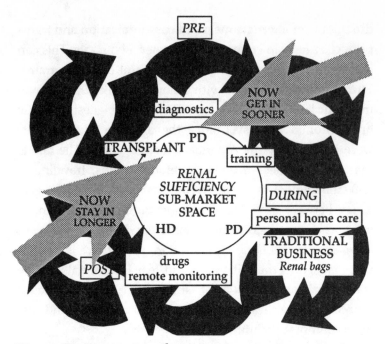

Figure 13 Baxter Renal: getting in sooner, staying in longer to get lifelong customer value

service, it provides patients with additional diabetic and cardiac drugs which are typically complementary to the patient's overall needs. This, plus its various value-add services and investment in transplants, gets one integrated experience to patients in the *renal sufficiency* sub-market space, and Baxter gets the entire 30-year lifetime of customer value (see Figure 13).

WALKING   To facilitate all forms of personal mobility in the *journey*
THE TALK   *management* sub-market space, the RAC has gone to great lengths to collaborate with industries and institutions previously considered competitors, e.g. taxi firms, railways, the underground and other transport companies. It has developed a transport smartcard to enable members to pay for journeys by all forms of transport, not just automobiles. In 1997, it launched a £500,000 campaign calling for more investment in the London Underground system to put pressure on politicians and planners and demand a well-funded,

efficient public transport system and thus obviate Londoners' suffering as pollution and congestion reached intolerable levels. Also on its list was to delineate priorities for bicycles (which it now makes and distributes itself under its own brand), buses, motorcycles, trains, areas for walkers and joggers, and more public spaces and protection for pedestrians. It has lobbied for a London business rate levy to raise money for public transport and more effective targeting of the vehicles responsible for the worst pollution offenses.

Complementors can be competitors in one enterprise space and collaborators in another. Nalebuff and Brandenburger neatly expound:

> *Your relationship with competitors is* prima facie *competitive, or win–lose. You lose when they enter the game. But you don't have to lose as much if you recognize that, once competitors enter the game, you can have win–win interactions with them. It's not all war with competitors. It's war and peace.*

The nature of the transaction card business is one example of simultaneous competition and collaboration because the receiving and paying parties usually clear with different banks. However, the difference comes when banks actively work together, giving each other access to their infrastructure, knowhow and resources to build new markets and increase wealth **all round**. That's what enables a species to survive. NatWest had a choice with Mondex. It could make the technology proprietary, confining it to its customers only, in which case all banks would do the same – a variation on the same diminishing theme. Or, as in fact happened, it could try to create one interoperable technological platform so that banks across the world could work together to create one global standard.

Blueprint for complementarity

The point is that with customer capitalism, the new enterprise collaborates with whomever is necessary to get the best result to customers. It is then, and only then, that it sees that the forces of increasing returns go into effect to both lock on customers and lock out competitors, with returns increasing for all involved.

Complementarity succeeds when there is:

CRITICAL
SUCCESS
FACTORS

Reciprocity

More of one thing doesn't mean less of another, or less gain for others. For example, it is said that with information technology people will be able to work anywhere – the mountains, the seashore, their homes. However, this doesn't mean that cities and international business centers will become redundant, any more than happened through the successive waves of telephone, automobile or rural electrification technologies. Instead, international cities become the nodes for the communication networks that make virtual infrastructures possible.

As Don Tapscott says in *The Digital Economy*, the fact that travelers will substitute multimedia workstations for air miles and face-to-face meetings doesn't mean that they will travel less:

> *They will enjoy sights around the world from the comfort of their armchairs. The 'vacation chamber' will certainly exist in some form, but so will international travel for pleasure. In fact, virtual reality travel will only increase the demand for the real thing.*

FALLING
INTO A
LOOP

Hollywood thought that VCRs would signal the end for it by pirating its products, and it went all the way to the Supreme Court to try to stop them with a tax levy. The fact that it lost the case was massively to its advantage because it created positive reinforcing loops – the market for movie rentals fueled the demand for movies, which fueled more demand for movie rentals, which kept on multiplying demand and revenues for movies. With foresight (and hindsight), working with the principles of customer capitalism, movie companies could have worked consciously to make this complementarity happen instead of trying to resist it.

NewsWorks works because embedded in its strategy is market growth for everyone – from itself, to its interactive media collaborators, to the international and national press; from the metropolitan-printed newspapers to the local media that have intimate knowledge of their specific communities. While Web audiences have increased, circulation for existing newspapers and magazines has remained intact – online audiences have proved to be among the most loyal print readers, looking to each medium for different purposes. Bookstores were concerned that videos would take their markets, but as demand for videos grew so too did the demand for books.

So far, experience shows that with the Amazons of this world and other new approaches, the whole market for a particular product can expand. What's more, by using the principles of customer capitalism, everyone involved can get the advantage of positive feedback – including customers. As one book industry figure, Mary Westheimer, puts it:

> *If, instead of fighting futilely, these threatened book sellers should try looking through the other end of the telescope, they might see what they perceive as competition is actually a complement ... Together, we can create an appetite that feeds our industry ... if all of us – booksellers, publishers, distributors, authors – do a good job of selling, more people will buy more books. And if we all work together towards the goal, we and our customers, the readers, will be that much happier.*

Sharing

Sharing is what Apple didn't do when it kept its operating systems proprietary, but what Microsoft did do and what IBM and Apple have subsequently done. It is also what Microsoft and Apple now do – finally, Apple machines also have Windows operating systems – and what Microsoft and Netscape could have done. What AMEX didn't do but is now doing, Mondex did from the start. Sharing is also what VHS (Matsushita and JVC) did when they allowed manufacturers to use the VHS standard for a very low royalty fee.

By the way, let's remind ourselves why VHS was victorious over Betamax. Betamax was technically the better system, and should have won by classical economist standards. However, with VHS customers could record for two to three hours (enough time to tape a football match or a movie), whereas with Betamax they could only use the machine for an hour at a time. Because of this, VHS-compatible players proliferated, the market grew and unleashed demand, which caused video rental stores to stock more and more, so customers locked on in one giant looping dynamo.

An Anglo–US joint venture could revolutionize the music industry to get high-quality music to as many people as cheaply as possible by using this principle of sharing. The Musicians' Union in the UK, and others elsewhere, have waived restraints on use of their members' work, and some record labels have allowed their exclusive artists to appear in recorded performances on the Global Music Network (GMN). Live music is delivered to the customer's computer, free of charge. With the new mind and spirit of customer capitalism, these players realize that cyberspace connection with the audience can attract new concert goers and CD buyers, and thus create a larger market for everyone.

JAPAN'S SOFTWARE LOSS   Customer capitalism doesn't tolerate closed systems that prevent customers from getting the value that we've talked about. For example, until 1993 NEC in Japan, unlike IBM, did not adopt an open architecture to encourage third parties to add value to its products with other complementary machines and add-ons. This decision narrowed its market, even though its brand is well known in Japan. Even more damaging was the fact that this decision lost it the valuable exponential growth that it would have gained on world markets. Add to this the knock-on damage to Japanese software companies, becoming isolated as they did from the rest of the world, and you have a pretty good picture of diminishing returns.

Citibank didn't use new logic either with ATMs when it first introduced them in 1977, and it suffered the consequences. Had it opted for complementarity then and involved others, everyone's ATM cards, including Citibank's, would have been more valuable. As it turned out, even though it had the technology first, other networks took the lead and Citibank and its customers lost out. (Citibank reversed its decision in 1992.)

Bertelsmann Venture Group, part of the Bertelsmann publishing and retailing empire, despite working hard to topple Amazon in the online book market, has nonetheless involved Amazon, with its huge customer base, in Nuvomedia. Nuvomedia was the inventor of handheld devices for the delivery of reading material via the Net. Presumably, Bertelsmann has learnt from Apple, AMEX and others that exclusivity is not the way to go. Prevalence is the goal and customers want linked benefits instead of being faced with a whole variety of technical standards.

Compatibility and interoperability

Customers just won't buy goods restrained by proprietary standards any more because they know that they can't get totally integrated results and that, ultimately, this costs them more in time, money and effort. As Nobel Laureate Arno Penzias explained in an interview with *Fortune*, we are entering an era in which the products made for ease of networking (linking customer benefits) will be far better off

NO
PRODUCT
IS AN ISLAND

than those goods that are good only in and of themselves.

What Penzias is saying, and the new enterprise is rapidly finding, is that new wealth occurs when everything comes together for the benefit of an integrated experience for the end-user customer. The range of issues involved in this compatibility and interoperability statement, fundamental to getting the rewards of customer capitalism, is enormous and can vary:

➡ from the missed possibility of Microsoft and Netscape not having worked together

➡ to the RAC ensuring that customers can use the same hardware, software and processes to get traffic information, whether from their TVs, PCs, cars or phones (mobile or fixed)

➡ to compatibility in policies, for example in the synchronization of publication dates and prices between countries in different editions of books, driven by Amazon and other online Internet ventures

➡ to standards set by Direct Line so that its 140 repair garages treat customers to the common service levels they demand once a call for repair comes through.

Mondex, in its quest to create a new world standard for customer payment of small items, has made compatibilty and interoperability a cornerstone of its strategy from the outset. Whereas VisaCash has several technologies in different regions that cannot work together, Mondex has a single technology, interoperable around the world. In the design of the hardware and software, special consideration has been given to making sure that competing cards can be used in devices and dispensers made compatible for this purpose, in one common and integrated, open, global system. In New York, to make sure that competitive systems could be used side by side, a pilot test was run with MasterCard and Chase Manhattan Bank using Mondex, and Visa and Citibank using VisaCash.

The move to multibranding is another way of looking at
compatibility and interoperability. For instance, in the *short-*
haul or *personal mobility* market space, customers may want
several kinds of vehicles and brands over a week, a month,
a year or a lifetime, but the automotive franchise system was
never structured for that. If one dealer didn't have a particular model in stock, the customer had to go around to find
it at another, or wait. Thus the major changes we now see as
dealers try to embrace the customer capitalism model,
driven forward by new entrants like Auto-by-Tel, is that
more and more are going multibrand, learning to connect
not just with customers but with each other.

GOING
MULTIBRAND

PART SEVEN

LOCKING ON AND ROLLING OUT

CHAPTER 20
FIRST PREVALENCE THEN PROFITS

PREVALENCE IS NOT ABOUT MORE AND MORE OF THE CORE ITEMS being made and moved. It's about creating and gaining mastery over a standard-setting new way of doing things, and getting it adopted by a market first. The more individual customers see, use and get value from the new way of doing things, the more prevalent it becomes, and the more compelled customers become to be part of it. This makes it infectious to others, who then get drawn in.

The new way of doing things effectively becomes the standard. The more advantage it gets, the more it is accepted, the more it accumulates advantage.

This prevalence doesn't happen because a technology is technically better (Betamax was better), or because it is first (Apple was first), though by definition increasing returns do favor the early. It is a conscious strategy on the part of the new enterprise to use the principles of customer capitalism to build demand and unleash the reinforcing behavior that gets an accumulating and compounding advantage. Branson is a prime example. The Virgin brand has become so prevalent that market research reveals that people say 'if the right product comes along from Virgin, we will buy it!' As the brand becomes more prevalent, it assumes even greater importance. It becomes the unifying link that attracts customers to companies within the group, and also attracts outside investors.

BEING BETTER OR FIRST IS NOT ENOUGH

In this new model for competitiveness, as profits gush from new ideas and technology that produce new ways of doing things for and with customers, developers respond by innovating at a faster and faster rate. Complementary products, services, extensions, upgrades, new applications and breakthrough inventions are constantly propeled on stream. The more this happens, the more value customers get, and so developers continue to invest even more rapidly in an upward spiral of progression and expansion. As Amazon took off, it attracted constant innovation from developers, from one-click payment systems so that customers don't have to keep entering the same information over and over again when they order books, CDs, videos or anything else, to handheld reading devices able to download material directly from the Web and with the potential to bring to an end book buying as we know it.

The new enterprise knows the importance of attracting and working with these developers, and adapting its offerings to incorporate these innovations and so retain its leadership as provider of new ways of doing things for its installed customer base, even if it means building obsolescence into its current offering. Whether Amazon stays out front in the *information and knowledge discovery* market space will very much depend on whether it works with developers to keep ahead, or at least apace, with the joint counter-moves being made by book retailers and publishers to deliver books and information directly to customers' screens.

With an increase in the number of participating players who supply the products and services that produce the integrated results during the various stages of the customer activity cycle, more developers will be drawn in. Demand generates more demand as technological breakthroughs become feasible and cost effective, opening up ever-increasing and multiplying opportunities, which in turn accelerate the speed and spend of developer innovation.

This applies to independent developers but also to investment from within the company. For instance, Baxter

Renal is now getting more and more internal R&D funds channeled to the enhancement of renal patient life extension.

Prevalence lost

If Steve Jobs had understood these new dynamics, he would have licensed Apple's innovation out, because top of his list would have been the creation of prevalence in the market-place. Together with other strategic moves, this would have dominated long-term relationships with an ever-expanding Apple installed base of users, with all the added and multiple prospects for taking customers and the brand into wider terrains.

APPLE'S BLUNDER TO CHEW ON

With perfect hindsight, Jobs would not just have got customers to lock on, but got developers drawn in as well. IBM decided it could live with clones and thereby achieved prevalence for the IBM and IBM-compatible personal computers which used Intel and Microsoft systems. Apple didn't want anything to be compatible with its machines and this restricted its growth among customers as well as interest among developers. By the time Apple changed its mind in 1994 and allowed Power Computing and others like Motorola to clone its operating system, the damage had been done. Far from growing the Apple market by converting IBM and IBM-compatible Windows and Intel customers to Macintosh, less than 1 percent of the new cloners' sales came from non-Macintosh users.

On the other hand, Microsoft became more prevalent. Software applications for Windows accelerated and multiplied, tightening its grip (can any of us ever forget?) on almost the entire market. Meanwhile, back at Apple, one of Steve Jobs's main tasks was to persuade software developers to continue to innovate for his new Macintosh machines.

What he (and we) didn't yet know or fully understand was that, with a new business model at work, creativity and technology are not enough unless they attract more creativity and technology. Apple ended up dominating its own Apple-based systems rather than achieving prevalence and dominating the overall personal computer market – what the *Wall Street Journal* termed '*one of the seminal blunders of business history*'.

More importantly from a strategic standpoint, Jobs failed to get customers in the market he had so carefully crafted to lock on. Apple had two really important things going for it. First, it was strongly positioned in education, supported by students, schools and universities. Right from the start, Jobs had pumped money into promoting the imaginative use of technology in teaching. That, plus the fact that his machines were more user friendly, cheaper, easier to maintain and more powerful for multimedia, should have earned Apple a lifelong position in the education market. Second, Apple users were ferociously loyal. Yet the 'Macintosh flock' did not protect Apple from competitive entrants. Why? Because Jobs missed a huge strategic nuance in keeping the education and work of his customers separated, even though they formed a single household's or individual's lifetime activities.

From the Apple perspective, it was OK for the personal computer technology used in schools to be very different to that used in the workplace. However, many parents (myself included) argued that the work done on a disk at school should be compatible with personal computer equipment and systems at home. It's just more convenient, cheaper and less hassle if kids can pop their disk into your machine when they do their homework and get stuff printed out on one printer. In addition, parents became concerned that the personal computer experience at school should prepare children for the real world – and the real world was Windows.

Prevalence regained

So the problem was not a lack of new technology for core items or that traditional marketing wasn't doing its job for Apple. Sales, promotion and distribution were good, product and pricing competitive and strategic positioning strong. The problem was that Apple lost out in a market it helped to create and grow because the decisions it made cost it prevalence. This could be seen not just in the overall market but even in its own segment, leaving others like IBM to come galloping in.

For example, in the higher education segment in the US, IBM has launched the Global Campus Program, extending to over 30 colleges, spreading the concept of Thinkpads and Lotus Notes for collaborative and distance learning. It has also sponsored the development of virtual, digitized libraries in order to capture and distribute multimedia material and information. In parts of Europe, like Spain, it is pioneering multimedia education in 140 secondary schools, equipping them with personal computers and Internet servers. In Italy, with Olivetti, it has developed a network to connect Italian schools. And in Vietnam it intends to equip all secondary schools with computers, with special programs to learn English, by the year 2000.

IBM is gaining prevalence in the education segment by targeting the even younger end of it. IBM and Little Tykes, initiated after one entrepreneurial mother of two observed the use of personal computers at her son's nursery school, have jointly developed and commercialized an all-in-one unit. This unit includes a child's desk with a built-in computer system for nursery and primary school use. The look and design of this Young Explorer are made to appeal to young customers and the system is therefore kept simple. Built-in software, maths and reading programs can be started up with one click of the mouse for this future generation, who are much more enthusiastic than their teachers about a high-tech experience!

IBM AND LITTLE TYKES

Ubiquity is (not) all you need

WILL
MCDONALD'S
PROVE THE
POINT?

If customers who want fast food see McDonald's all over the place, will they want to buy more of its hamburgers? Some people argue yes, being all over the place is enough to increase your market. The more places you have, the more ubiquitous you become, the more customers want to eat there, the more you get increasing returns.

In fact, being ubiquitous is not enough for the prevalence needed to generate the durable success and positive disproportionate gains that customer capitalism can engender. This requires that customer lock-on, and what that represents, is central, clear and ongoing on strategy, with constant innovation driven by the corporation and its collaborators.

McDonald's, despite its obvious ubiquity and continued global expansion, persisted in defining rigid standards, not only for its products but for the processes that deliver them. At times this has even conflicted with the entrepreneurialism of its own franchisees. It never got out of the traditional capitalism treadmill of mass production, distribution, promotion and discounting to gain market share. Neither did it personalize its offerings for the changing tastes and preferences of individuals to build an installed base – those people who want the firm or institution as their dominant or sole choice on an ongoing basis – until diminishing returns set in.

So, despite owning one of the best-known brands on the planet and a global string of fast-food restaurants, this phenomenon of the twentieth century suffered all of the malaise of diminishing returns in the world's advanced countries. Top management persisted in intensifying distribution to build ubiquity to push market share up, increasing its US outlets by more than the average industry expansion rate. However, unlike its new-thinking competitors, its per-store performance went down.

No, ubiquity is not enough to get growth, sustained competitiveness and increasing returns, and McDonald's has been testament to this. Any attempt to reinvent the corporation would need to be driven by the principles of customer capitalism, articulating new market spaces and pushing for customer origination and mastery over *new ways of preparing and distributing food*, gaining prevalence and lock-on from people in a very different world.

CHAPTER 21
INVESTING UP FRONT FOR INCREASING RETURNS

To achieve prevalence, classic lifecycle curves and frameworks must be reversed. With traditional capitalism, competitors would come into the market and undercut prices, not having had to make the initial investments. So corporations would try to recoup their outlays early on (see Figure 14). The higher the profit margin, the quicker the leader could recoup an investment, but the quicker competition moved and cashed in on the early and late mass market, leading to diminishing returns.

The reversal in thinking is this:

➡ With **traditional capitalism**, the corporation had to recoup technology and marketing investments quickly.

➡ With **customer capitalism**, these costs are regarded as investments in getting prevalence and potential for becoming the standard, accumulating advantage and increasing returns.

A NEW
ALGORITHM
With customer capitalism, the enterprise is not looking for a quick win because the new market and economic dynamics change the algorithm:

➡ With the new market dynamics, multiple gains are accrued because of difficult-to-imitate relationships that, once established, get customers to lock on to the organization.

➡ With the new economic dynamics, costs are inverted for several reasons (more on this later), enabling invest-

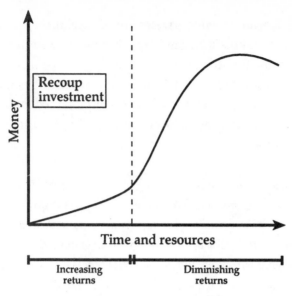

Figure 14 Diminishing returns – profits come first

ments to be amortized over more customers and customer opportunities over longer periods.

Investment as a state of mind

The mindset needed to invest up front to get prevalence, become the standard and get all the ensuing positive disproportionate gains is different from trying to grab high profit margins at the outset of an innovation or investment, which is how it was often done with the old business model. The new thinking belongs to those enterprises, large and small, who don't just want to be ahead, but also want to gather market momentum so that barriers to competitor entry rise, making it difficult for others to catch up.

Such action invariably means no, or low, profits (in the conventional sense of the word) for a time, which old minds and spirits find difficult to grasp and accept. During the first 10 years of Microsoft's existence, its profits were negligible and its share price paltry until 1990, when both took off exponentially. The same with Federal Express – it took

VYING FOR THE LONG TERM

years for its massive investment in technology and customers to take effect. Similarly, there is no way that Lego's enormous investment in parks can guarantee a short-term payoff, especially on Disney's home turf. Amazon has shown no profits yet. It could have, but it has chosen to continue to invest heavily in new innovations and marketing. Says Bezos:

> *We spend marketing dollars [on advertising and to get premier positions and gateway sites] which is disproportionate to a company of our size. And we do that because we believe this is a critical category formation time where, roughly speaking maybe a dollar spent on advertising today is worth ten dollars spent on advertising next year.*

The point is that if it waited to make this expenditure, there was a huge opportunity cost in terms of the prevalence that Amazon could get with all of its exponential gains by becoming the standard.

Branson insists that in any event profitability is an unfair measure by which to judge a modern growth company's performance. The Virgin Group's subsidiaries are encouraged to invest most of the cash they generate in new innovations, many of them – such as the V2 record company, the Virgin Active chain of health clubs and Virgin Direct – being long-term investments. Branson claims that trains are so bad, having had minimal government investment over the last 30 years, that he has had to invest heavily in them to the tune of £2 billion, knowing that profits will suffer in the short term.

CHANGING THE
TIME HORIZON

What new enterprises have in common is that they look at investments differently over different time horizons. They know that every investment wave takes time to build the prevalence that thereafter brings them exponential rewards. Diminishing returns or no returns at all are acceptable at the beginning of an innovation (see Figure 15),

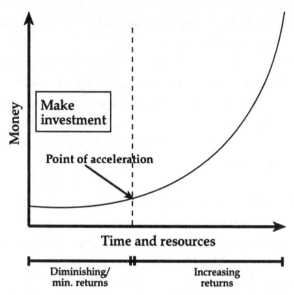

Figure 15 Increasing returns – exponential returns come after

because of the consequent upward-arching returns when the positive loops start to feed off themselves; just as we saw when we discussed investments in relationships in the Citibank example (see Chapter 15). So:

➡ If the Mondex International investment succeeds in making its unaccountable electronic cash system the global orthodoxy, or the platform for further innovations, it could continue to get royalties *ad infinitum* from its franchises and collaborators.

➡ If the RAC investment succeeds, it could get a pool of customers who use it more routinely and widely on a global basis through any of a variety of new electronic media. It also aims to draw others in by getting customers early on through its new driving school or via the Web.

➡ If Monsanto's investment succeeds for standard *new ways of farming*, there should be no reason that it couldn't get customers to lock on and share with farmers the yields that promise to increase exponentially with every new innovation.

➡ If Amazon succeeds in staying ahead by virtue of the investments it has made to establish an installed customer base, ever increasing, ever more lucrative, it could gather the kind of market power that will enable it to produce the profits needed to ensure still more investments to keep it ahead.

Though Microsoft refuses to put a figure on how much it has paid to enter the travel business through its MSN Expedia site, within the first year it was already earning revenues in excess of $1 million per week from online bookings for air travel, hotel rooms and car hire. If its predictions are anything to go by, it could continue to achieve substantial growth rates at very little extra cost as more and more customers lock on.

WILL MONDEX WIN–WIN? While we still can't tell the outcome of its innovating mind and spirit, Mondex is a particularly good example of acting out the principles of customer capitalism. NatWest Bank sought to ensure that it would get worldwide prevalence, not just another new product for itself that others would soon copy.

Its attitude to the initial investment was thus very different from what it might have been with traditional thinking. To start with, Mondex would never have happened with traditional thinking. Rewards were only likely to come well into the future and were uncertain, difficult to quantify and based on a market opportunity that was yet to be created, rather than a set of market statistics that required a response. For a conservative bank this was unusual enough. Second, its new way of doing things was an ambition that went way beyond a new product – the object was to build a global standard-setting electronic payment system for small-ticket items, offering customers value at each critical point in the activity cycle.

Other players in the customer's experience were included in the initial investment, such as competitor banks and telecommunications firms with which NatWest worked to develop point-of-sale payment equipment. It also involved hardware and software system makers in order to facilitate ease of customer use. For chip card reading it got developers on board so that Mondex would go into standard equipment, from personal computers to parking meters. It also designed a digital device for installation in cabs which could fill and spend the electronic purse. This was linked to other communication electronics being made by auto manufacturers. Additionally, it worked with local terminal and telephone companies to encourage development to support its payment systems. And with suppliers, NatWest ensured that if a bank chose the Mondex option, every part of the implementation process was available to it with the relevant support and services.

Third, from the conception of its idea the bank knew that, in order to build prevalence, the innovation would have to have win–win benefits for all parties. Mondex would also have to do this without holding anyone up by attempting to cover the initial investment quickly. Banks could immediately do away with the cost burden of collecting transactions and taking hard currency through complex systems. Merchants could immediately reduce the risk of burglary and currency forgery by not having to deal with cash, and get their money into their bank accounts instantly, instead of having to wait the average three days.

As for customers, the object was to use price and access to get them on stream as quickly as possible, not at a pace convenient for suppliers or most effective for covering Mondex's up-front expenses. Customers could have funds credited to their cards in their homes or offices from their PCs, TVs, Mondex terminals or phones. They could also make their payments, especially on small-ticket items, with e-cash more simply and time efficiently than having to use paper bills and coins, and more privately than with credit or debit cards.

Having made the investment of some £106.5 million up front, NatWest made a deliberate decision early on only to cover costs, rather than to try to make profits from the sale of 51 percent of its equity to Mastercard to form Mondex International. This was intended to get the prevalence that would bring about long and lasting rewards, rather than to make a quick buck.

Before anyone else, Mondex saw what would make its new way of doing things happen - a multi-application platform. Hence it developed MULTOS, which enabled an infinite variety of applications to go on the Mondex card, e.g. transport, theater tickets, loyalty cards etc. This, too, was a long-term goal and non-proprietary. MULTOS was 'donated' to the banking industry and is being run by a consortium of competing institutions including Mastercard, American Express and the Discovery Card.

The business case for e-cash can be difficult to justify, given the costs of implementation, especially in the US where e-cash has been slow to take off. With the multiple-application platform that Mondex offers, the investment for customer corporations can be spread more widely, the object being to accelerate market take-on.

CHAPTER 22
THE CRITICAL VALUE OF CRITICAL MASS

FROM PHYSICISTS COMES THE NOTION THAT A MINIMUM MASS IS necessary for a chain reaction to occur. In many ways, creating a new market, and prevalence within it, is a chain reaction. If enough of the right people take on a new way of doing things, they become 'demand generators' and the rest follow.

The exact size of the critical mass needed to set a company sufficiently ahead is difficult to say. Each circumstance is different. But what is important is that people, both on the demand (customer) and the supply (player and developer) sides, quickly get involved in the new way of doing things. This drives the corporation beyond a threshold, at which point customer lock-on and the looping mechanism of increasing returns begin to take effect.

Building the market momentum

To join forces with other banks early on, NatWest sold 51 percent of Mondex's equity to MasterCard to form Mondex International. Around the world, from Japan and Hong Kong to Canada – where Mondex has consolidated the support of 90 percent of the financial community – from France and Norway, to Costa Rica, Chile and Uruguay, from Australia, New Zealand and South Africa to Israel and to the USA, some of the world's leading banks, which could 'see' the potential and could act as catalysts to draw others in, were involved in piloting the system. In all 56 territories participated, together reaching a marketplace of over three billion people.

FINDING DEMAND GENERATORS

Going into an area of cash issuing that up until then had been the exclusive domain of governments, Mondex International faced unique challenges in each country that needed to be consciously managed in order to get the critical mass to create prevalence at local level. It deliberately worked with local personnel in order to diffuse its cash payment systems into individual environments, modifying according to conditions to get local buy-in. At the same time it kept the brand and systems universal and interoperable.

Early on, Tim Jones and his colleagues, having done their research and become confident and familiar with the concept, began to look for collaborators, not least of whom was someone who could manufacture the chip. For nearly two years they worked with one Japanese manufacturer, talking, giving assurance and jointly building specifications, getting commitment for the investment without any definite orders. *'Enthusiasm is all important,'* said Jones, *'but at the end, you have to trust and like each other.'*

Rather than experiments hidden for fear of failure, all the necessary resources and infrastructure were harnessed to make tests work in completely transparent environments around the globe. A new payment infrastructure was developed for each setting for the entire participating enterprise space, involving key retail chains and banks, setting up Mondex ticket machines in parking lots, card readers in buses, taxis, pay phones and so on. Mondex, as a global, multicurrency system, had distinct advantages for the multicultural community of Hong Kong over single-currency, stored-value cards. It also appealed to the young technophile community interested in cash substitutes and the huge cash transfer potential there: HK$30 billion is spent annually on retailing, of which 80 percent is in cash. Mondex International therefore chose Hong Kong as its first launch, considering it a microcosm of the way the payment system would evolve worldwide to supplant currency.

Success factors that are critical

Getting critical mass requires the following:

It must be easy for customers to adopt a new offering or standard, take it on, use it and be successful at getting results

Rank Xerox invented the mouse/icon workstation in the 1970s, but it was difficult to use. It wasn't until Apple adapted the technology and made it easy for people to buy and use that the point-and-click technology actually reached critical mass. Similarly, Prestel launched a video-text service using phone lines in the mid-1970s, but it didn't work. Prestel was the first in the world but the apparatus was too complex for the customer to find and operate. The French PTT, on the other hand, launched Minitel, an electronic information and home-shopping device (originally intended for phoning directory enquiries). This got a rapid response because households got the equipment free and it was easy to install and use, plus they received training to be able to use it. Today there is a Minitel in most French households, over which a quarter of a million sophisticated services are sold.

Having gone on to the Internet, Minitel made the transition for customers as easy as possible 'to bring advanced communications to ordinary people'. France Telecom has taken responsibility for maintaining and upgrading the software on customers' terminals, and intend to have as wide an array of terminal manufacturers as possible to keep the system totally open.   TAKING MINITEL INTO CYBERSPACE

Amazon achieves ease for customers through the design of its Web pages and easy access to its site. A good deal of Amazon's investment has been to ensure its presence on as many different, much-trafficked portal sites as possible, like AOL, Yahoo! and AltaVista. The strategy, although expensive, has been a conscious intention to make it as easy as possible for customers to link into Amazon quickly and seamlessly from almost anywhere on the Web. Similarly, Insweb has 15 partnerships with leading Internet gateway sites which together account for more than half the traffic on the Internet.

Lotus Notes, now part of the IBM contingent, positioned itself as the lead player in the growing *electronic collaborative group support* market space. Its strategy is a deliberate attempt to become the enduring worldwide standard for *new ways of managing a virtual office environment*, enabling employees in one company, or from company to company, to co-exist virtually and at any place, in real time. Take Publicis Technology, an advertising agency that is part of the French international communications firm and one of Lotus Notes's clients. In this company, people don't send messages backwards and forwards to each other and to their customers. Instead, they create reports and advertisements together, sharing ideas, amending, annotating and editing, simultaneously and instantaneously. The savings all round on costs, time and effort have given Publicis Technology a real edge with its end users, whom it gets to know better each day.

Getting enough people linked and using its system was part of Lotus's early strategy to get critical mass for electronic group collaboration and prevalence for Notes. Consciously, various moves were taken to make it easy for users to convert to the system which attracted still more users, expected to top 50 million by the year 2000. Lotus has discovered that when customers find it easy to work in this new way, they begin to install Notes themselves, which accelerates use and networking effects even more.

To achieve critical mass, Lotus has:

➧ made it easy for customer functions to become connected and involved and build on each other's information and knowhow. For example, when people want to collaborate but are on different systems, Lotus allows them to use a standard Web browser.

➡ given easy access to firms who are not on Lotus but are connected in their daily dealings to someone who is (for example, a client company not on Lotus wanting to track its parcel being sent by a Notes-user courier). It also gives access to firms too small to afford the infrastructural set-up investment costs.

➡ given access to parties relevant to Lotus customers, such as their suppliers who are not necessarily on the Notes system.

➡ set up forums to train, discuss and share experiences with users, published white and academic papers and formed a university called the Lotus Institute which has accelerated understanding, use and knowledge of its new electronic team-support offerings.

➡ instituted its own consulting division, offering high-ground services to show customers how to get the best results from this new way of collaborative group working by integrating it into their entire business and knowledge-management system.

➡ involved other players, such as AT&T and BT, to run the telephone services needed to enable Lotus customers to link up easily with others in the system.

Sequential progressive pricing must be replaced by 'ease of decision' pricing

Conventional product lifecycle theory inbred in the traditional capitalism model had products and services priced as they moved through neat, discrete, diffusion categories. As enterprises sought to recoup technology and marketing costs, they priced high, assuming that early adopters would pay for getting something new first. With customer capitalism this no longer holds. In fact, the product lifecycle itself no longer holds, given that there is little protection of the actual core items to speak of any more, and no time to waste

PAYING FOR PRICE

when trying to make a new way of doing things prevalent and get customer lock-on.

Pricing, according to the conventional, sequential model, can, and does, seriously delay market acceptance and the achievement of the critical mass that the new enterprise needs to excel in our modern, fast-moving economy. The point is that pricing should never be the inhibiting factor in a corporation's efforts to create critical mass. Xerox set prices for the mouse exorbitantly high, so customers resisted the price and its new idea, while Apple adapted the idea and pulled prices down. Microsoft dropped prices even further. Microsoft went in low to become IBM's first customer and has continued to position itself as a high R&D spender which, nonetheless, keeps its prices down. This is in marked contrast to Postscript (Adobe), which was ahead technologically and chronologically, but never became the standard for printer page language originally because it was just too expensive. Printer and computer manufacturers resisted it and went with the Hewlett-Packard system instead. Since then, with its Internet strategy it allows browsers to download its software free of charge in the interests of changing *the way published information is moved and archived within organizations* using its various other products and services.

Prestel wanted customers either to purchase or to hire a television set that was twice as expensive as a normal TV and difficult to find, so it failed. Part of the Minitel success was that it gave customers specially designed terminals and training free of charge. With Minitel moving on to the Internet, the object is to try to keep the price of the new screen telephones in line with low and falling personal computer prices.

THE
WEIGHT OF
ENCYCLOPAEDIA
BRITANNICA

In the mid-1990s the threat of computers and CD-Roms became clear to Encyclopaedia Britannica. Encyclopedias such as Encarta were fast gaining critical mass, selling as they were below $100 and with all their additional advantages. In response, Encyclopaedia Britannica developed its own CD-Rom version. However, so as not to interfere with salesforce incentives (its single biggest fear being losing these employees), executives decided to include it free with each printed version of the product and charge $1000 to anyone buying the CD-Rom by itself. The consequences were devastating – revenues declined and salespeople left in any case. Pricing decisions had turned the market off and plunged one of the best-known establishments in the English-speaking world into a diminishing returns spiral.

Mondex, not wanting to make money out of the machinery that delivers the service but anxious to get critical mass for its new way of doing things, gave away terminals to customers at first and then, after six months, rented them out. Lotus purposefully links people up as instant temporary teams without undue costs of set-up to avoid price inhibiting take-up. In both cases, the object is to get lifetime and multiple value from customers without allowing short-term recovery of costs to get in the way.

Some corporations give their innovations away initially to break markets open, and to activate interest and use. The quicker their brand is seen and experienced favorably in the marketplace, by as many people as possible, they reason that the more likely customers are to take up the new way of doing things. This investment will be more than offset once customers lock on to the organization through the longevity, depth, width and diversity of their spend and due to the decreased costs of doing business together. WHEN PRICE IS FREE

For instance, Citibank gave clients free access to its Internet site for a year to encourage people to use it, which, together with transaction-free electronic banking, is how it intended to get critical mass for its new Citibank Internet Banking Services. Sun did this for its Java platform-independent programming language, which operates across all computing systems today, enabling the Internet to act as one giant computer. And Netscape did this initially when it gave away 40 million browsers, which in no small way contributed to bringing the Internet to the mass market. But

Netscape was a single-product company and it decided not to benefit from the existing standard and grow with it by signing a licensing agreement with Microsoft. Java did and gained prevalence in the process. Since then, Netscape has changed its strategy beyond a single-product focus and is becoming more prevalent at critical stages in the customer activity cycle.

Pricing can be used in several creative ways to get critical mass. Midas Kapiti International (MKI), the banking software provider of the giant Misys industrial conglomerate, offers preferential rates to customers who commit to its banking software innovations first. In other words, customers who come in immediately get a better deal than those who follow, in complete contrast to traditional capitalism, where the reverse is what often happened. Said one executive:

> *This is to build the critical mass so we can get to the general marketplace more quickly. People talk to each other and we are careful to choose those we know will not only talk, but be influential in letting other people know about it.*

Venturing together with some early-adopter customers is another way to give those in first a preferential price and so build market momentum. This is especially true when assumptions are difficult to make about outcomes with a new market application. Some of the banks which take MKI's new innovations initially become reference sites, where others can come to see the project working *in situ*. As future contracts are acquired by MKI from these endeavors, the initial adopters are given discounts. If an MKI customer wants a special software application uniquely developed for itself, the company will do so at a price, but as other customers take it on and critical mass is reached, MKI applies the same principle – the originating customer is reimbursed, sometimes pushing its initial costs down to zero.

PART EIGHT

IT'S THE THOUGHT
THAT COUNTS

CHAPTER 23
THE INCREDIBLE WEIGHT OF INTANGIBLES

TODAY IT IS OVERWHELMINGLY THE INTANGIBLES – IDEAS, knowledge and information – which are driving growth and prosperity, not the core items which, on their own, soon become commodities. Paul Romer, economics professor at Stanford, illustrated this in an economic context. He argued (and for the first time had supporting evidence) that it wasn't the scarce, tangible resources like labor, capital and raw materials that led to economic growth and generated wealth. Rather, it was the technologies, be they new or combinations of the old. What propeled these technologies were the intangible factors.

Products and services: like body and soul

The same principle held for corporations. While Romer was making headlines on the criticality of the intangibles in economic growth, those of us in academia and consulting were trying to get more emphasis shifted to the intangibles, insisting that value-add services were the vital component in an integrated customer experience.

SERVICES TAKE ON AND OFF Until then, products and services were considered to be distinct: a firm or institution was in either one or the other. This distinction was also seen in the annual listing of the top *Fortune* 500 companies, where the service sector had always been separated from manufacturing; only in 1995 did *Fortune* combine the two sectors. It had become obvious that the manufacturing/services distinction was meaningless.

Like body and soul, products and services were inextricably part of the same offerings needed to compete durably – products needed services and services needed products.

The market power was increasingly coming from the value-adding services in service and manufacturing companies because, in both instances, it was these intangibles that were making the difference, producing results for customers.

The corporations, in product and service manufacturing, that had moved into a diminishing slide were the ones trapped into believing that it was the core items that customers were buying. Consequently, they used the usual product–price–place–promotion formula to compete. Their diminishing returns slide was aggravated when, to protect margins on their core items, they often squeezed costs. And their service levels went down, as did their investments in intangibles, losing them even more precious, future customer ground.

Services and the intangibles driving them had clearly begun their domination of economies and offerings by the mid-1980s. By the mid-1990s, given advances in technology, there was no more doubt. Possessing the skills and knowledge, ideas, information and infrastructure to produce value-add for customers through services was rapidly becoming more important than owning land, buildings, machinery or other physical or financial assets. Those who saw the point quickly learnt how to accumulate and package their ideas, information and knowledge in order to take their corporations into the future.

Changing the axis to intangibles

SKF Bearings was a 'test case' used in the classroom initially, particularly in Europe, to make the point that services were all important. No company could have been more traditional than this Swedish giant, making and moving high-

SKF BEARINGS' 'TEST CASE'

quality bearings in huge volumes in over 40 countries at competitive prices. What the case demonstrated was that more and more resources put into the bearings by SKF was not what was getting the value out to customers. This could be seen especially in the after-market, where these excellent core items were being badly installed and lubricated 45 percent of the time. This caused customers huge downtime costs and aggravation.

Goran Malm, CEO of the newly formed bearing services division, redefined the business for the after-market as 'trouble-free operations'. Customers didn't want bearings, he said to the shocked 2000-strong worldwide bearings salesforce that he tackled early on in 1986. They wanted to predict and plan and preferably prevent any downtime altogether. For that, the customers and SKF needed value-add services.

So began a two-year transformation at SKF to develop, deliver and support a range of services, which included special installation kits, automotive body shops, lubrication services, cleaning programs, remote conditioning, monitoring systems and maintenance services and installation for corporations using bearings in their machines. The company has undergone several changes since the transformation started – bearings have been rocked by recession and other outside interference – but services have remained a bedrock of the SKF strategy, fostering the customer lock-on that has helped to block competitive entry.

Statistics and research of practice show that worldwide, services are more significant in both input and output terms. Even in high-tech manufacturing where hardware and software may remain the money makers in the near future, demand for assistance, advice and follow-through is making services the top priority. This side of the business is expected to grow by 144 percent and to generate worldwide revenues of $303 billion by 2002.

GE: NOW A SERVICE GIANT   Examples that make the point abound. When Robert Nardelli took over as president of the power systems unit at General Electric (GE) in 1995, it was facing deflationary pressures brought on by deregulation in the electric utility industry that it sells to. Instead of cutting prices to get market share, Nardelli turned to services: advising customers on the nuances of doing business in the diverse environments of Europe and Asia; providing maintenance staff for equipment upgrades rather than just fixing problems; moving engineering time and expertise from new product development to new service development. In the process, GE signed up contracts carrying revenue commitments of billions of dollars for a decade and longer. These commanded higher margins and access to other lucrative customer opportunities.

GE is among the world's top financial service providers today – high on the *Fortune* Service 500 listing. As traditional manufacturers continue to cut prices in response to pressure, they turn to services. For example, in managed healthcare institutions, GE continues to introduce more and more services such as diagnostics to pick up and fix machines remotely, or outsourcing non-strategic customer activities, leaving them to concentrate on their customers. GE Capital Services is the fastest-growing part of the business, expected to top 50 percent of the mighty corporation's profits by the year 2000, operating in 23 countries around the globe.

Europe is now the center of GE's growth strategy, where it claims that, among other things, it will revolutionize European logistics through Penske Logistics Europe. Taking on the old-style hauliers, Penske will cater to multinationals seeking a single, integrated Euro-logistics experience. The new venture is *'not interested in straight transport or storage'*, as one executive put it. Its object will be to cover the entire customer activity cycle, including getting involved in the customer's production process early on, taking over inventory management, subassembling components and scheduling inbound material, all in the interest of putting value in

PENSKE TAKES ON 'OLD HAULIERS'

and taking non-value out. Other services will include advice on working capital optimization, debt collection, tax representation and product testing in order to get companies headquartered outside of Europe to lock on.

Obeying different laws

The significance of services, and the intangibles within them, as the value-generating vehicle for giving and getting the superior offerings that bring about lifelong customer value is irrefutable:

➡ It is the ideas that produce the customer origination.
➡ What produces the innovations that create standards for new ways of doing things for and with customers consists in the knowledge and skills needed to turn what is known into new markets and customer opportunities.
➡ It is the knowledge- and information-loaded services that are gaining the high-ground 'pre' opportunities in the customer's experience when decisions are being taken about what to do.
➡ It is these intangibles that enable the new enterprise to upgrade and extend products and services in the all-critical 'post' stages of the customer activity cycle.

All of this contributes to the generative behavior that leads to customer lock-on.

RIDING THE INTANGIBLES WAVE

But to get this into an increasing returns context, let's go back again to the big economic picture. What was so astounding about Romer's declaration and the reason that he '*busted the study of economic growth wide open*,' to quote the words of one journalist, was not that he said that it was the intangibles rather than the tangibles that caused economic growth. What was significant was that he made people realize that the market and economic dynamics changed as a consequence. Intangibles – the ideas and knowledge that people have, the skills to use this knowledge and the information they hold – differ in one hugely significant way from the scarce and discrete resources of the old economic era – they grow as they are used. They therefore obey the law of increasing, not diminishing, returns.

CHAPTER 24
THE ABUNDANCE FACTOR

THE MOST SIGNIFICANT THING ABOUT THESE INTANGIBLES IS THAT they are abundant rather than scarce, and infinite rather than finite (see Table 11). The modern enterprise is therefore not constrained by fixed quantities of productive resources with which to work, as was the assumption with classical economics and management theory. Paul Romer argues that there is *'essentially no scarcity to deal with,'* because the number of ways to create something of value is so vast – a combinatorial explosion (his metaphor). Wealth can be created almost out of nothing, by the intangibles – ideas, knowledge and information – all of which are boundless. *'Take for instance all the possible bit-streams you can turn into a CD-Rom.'* Romer notes that this is something in the range of 10 to the power one billion, ensuring that we'll never run out of software to discover!

The Internet encapsulates this theory perfectly. This 'network of networks', with prospects for linking a billion people early in the twenty-first century, has no substantial physical body underlying it and it comes from no fixed tangible assets or capital. The World Wide Web was an idea that sprang from the mind of a scientist in Switzerland and the key technology for using it emanated from an idea that a student had in his early twenties. In addition, innovations keep coming as more and more ideas, knowledge and information are pooled and shared, making it the fastest-growing economic and social medium in human history.

➡ They are abundant and infinite, not scarce or
finite.

➡ They grow as they are used – in fact, if properly
stimulated they self-generate and grow
exponentially.

➡ The more people interact and share them, the
more there is in it for everyone.

➡ They can be linked in infinite amounts to infinite
numbers of people.

➡ They can't be consumed, or used up, or lost.

➡ They feed off themselves and therefore compound in value.

➡ They reside in people's heads and are therefore
portable.

➡ They travel instantly at high speed.

➡ They can be converted (and reconverted) into
value in real time.

➡ They cost nothing or very little to share and
spread.

Table 11 The peculiarities of intangibles

Having your cake and eating it

What this boils down to is that the prospects for economic
growth, product, service and market creation are far greater
today with customer capitalism than traditional capitalism
had us believe. The intangibles that produce customer value
are theoretically limitless. They grow as they are used
instead of getting used up. Not only do they grow but, if
kept alive, they never need become obsolete.

As they grow in value, they become the platform for
standards for new ways of doing things on which other
standards can be built. This is what makes whole new
industries, with infinite possibilities for both customer and

LEVERAGING
FROM
ABUNDANCE

corporate value, an ongoing and exponential phenomenon.

From the multifunctional Java technology, for instance, has come the capacity for smartcards to have all of the capability of the original IBM PC, making the card a computer today. The smartcard is able to transact and integrate services for customers across an infinite number of different sectors, from frequent flier points to health insurance information, from passport data to grocery loyalty card updates. It can also receive the news anywhere, anytime. And the possibilities for giving and getting value expand exponentially daily, dependent solely on the speed with which people can come up with more relevant ideas and services to add.

Thanks to today's technology, intangibles are also increasingly transportable, accessible and easily communicated. Because of this they can be used by millions of people simultaneously and globally, instead of being limited by time, distance or space, as was the case with the scarce, discrete, tangible resources of the traditional business model.

As Thomas A Stewart, a leading proponent of knowledge management in the business press, puts it in his book *Intellectual Capital*:

> ... *like quantum particles, the [intangibles] can be in more than one place at a time. Sell me a cake and you no longer have it. Sell me the recipe and we both have it. Where intellectual assets and intangible outputs are concerned you can have your cake and eat it too.*

The implications for business are vast.

Changing the arithmetic

The economic principle of Ricardo and Keynes that value resided in the scarcity of core items is now irrelevant. But the principle – that adding yet another resource, be it a piece of land, a machine or a unit of capital, would only bring about diminishing returns – is deeply embedded in old management theory.

It is not just the manufacturers of high-tech products which can use the exponential characteristics of intangibles to produce new wealth. They can be used by all companies which seek to produce superior and personalized value for their customers. Who today can afford not to be such a company?

For these enterprises, the abundant intangibles are the prime source of wealth, a central and key principle of customer capitalism (see Table 12). Value appreciates disproportionately to resources employed due to the abundant nature of the intangibles, causing a change in the arithmetic – with traditional capitalism, the arithmetic is **addition**; with new capitalism, it is **multiplication**.

Intangible resources are able to build on themselves and returns increase as these resources are used and reused. New ideas beget new ideas; new knowledge begets new knowledge; new information begets new information:

➡ When a good idea for a customer by one employee at PricewaterhouseCoopers in Toronto is communicated to another in Singapore and used (and improved on), it appreciates in value exponentially.

➡ As the knowledge that Baxter gathers on the collective intelligence acquired on renal cases is accumulated and shared daily, so it appreciates in value exponentially for Baxter, hospitals, doctors and individual patients, health authorities and insurance companies.

➡ As the information that the RAC uses in its traffic system interacts, going backwards and forwards from corporation to corporation, corporation to customer, it appreciates exponentially. (Note: the same occurs in the commodity business, as traders learn, for example, more about what bulk chemical commodities have been traded.)

	TRADITIONAL CAPITALISM PRINCIPLES	CUSTOMER CAPITALISM PRINCIPLES
1 **AIM**	Maintaining the status quo	Fundamentally transforming
2 **LEADERS**	Replicating and improving products and/or services	Finding new ways of doing things for and with customers
3 **INNOVATION**	Inventing new technologies	Originating for and with customers
4 **OBJECT**	Optimizing margins on unit transactions	Maximizing the time value of customers
5 **MEANS**	Increasing market share in product/service categories	Dominating activities in market spaces
6 **VALUE**	Making and moving more core items	Linking benefits in an ongoing integrated experience
7 **TARGET**	For markets and average customer	For individual customers in an ever-increasing, ever-lucrative installed base
8 **UNIT OF** **COMPETITION**	By units/companies/ countries/industries	With win–win for all contributing players in new enterprise spaces
9 **RESOURCES**	Relying on the scarce tangibles	Relying on the abundant intangibles

Table 12 Principles of traditional and customer capitalism

These are not special cases. They are everyday illustrations of how, through the use of intangibles, the new market and economic dynamics of customer capitalism follow a multiplication path.

The thinking structure is fundamentally different from the old:

➡ With **traditional capitalism**, thinking was about allocating finite tangible resources that were scarce in order to optimize corporate assets.

➡ With **customer capitalism**, thinking is about processing intangible resources that are abundant in order to optimize customer value and so multiply corporate wealth.

Corporations which know how to leverage from this fact get the positive disproportionate gains and reinforcing effects of increasing returns. The more ideas, knowledge and information are shared between customer and corporation, the more proactive and precise are the offerings and the lower the cost. The more ideas, knowledge and information are shared between customer and corporation, the closer and deeper are the trust and the bond, so the stronger and longer the relationship, and the more what is known can be leveraged and exploded into wider market opportunities.

CHAPTER 25
MOBILIZING MINDPOWER

INCREASINGLY, THE ABUNDANT INTANGIBLES ARE THE MAJOR productive resource for the new enterprise. They also are the offerings themselves, its stock in trade. As they grow, accumulate and mutate, they become the assets, and count more than the ability to make or sell the core items.

But let's not misunderstand. In and of themselves, intangibles don't get increasing returns unless they become a steady flow, easily transferred from person to person, company to company, when and where needed. Intangibles must be readily convertible into decisions that result in relevant, not-easy-to-imitate value for the individuals in an installed customer base at critical points in the customer activity cycle.

Managing the stock and flow

WHAT'S IN PEOPLE'S HEADS Information is objective and easy to codify. It can be made tangible in databases, directories and software. In contrast, ideas and knowledge are subjective, in people's heads. They are human, mind-centered creations, dependent on the talent of individuals, but these are the intellectual assets that got and delivered the billions of dollars worth of long-term contracts for GE power division, when prices of core items were drastically falling. Such intellectual assets conceived the idea for an Auto-by-Tel, a Peapod, a Virgin and an Amazon, and leveraging from the lifelong value of renal patients rather than just selling more bags. Intellectual assets invented the software that got £259 million for Lotus from IBM, 14 times its book value. IBM didn't pay for the past revenues generated by Notes and other Lotus products, or for its labor hours, factories, machines or buildings. Neither was it paying for its manufacturing, distribution or sales facilities. Rather, it paid for the accumulated expertise, experience and cognition in the firm and the imagination of its people, which made it number one in the fast-growing *electronic collaborative group support* sub-market space. This was what Gerstner and his top executives believed that IBM needed in order to dominate the *global electronic networking capability* market space.

Acknowledging the role of intangibles in offerings, and the significance of ideas and knowledge in those intangibles, a chief task for the new corporate leader is to make sure that the company has the 'mindpower' or collective intelligence that it needs in stock and, if it hasn't, to get it or target it for investment. However, even though intangibles have potential for exponential returns once created and harnessed, they must still flow to and from employees, corporations, collaborators and customers if they are to be turned into money.

So, in a world of customer capitalism, the following top-of-mind questions should be constantly asked:

➡ What are the ideas and knowledge needed to provide offerings for customers?   ASK THESE QUESTIONS

➡ What ideas and knowledge do people who provide these offerings, or deal with others who provide these offerings, need?

➡ From whom do/will these ideas and knowledge come?

➡ How can they be captured and transformed for use/reuse?

➡ How can they be communicated and disseminated for real-time action at critical points in the customer activity cycle?

➡ What kinds of learning and reward environments do we need to keep them flowing, constantly growing, relevant and productive?

Making mindpower productive

One of the supreme ironies that we should keep in mind is that the very resources and assets that the modern enterprise needs in order to generate increasing returns are not owned by it and are beyond its control. Compare this with the traditional capitalism model, where corporations both owned and controlled the tangible assets, though they nonetheless brought diminishing returns. In his inimitable way, Charles Handy reminds us of this in an article in *Rethinking the Future*:

> *Who owns the capital? It's not the shareholders. It can't be in any real sense. The people who own the intellect are the core workers of the company. In other words, it's the assets who own the assets. Because we can't in any real sense own other people. They can always walk out on us.*

ASSETS
AS DEBTS
Given that today's value-generating resources belong to the people in whose heads they reside, they can be seen as more of a debt than an asset to the new enterprise. Consequently, these intangible assets cannot be managed in the same way as tangibles were in the past. Managed they must be, however, if they are to be leveraged for a durable advantage and kept alive in corporate memory banks. First and foremost, the new enterprise must get hold of them, a problem not previously encountered when a firm owned the tangible productive resources, raw material and a given amount of labor's scarce time. Second, it must spread them in order to grow them, a feat that conventional wisdom held to be impossible, since people could only be in one place at a time, doing one rote task at a time.

The consulting profession has some good examples of new practice. When KPMG Peat Marwick New York consultants go to a customer's office, they take their 75,000-odd colleagues with them. Everyone has access to the firm's 'brain trust' (as one executive referred to it), a giant mindpower machine accessing the ideas, information and knowhow, i.e. collective intelligence, of employees from around the world on practically any topic related to the client or its business. Expanding on this, a member of top management said:

KPMG PEAT MARWICK'S 'BRAIN TRUST'

> *Down there on the battlefield every professional that stands in front of a client is [the whole of] KPMG Peat Marwick. We are directing the combined intellectual assets of the firm down to a single point.*

His message is strong: the customer doesn't just get the best that a particular employee can offer, but if the intangibles are harnessed and the collective mindpower is made accessible, the customer can get the best that the whole corporation can offer. And through advanced technology, the KPMG Peat Marwick system can connect ideas, knowledge and information in the same way as linkages are built in the brain, creating what the company's executives call *'thought optimization'*.

The new enterprise can only get compounding leverage when people consciously apply its mindpower in their day-to-day dealings with customers. Andersen Consulting acknowledges this and actively targets employee behavior to avoid having ideas and knowledge just sitting in a static database. To achieve this end, offices have deliberately been made less and less relevant. In Paris, for instance, the company's move out of its old facilities to new ones has removed any vestige of personal employee space. This has been replaced by very sophisticated systems that allow consultants to log into its intelligence bank. Each consultant now

ANDERSEN CONSULTING: 'SPEAKING WITH ONE VOICE'

has a tiny filing cabinet with wheels designed to house as little paper as possible. This means that the only real link they have with the company is through the interactive electronic system, except for a number of large communal lounges on the premises where people meet, talk and discuss (a little like in airports).

Putting loops into global action

This emphasis on mobilizing mindpower at Andersen Consulting goes beyond the obvious. It is part of the company-wide objective to create a common language and set of experiences so *'it can speak with one voice to its growing numbers of worldwide customers'*. It also enables employees and their knowledge to be easily transferred from one project to another or one country to another for increased customer value creation. In addition, segments can be broken down into individual relationships while unifying the global audience.

Thanks to advances in the World Wide Web and private intranets, not only can huge quantities of unstructured information be collected, connecting people's technical and social networks, but additionally what is in people's heads can be made explicit as computers 'learn to learn', daily coming to a greater understanding of the meaning of information, which can be input to a firm's knowledge bank.

MOBILIZING
COLLECTIVE
INTELLIGENCE
GLOBALLY

Mobilizing collective intelligence is particularly important as customers, both private and corporate, demand that offerings are integrated and global. Not only can enterprises move their mindpower instantly to any destination around the planet, but they can also give customers the full impact of their collective mindpower without having to incur costs in time, money and energy moving staff around. This triggers the looping effects of customer capitalism:

➡ Customer **relationships** are enhanced by virtue of taking superior local offerings wider afield more quickly and cheaply, so strengthening global relationships.

➡ As more people and machines are connected by a particular technology worldwide, the value of the offering for customers is pushed up, globally as well as locally, as is the value of the **networks**.

➡ Investments in intangibles can be spread globally, cutting down the **costs** of doing business with customers, both locally and across the world.

➡ The more the **intangibles** are shared globally for local application, and locally for global application, the more productive the existing knowledge becomes and the more new knowledge is created, making offerings increasingly superior without undue added expense or time.

➡ As **players** do their part in the integrated global experience for customers, anyplace, anytime, so the value of offerings is enhanced locally, attracting more global customer spend and players.

➡ Due to global reach, investments are made by **developers** that place the infrastructure ahead, accelerating local advantage, expanding potential for further global reach and attracting still more innovation.

PricewaterhouseCoopers (PWC), which employs over 130,000 employees in 120 countries, is one of many examples of professional service organizations which leverage from these positive effects, having invested many years back in a powerful global, neural network. On a minute-for-minute basis, what is collected from the experiences of employees with local customers is fed into three global category-knowledge banks: business line, target segment and major clients. Each person in the organization has access to all of these. They are able to find out if a particular problem has been tackled before, and whom to contact to get the best expertise on that subject. So, for instance, a

NEURAL
NETWORKING
AT PWC

partner in Helsinki leading a project to apply computer systems to a mining house in Russia may find the mining expertise in Toronto and the computer expertise in California. PWC's network can bring it all together to present an optimum and cohesive picture to the Russian customer instantly in an extremely cost-effective way.

In much the same way, Citibank communicates its experiences with local customers globally to all concerned in its vast organization. As a matter of routine, all call schedules and reports go on to its intranet. Says one executive:

> *The object is to obviate old country reporting systems which are cumbersome and slow. This way people talk to others whom they would not normally do so on the conventional organization chart. Time and resources can be saved and the knowhow accumulated is used to anticipate the needs of customers locally, rather than wait for a request from them. In other words, we know what other parts of a customer organization are doing in other countries before they do, and we tell them.*

The new enterprise also shares ideas through its electronic networking systems to consciously extract and disseminate new thoughts for breakthrough innovations. Says a partner from PricewaterhouseCoopers:

> *Great ideas come from various strands of the business but have to be pulled together so that everyone benefits. When one country does something or has an idea, another can build upon it and there is a constant leapfrogging effect which is transferred directly into the marketplace.*

But needless to say, technology isn't enough.

MINING
MINDPOWER
AT BP

In addition to interactive electronic systems, getting increasing returns from the intangibles requires new, high-performing environments and organizational forms. British

Petroleum (BP) is renowned for this. CEO John Browne's strategy has been to jump the commodity chasm, moving the company from producing and distributing fuels and lubricants to providing various products and services in the *total supply management* market space for customers on the move – either traveling, or going by car to and from work. This has taken BP into convenience stores and various other domains, and who knows where else it may lead?

A great deal of energy since Browne's arrival at BP in 1995 has been about mobilizing collective intelligence inside the company and out in order to create customer value in this market space. With true innovative flair, he demolished the existing hierarchy and arranged BP into a series of virtual communities. These networks are linked by technologies and eagerly share ideas and knowledge.

In one huge global electronic environment of virtual teamworking, BP extracts the intangibles and gets them working effectively and exponentially. The explicit (exact) knowledge is captured and put into a database, while what is more implicit (experiential), for example the creative solution to a problem, is recorded. After-action reviews, borrowed from the US Army, are one technique used. Individuals meet informally to discuss their experiences following an event or customer project. Learning histories is another – employees are interviewed and their responses are formalized into a central repository with summaries, making what they know easy to find, understand and use, instead of people having to struggle to interpret them.

At Monsanto, knowledge teams are dispersed throughout the organization, creating and maintaining an online and video-conferencing 'yellow pages' guide to the company's knowledge. This guide then serves as a point of contact for people seeking information on different topics. Playing this role has much more to do with having the right instincts or inclinations for making sense of information and markets than with any notion of an individual's formal title. 'Topic experts' come from all walks of the organization, acting as conduits to and from other networks and sources of knowledge inside Monsanto and out.

Giving credit where debt is due

DRIVING
SHARING
BEHAVIORS

In all cases discussed, executives agree that the use of technology and systems is so strong as to be second nature to employees today. That is no longer the issue. What is the issue is changing employee behavior to reflect their contribution to the stock and flow of the intangibles that are effectively in their heads. To drive the sharing behavior that turns intangibles into the positive reinforcing looping that generates superior customer value involves new incentives and reward systems. Much of this is done through performance contracts and bonus schemes at BP. However, according to Hum Vainerie, a director of BP Oil, sharing behavior also happens because of BP's peer-to-peer structure. People at the same level doing the same things in different countries connect electronically and meet regularly face to face. The pressure that comes from colleagues working together in this environment of trust and reciprocity to achieve common goals produces effects that no formal system or diktat can do.

Five years ago, partners at what was then Price Waterhouse could maximize their profit share by being promoted to a management job – so that was the behavior bias. Today, the situation is quite different. The new reward system is deeply customer centered and bonuses are related to the contribution of knowledge and new ideas passed on that have gained ground for the enterprise in a segment or for a specific customer. Constant sharing and using of accumulated knowhow are critical to achieving this, which is why the use and reuse of this knowhow is what now drives behavior.

Japanese electronics manufacturer Fujitsu goes one step further to get the knowledge moving among its 70,000-strong workforce. It has developed an 'internal knowledge market'. Employees can sell knowledge to colleagues at a price, determined by the cost of knowledge generated, divided by the number of times it is expected to be reused (such costings are continually compared to the outside market price). Billings are made automatically and are currently heading for the $2 million mark. Every six months, each employee gets an income and expenditure statement and any net income made from knowledge sold is credited to that person's budget, which they can use to buy knowledge from other departments. FUJITSU'S INTERNAL KNOWLEDGE MARKET

As with stock markets in shares and other financial instruments, NatWest intends to go into knowledge markets, what it calls a global knowledge exchange. How it will trade this knowledge remains intriguingly uncertain, but the idea fits perfectly with a modern economy and customer capitalism, especially if it relates to growing markets and building new wealth. NATWEST'S KNOWLEDGE EXCHANGE

IBM Product Support in the UK recently made a radical shift from a reactive maintenance arm to a fully fledged, proactive business. With skills short and expensive, but opportunities abounding to help customers succeed with complex technology in increasingly resource-constrained environments, a management system has been built expressly to incentivize the growing and sharing of knowledge. Previously, productivity and profit potential were based on a consultant's daily utilization, i.e. billed time; they now depend on the extent to which the person's knowledge is reused and on its impact on productivity and performance. The object is to try to make professionals feel responsible for getting what they have learnt reused, even though it requires time and effort in activities they previously didn't have to do.

Rewards for consultants have been incorporated into their management and evaluation systems on a royalty-type basis, with employees encouraged to: IBM'S ROYALTY

➡ deliberately record what they have done and achieved with customers

➡ set out these experiences in a road map so that others can reuse this knowledge

➡ feed this into the database

➡ update when applicable.

This is accessed by colleagues who apply it, reuse it, refine it for their purposes and add to it, thereby making the knowledge more valuable and more widely known. As consultants spend time packaging their ideas and expertise for use by others, their profit on single engagements or for a period of time inevitably declines. However, if that person has been consciously building knowledge that contributes to growing the market or share of customer spend or bringing new customers into the installed base, credit is given on the basis that IBM will leverage the investment multifold.

PART NINE

ECONOMICS OF
CUSTOMER CAPITALISM

CHAPTER 26
SPREADING THE COST OF LEARNING

BJORN WOLRATH, CEO OF SKANDIA ASSURANCE, AND JAN Carendi, head of Skandia AFS, the Swedish-based financial company, had this compelling idea. They would create an independent network of local agents, financial advisers, brokers and bankers across the globe and make their collective mindpower accessible to Skandia employees. Skandia would be able to use this to build superior offerings for customers and leverage from the increasing returns of customer capitalism.

They succeeded.

The multiplier effect

MULTIPLYING KNOWLEDGE AT SKANDIA

Ever since they built this constellation of alliances in 1990, the company has been growing globally because of the compounding characteristic of knowledge. With a growth rate of nearly 50 percent per annum, it is now one of the top three providers of variable annuities (savings-cum-insurance) in the world. Describing itself as a *'specialist in cooperation'*, the company employs only around 2200 people, but it uses the collective learning of the 70,000-strong giant 'federation network' which it converts into ongoing and exponential customer value. Says Leif Edvinsson, director of intellectual capital at Skandia and author of several books on the subject:

Skandia leverages off this knowledge without all the costs of ownership. We used to own a huge expensive mainframe in the back room with which we did the financial planning for customers; now we get the knowledge and information of the entire network. We can leverage 40 people on average for every full-time employee that sells our financial services.

No explicit theories exist to explain how knowledge behaves INFINITE as a resource and how it affects the economics of a business. SCOPE However, what we do know is that, if managed correctly, the new enterprise gets a multiplier effect when the abundant intangibles are being productively used and reused, which gives the firm the infinite scope that has never before been encountered. This portrays yet another distinction between traditional and customer capitalism:

➡ With **traditional capitalism**, the more of something that was used the less valuable it became.
➡ With **customer capitalism**, the more something is used the more valuable it becomes – exponentially.

Quite simply, with customer capitalism the enterprise can create resources by reusing and renewing those it already has. At Skandia, the collective intelligence of the network is deliberately turned into a tangible format. Edvinsson's point is that you can't borrow money on the strength of your employees because they can walk away, but you can borrow money if you can create a tangible representation of what the organization knows. So mindpower in people's heads, like organizational capability or information technology systems which can be made tangible, is quantified at Skandia so that the company and others (like employees and investors) know what they have got. This enables them to get superior offerings to existing customers and new markets better, quicker and more cost effectively and so leverage from the positive disproportionate gains of customer capitalism.

Planned knowledge management

We have known for some time that knowledge grown exponentially comes from the continuous learning processes that people go through. Tasks get easier the more frequently they are done, the impact of which is well documented in as much detail as corporations desire. As productivity goes up, the cost of making and moving products or services goes down.

MOVING
THE LEARNING
CURVE ON

However, using the learning curve formalized by Boston Consulting Group almost exclusively for cost purposes to increase market share and profits per item is what made learning curves part of traditional capitalism thinking and a victim of diminishing returns. Yet this has occurred for decades in both the manufacturing and service sectors. So much so that learning in the interest of producing superior cost-effective offerings was often ignored in agendas and day-to-day activities. In fact, some writers suggest that the whole idea of calling it a learning curve was probably a misnomer, since it had less to do with learning and more to do with getting high volumes of the core items out of the system.

With Peter Senge's book *The Fifth Discipline* came the popularization of the notion of the 'learning organization' in the 1990s. Learning came to be seen as more of a strategic than just a cost tool and enormous amounts of time, money and effort were directed into learning systems. But this often was too much for the sake of learning and not about translating this learning into customer value and new market opportunities.

HERE'S THE
DIFFERENCE

Here's the difference with learning in the new customer capitalism model:

➡ When learning becomes a device for acquiring and applying information and knowledge about individuals to serve them more effectively, the positive reinforcing loops go into motion, engendering customer lock-on with all its accelerating and multiplying benefits.

➡ When learning is used for planned knowledge sharing with others in the enterprise space – the units, divisions and corporations delivering the customer results – the value of the knowledge rises exponentially for all. Authority James Brian Quinn expands on this in his classic work *Intelligent Enterprise*:

As one shares knowledge with colleagues and other ... organizations, ... these units gain information ... They usually feed back questions, amplifications, and modifications, which instantly adds further value for the sender. As each receiving group learns and creates from its new knowledge base, the base itself grows, opening totally new exponential growth possibilities. Since learning feeds knowledge back to the base, the next step ... will spring from a higher base and be a larger absolute increment. The process itself is exponential – exponential growth occurs in the value of each sharing group's knowledge base. As the groups share solutions with each other, the interactive potentials of their knowledge grow at an even steeper exponential.

The point is that customer capitalism uses learning curves to assist corporations to get to know more about customers and how to deliver value to individuals better than anyone else. The learning becomes the new form of labor, as Shoshana Zuboff so aptly states in her work *In the Age of the Smart Machine: the Future of Work and Power*. However, unlike the labor of traditional capitalism, limited and discrete in time and energy and by rote in output (and therefore scarce), this learning — or new form of labor – provides the opportunity for infinite scope and variety, constant innovation and the flexibility to make changes in real time where and when necessary.

Skandia selects, combines and refines the learnings of its 70,000-strong alliance and employees to produce high-quality, personalized offerings geared to suit the unique and changing needs of its customers. Ideas, knowledge and information are plentiful rather than fixed (as regimented labor was before), which means that Skandia can keep on producing better offerings at no extra cost. This is why and how it creates the generative behavior that gets customers to lock on, thereby avoiding the one-off, price-driven transactions that produce the diminishing returns characteristic of its industry for so many decades. Specifically, Skandia manages learning by:

➡ packaging it for transfer to others
➡ deliberately getting it shared to be reused over and over again
➡ changing it continuously, keeping it updated and in constant flux
➡ recirculating it, through technology, in real time.

It is not to be forgotten that these learnings represent an invisible, virtual production process with customer capitalism. When more of what is known is applied, more value accrues for everyone — customers, corporations and collaborators. However – and this is essential – what is 'seen' and 'felt' to get customers to lock on is the flair and force of the modern enterprise. In the case of Skandia, the 2200 employees use the intangibles to create the customer link and bonding, constantly strengthening their brand equity.

Mass customizing knowhow

Whereas in the past the corporation sought to get economies of scale from its resources, which it did by producing the core items in volumes, the new enterprise seeks to make the most of what people have learnt and know. As the spreading and sharing of knowledge are increased, costs decrease which, together with superior offerings, reinforce customer lock-on. Moreover, from unique encounters with unique customers, unique value is extracted and converted into widened possibilities for spreading skills and costs across new customers and new market spaces.

By consciously looking for those parts of the experiences that are replicable and getting these learnings into working processes and practice, the stock of mindpower multiplies, economies of skill are built up and time, energy and expenses are reduced. Says John Browne of BP:

> *No matter where the knowledge comes from, the key to reaping a big return is to leverage that knowledge by replicating it throughout the company so that each unit is not learning in isolation.*

Getting this learning into a form in which it can be leveraged as an intellectual asset for future growth potential is critical. IBM has made special investments in this in its global consulting division. Executives say that learnings should:

LEVERAGING FROM LEARNING

- ➡ be reusable in a variety of contexts
- ➡ exemplify a unique, innovative approach applied to a customer situation
- ➡ create or enhance a methodology, technique or architecture
- ➡ provide a unique visual representation of a concept or process
- ➡ present a comprehensive update or summary of information.

As John Browne reminds us, the wonderful thing about knowledge is that, unlike tangibles, once it is captured it is relatively inexpensive to replicate. And miraculously, in complete contrast to traditional capitalism, not only does stock go up but costs go down, adding quite considerably to building the multiplying and durable advantage for corporations which use the principles of customer capitalism. Without these principles, it would just be another ploy to save on cost per unit made and sold.

But let's not oversimplify. No learning can be completely routine and replicable, even learning that can be replicated – it depends a great deal on the type of business. One way or another, learning modules need to be built so that what is replicable is easily repeated and the rest can be adapted – call it mass customization of knowhow.

STARTING WITH END USERS Taking BP as an example, it starts with the end-user customers and works backwards to decide on processes needed to, let's say, globalize a range of merchandise in its convenience stores across the world. What can be replicated on a country-for-country basis become generic modules. The rest can be adapted in part or whole to suit local conditions, like environmental regulation or consumer preferences. As long as the generic processes are replicated by individuals in their respective countries, the actual offerings can be modified, says Jorge Tavares, head of the globalization project.

People doing similar functions in different countries are brought together with the express purpose of sharing what they have learnt, as BP tries to create prevalence for *new ways of providing supplies to customers on the move* simultaneously in all of the advanced, emerging and developing countries of the world.

Tavares expands:

> *They question each other, take note and look for what is common to take away and replicate, rather than what is different which is what they did in the past. These learnings are then transferred, increasing the value of what is known on that subject to individual countries and to the BP network as a whole.*

Growing and expanding knowledge by making it replicable
also enable the new enterprise to get into higher value-add
ground in the customer activity cycle, which often requires
skills that are expensive and in short supply. By applying
and spreading learning, the new enterprise is able to operate successfully in these new, complex environments without cost becoming a huge barrier to it or its customers.

On this higher ground, making knowhow replicable is
not that easy, however, as tasks are complex and often one-
off applications. Getting the benefits of mass customization
is possible, but less obvious, requiring proactive management of the process. For instance, executives estimate that
for IBM's Product Support Group only between 25 and 30
percent is replicable – the rest are specialized applications.
However, this 25–30 percent is actively reused. At the same
time it is reworked, put into the data banks with modules
kept flexible, modified where and when necessary and
updated continuously with new experiences in order to
avoid obsolescence.

As enterprises share and grow their knowledge, and
people learn how to learn from each other, they accelerate
market acceptance and prevalence for their new ways of
doing things. Revenues come in more quickly and projects
are more cost effective to set up. In particular, getting what
works in one country speedily implemented in another
requires a search for generic concepts that get altered at the
margin, instead of the other way round.

Citibank has used 'model concept' branches as a physical manifestation of its learning to accelerate its globalization strategy. These model branches are built so as to follow
the customer activity cycle from the beginning to the end of
a person's experience with the bank in the *global financial
management* market space. They also allow customers to get
the same service electronically in their homes, offices or
cars that they would experience at the branch. Having
begun in Chile, this model concept was taken into Europe

where it was started in Greece and then moved further afield. It acts as a live laboratory and reference point for colleagues throughout the organization so that learning can be passed on in a tangible way.

What this all boils down to is that learnings drawn from countries, and shared, change the economics with increasing returns implications. They dramatically alter the speed at which projects can take off, and accelerate cash flow as well as lowering the cost of implementation. Tavares of BP gives two statistics to demonstrate: building a service station is 60 percent less expensive today with planned knowledge sharing; and it now takes only 10 weeks to finish one, whereas in the past it could take up to three to four months.

Skandia has had the same experience. Reusing the learning, bringing it consciously back into the system, has sped up the opening of offices worldwide from seven years to seven months, giving the company worldwide market presence and prevalence at quantum speed. *'It's easier, quicker and cheaper to swap recipes than to keep building cookie factories in every locality,'* says Edvinsson.

CHAPTER 27

THE 'FALLING COST PER UNIT' PHENOMENON

THE COSTS OF MAKING AND MOVING OFFERINGS WITH CUSTOMER capitalism in no way resemble those of traditional capitalism. In the latter, the marginal costs of the core items, be they loans or seeds, car repair or personal computers, were what was important in assessing profitability. The main way to get profit up was to get the marginal costs of the core items down, and the way to achieve that was to increase volume, to get the core items sold, i.e. to increase market share.

The problem was that this formula only worked up to a point. At that point, marginal costs began to rise again, meeting marginal revenues head on and producing diminishing returns.

Marginalizing marginal costs

All that changes with customer capitalism. Offerings that provide customers with results and corporations with potential for customer lock-on and growth are high in intangibles – ideas, knowledge and information – and investments in these are made up front, long before the production process begins. The result is that cost becomes marginal, a non-issue. This is another important distinction between traditional capitalism and customer capitalism:

➡ With **traditional capitalism**, financial success was inextricably bound up with the marginal costs of items, related to the number of units produced.

➡ With **customer capitalism**, the marginal costs of the important parts of the offering are so low as not to be relevant to financial success and, if relevant, are not related to volumes of units produced.

Costs fall because...

Costs are inverted with the new market and economic looping dynamics of customer capitalism because:

➡ The cost of doing business between a company and the customer goes down as ideas, knowledge and information are shared.
➡ The cost of delivering a linked benefit in the new enterprise space goes down as resources are shared and duplications are eliminated between players.
➡ The raw materials, the intangibles, are abundant and grow as they are used, further reducing cost of stock.
➡ Customers give productive input, which additionally reduces costs.
➡ The high dominance of intangibles and technology in offerings leads to what is known as the production 'falling cost per unit' phenomenon.

Let's look at this final point in more detail:

Offerings increasingly high in intangibles have a low, if not trivial, marginal cost

The first Microsoft Windows probably cost $150 million to make, whereas the follow-up version cost next to nothing. This was because most of the investment was made up front (silicon chips are made from small amounts of cheap, essentially sand-based derivatives). Distribution, i.e. copying the piece of software on to a disk or putting it on to the Internet, costs just a few dollars, if that. The cost to Encyclopaedia

Britannica of producing – printing, binding and distributing – a set of encyclopaedias went as high as $3000. In contrast, the cost of producing a CD-Rom, embedded with intangibles and low in scarce resources, is only about $1.50.

Software is an intriguing case. What is it, a product or a service? This was the big question that was being asked in the mid-1980s when the merging of products and services occurred. The more advanced offerings became, the greater the customer's appetite grew for value-added services. But here was software, caught somewhere between a traditional product and a traditional service, tangible and manufactured, yet with intangible real value. Costs were incurred long before a production process began, so what pricing pattern would it follow?

THE HARD SIDE OF SOFTWARE

It became obvious that with these information products, there was not just another pricing strategy to think about but a whole new economics going on. As the heavy component in software was intangible, the marginal costs of production were so low as to make them irrelevant, which meant that they followed the pattern of increasing rather than diminishing returns.

No one is immune

This phenomenon does not just apply to software and high-tech information products. First, there isn't a single corporation today that can operate without technology, and this includes bulk producers of commodity products; no one is immune to the new economic dynamics.

Second, we should not think of software as just being a computer disk. Any part of an offering that gives instructions about use is software: the gene inside a Monsanto seed is software when it tells the wheat seed how to react and behave under different circumstances, i.e. resist frost, bugs or disease, grow faster, slow down, protect itself, or when it enables the seed to produce special attributes for end-user markets, like less starch content for bread makers or more digestibility for animal feed.

And the talk is that soya beans will soon be able to be instructed to make a natural compound to fight cancer or reduce the saturated fat in the eggs of the chickens that eat them. Future generations of drugs or vaccines will be able to adjust to suit the unique features and circumstances of a particular individual patient's unique metabolism or pathology as part of their own made-to-measure medical program. That's all software.

PUTTING
INTELLIGENCE
ANYPLACE,
EVERYPLACE

Third, software or intelligence is going into almost all products – automobiles, consumer electronics, appliances, wallets, toys. Therefore the dynamics of increasing returns will accrue to enterprises that use information and computer products to drive lifelong customer value, rather than those that simply make and move more and more of the high-tech core items.

The metal parts in cars are being replaced by intelligent systems and advanced safety features through built-in computers and software. When these are combined with other value-add services through the customer activity cycle, the customer gets a superior and linked experience.

Having switched from 'automobile guaranteeing' to 'mobility guaranteeing' in the new *personal mobility* market space, companies like Toyota are filling their trunks with computers and multiple sensors that operate nearly 20 safety systems. They have cameras that enable drivers to see around corners and SOS buttons so that they can stop the car if they feel ill. The cars also have radar technologies to warn of solid objects up ahead. The car can predict how its driver will behave, inform cars nearby and, if an accident is likely, alert the driver so that they can take evasive action.

In Japan, Toyota is putting terminals into vehicles that are increasingly becoming extensions of the driver's work and leisure space. Drivers and/or passengers can navigate, watch videos, listen to CD-quality music and tap into the

Internet and e-mail by subscribing to the Nihon Mobile Broadcasting Corporation (NMBC) multichannel service, a joint venture between the broadcaster, Fujitsu and Toyota. Knowing the Japanese reputation for sharing knowledge and spreading it across nations, it probably won't take long before we see this globally.

In an attempt to dominate activities in the *short-haul mobility* market space for its installed European customer base, Mercedes is building software into its vehicles to tell drivers when they need oil and transmission fluids, instead of having to watch the respective gauges. It is also connecting cars' software to the Internet to remotely diagnose (and so prevent) a problem while the car is on the road. Mercedes also offers onboard computers whose software gives audio navigation instructions. In other words, the software is being used as part of one totally integrated experience to get customer lock-on.

BMW is ready to sell cars with voice control systems, meaning that the driver can verbally give a destination address to the car, which will then call out when and where the driver should make the turns. In time, motorists may be able to climb into the back of their car and simply order it to drive itself home, thanks to Visteon, the Ford-owned components group that has developed the complex new software technology.

What is amazingly different and significant is that no identifiable additional expense is expected to go on to the marginal cost (or price) of these cars. This is because the investments have been made up front, before the vehicles get to the production line.

Modern service enterprises obey the same rules, in that they don't necessarily need more resources to produce more. Knowhow and information content are high and investments are made up front, with all the opportunities for use and reuse that we have discussed. All of this adds up to the fact that their marginal costs go down or are unaffected by numbers of customers. This is distinct from a McDonald's which, once it has millions of customers queuing for

SERVICES OBEY THE SAME RULES

hamburgers, must also have more tangible resources and labor (doing repetitive tasks) to meet the demand.

Another significant point is that the cost of expanding services into wider markets decreases quite dramatically once the initial investment in intangibles has been made. IBM Europe, for example, has invested hugely in knowledge, skills and information to outsource for the insurance segment, among others. Its venture with the Perth branch of General Accident Insurance was the first step in a new, long-term competitive strategy to build a center of excellence for customers in personal and corporate financial risk management. It then sought to lever its ever-growing experience and knowledge into a wider market at low marginal cost. Said one IBM executive:

> *Having done it once for General Accident, the initial costs have been spent. Gathering together a community of technological and industry specialists and making that system work was the difficult and expensive part – now we can leverage that by providing services at a much lower production cost, attracting more customers and new markets, pulling down costs even more while continuing to grow our expertise and improve our offering, accelerating market take-on even more.*

Once Baxter Renal had made its up-front investment to become the provider of renal care in the customer's home, it was able to spread these expenses in several ways and get the consequent gains. Such gains included longer-term agreements with buyers that cost less than the old contract system, which involved huge renewal expenses. From the initial investment, it has been able to stretch its brand into HD (the treatment that usually follows PD) and provide other drugs and services related to renal diseases that patients need for a fully integrated and longer experience at home; all at very little extra marginal cost.

Economics of the Internet

In the traditional capitalism model there was constant tension between spending time with customers and saving money by working faster, reducing interaction and so maximizing margins and returns per transaction. Resolving this conflict was a continuous battle, which many a service company or institution in particular simply resolved to live with, much to their diminishing returns. Things have changed.

The use of interactive technology in offerings dramatically reduces costs

With interactive technologies a way of life, and a critical mass of the population poised to use the Internet and whatever else may follow, the economics at the point of customer contact change. The World Wide Web medium in particular means that costs of production, delivery and communication for an extra customer can even approach zero. This being the case, the new enterprise can increase its capacity at little or no extra cost, taking on ever more customers without the added expenses.

With the Internet it is not necessary to invest in a dedicated network (that is, people and machines connected by a particular technology belonging to a company) in order to get to customers. For example, from its Web site Federal Express can now allow the 40 percent of its customers who were not on its dedicated infrastructure in the past to track their own parcels and look up records of their dealings. This avoids the time and hassle of phoning in and the expense to Fedex of having an operator. Michael Janes, vice-president of electronic commerce and logistics management, insists that ultimately: *'We don't care if it's their network or ours. We just want the network to be everywhere.'*

All Fedex customers have real-time and detailed access to the movement of their goods, including exact times of arrival at interim stops. This improves the quality of their experience without Fedex having to make any gigantic investment. The essential point for the new enterprise is this: the production costs of connecting customers have nothing to do with volume. Irrespective of how many customers want the service at a particular time – one or a million – the expense to Fedex remains the same.

On the same theme, the marginal cost to Auto-by-Tel of having the customer stay online for another minute is extremely low compared to having to dedicate an extra minute to that person face to face or through a call center. In the first case, each customer would dominate a resource, preventing others from using it. On the Internet, millions of customers can now access the same site at the same time at practically no extra cost.

HOLDING ON TO CUSTOMER INTIMACY

So with customer capitalism, not only are we dealing with economics where there is zero or close to zero cost to adding extra customers, but with the Internet, the new enterprise can also sweep in larger numbers of customers at nearly zero cost without having to forfeit the personalization that creates individual customer lock-on. In marked contrast to traditional capitalism, tradeoffs do not have to be made, with customers on the losing end. Instead, customers gain. For instance, Auto-by-Tel doesn't have to get rid of customers as quickly as possible to save money. At point of contact, customers can stay online as long as necessary. In fact, Auto-by-Tel actively encourages this because customers feel happier that way and they make better, more informed decisions. This all saves time and money for auto dealers, keeping costs down, prices competitive and reinforcing customer lock-on.

In addition, with the changing cost dynamics of interactive technology, the new enterprise gets access to new markets that might previously have found the price of a service offering too formidable. IBM Product Support Services is one example: it now offers consulting-led management systems over the Internet to small and medium-sized businesses which are unable to pay high fees. Through a series of questions, IBM finds the problem and fixes it and then exposes these clients to the rest of its portfolio. The assessment exercise enables it to get into the customer activity cycle early on, at a price the customer can afford; and it gets to know users and their operations intimately, thus building a platform for new business and subscription revenue for other services.

Another part of the costs saved using interactive technology lies in disintermediation. Corporations learn to deal directly with customers quickly and effectively. They connect with others who provide the total experience in the customer activity cycle, instead of perpetuating the linear value (cost?) chains of the old model. With the Direct Line format now mainstream for many types of insurance policies and providers, 'middlemen' costs are eliminated, making offerings 30 to 50 percent cheaper than those of the conventional alternatives – travel agents, banks or building societies. But here's the point: the customer comes out with a better experience, not just a cheaper product, and money saved is channeled back into R&D and the infrastructure to constantly improve the offering.

Factoring in customer input

Costs are also saved by virtue of the input obtained from customers – a 'free good'. In other words, in reality customers pay not only in money but also in value-add opinions, experiences and commentaries with customer capitalism. They also provide solid information on a variety of fronts, including themselves, all of which can be used and leveraged on.

This value should be factored into the economic calculation of doing business with that customer. As already stated, in the future it is more than possible that these customers – especially the large corporations or organized virtual communities – could very well begin to charge for their

CHANGING
COSTINGS

input or the data they provide. At the very least, they could control the information disseminated about themselves.

One of the particular savings, though not the only one from getting this input, comes from delivering offerings through new technological link-ups. For instance, the questions that IBM Product Support UK asks over the Net when it consults small and medium-sized businesses feeds its database, which becomes self-perpetuating, ever growing in value. It can easily do this on a pan-European or global basis.

With new technology, it's also easier to access more information on more dispersed customers. This information on a wide variety of products can be obtained more quickly than was previously possible. It is also possible to get to customer histories across firms and industries (think of the added value in medicine or banking), which cuts down on the costs of fully integrating offerings.

CUSTOMERS AS PRODUCERS   Moreover, as customers become more familiar with the technology, they are able to participate more and more in the actual production process, extracting the value for themselves and sharing it with others. In other words, they become producers, not just consumers. For instance, as Fedex customers do their own tracking, they do real work that saves Fedex costs. Through the technology customers are becoming, as John Hagel and Arthur Armstrong put it in their book *Net Gain*, a 'key driver of economic value', with yet more potential for decreasing costs. This is especially true if it is combined with the promise of so-called electronic helpers or agent software that is designed to circulate on the Internet, helping customers find exactly what they need, further increasing their productivity, with potential for even more cost savings.

The new enterprise can also save costs through customer chat lines, because customers train and do things for each other. For instance, the installed base of customers who enter the Lotus Notes technical support database directly has become so large that not only do greater numbers get assistance from Lotus, but they also help each other. Lotus executives report that this pulls Lotus's costs down and pushes service and customer camaraderie up.

CHAPTER 28
MORE WITH LESS

THIS ALL POINTS TO A WORLD IN WHICH THE NEW ENTERPRISE can get more with less or use less to gain more, by working with the new market and economic dynamics of customer capitalism. Previously, gains came from managing scarcity; gains now come overwhelmingly from managing abundance. Intangibles are the dominant factor in offerings and costs decrease though value increases. We also see that the expenses of producing and distributing offerings, or reaching another customer, are driven down thanks to new networked technologies, while intimacy is retained and customers get better and more personalized offerings.

THE FACTS OF THE (NEW) MATTER
These are the facts of the (new) matter, or, more explicitly, of the non-matter:

➡ Factors of production and raw materials grow as they are used, applied and reused.

➡ The productive resource inventory is augmented, not depleted, in the production process.

➡ With offerings loaded with intangibles, the marginal cost of production is low or even zero.

➡ The new electronic technologies that convey these valuables can get to more customers, more quickly, at no or very low extra cost.

➡ Costs are saved because of value and input obtained from customers.

New economies for new economics

Economics reconstruct as the principles of customer capitalism are used to produce customer lock-on and intangible-dominant offerings become mainstream. The economics change from one dependent on volumes to get the marginal cost per unit down, to one where marginal cost is minor or features less in the financial algorithm. This, plus the use of technology, switches the economics for the new enterprise from economies of scale based on the volume of core items made and moved, to four new constructs, namely:

➡ **Economies of skill** – knowing more, growing and using and reusing this to produce ongoing, superior customer value at no or low cost.

➡ **Economies of stretch** — endowing the brand with power and elasticity so that it can quite easily stretch into other products and services within a market space or into new market spaces at no, or low, customer acquisition costs.

➡ **Economies of sweep** — through networked interactive technologies, the ability to get to large quantities of customers superior personalized value at no or zero additional cost.

➡ **Economies of spread** — creating prevalence, which makes new ways of doing things the standard, so enabling investments made to be spread over larger numbers of customers over longer periods.

Moreover, as the new enterprise learns to use new technologies over a wider variety of offerings and circumstances, not only do costs go down, but some of the familiar and formidable tradeoffs of traditional capitalism disappear. Offerings can be personalized for individuals because new interactive technology allows electronic intimacy, which

ELIMINATING THE TRADEOFFS

makes for lasting and deep relationships in many more instances than was previously feasible. The new form of electronic interaction sometimes eclipses human interaction and sometimes combines with it.

Intangibles, representing the bulk of the value in offerings and being front loaded, mean that money has been spent before the production process begins. The new enterprise can therefore amortize investments across rising customer volumes as prevalence is built, rather than having to hike prices initially, which can inhibit market acceptance.

Value is no longer constricted or constrictive since it is no longer produced by limited scarce resources like materials, finite labor or financial capital. Production is also free of these constraints. So however high, diverse or dispersed the market may be, supply should be feasible as demand fuels demand in a new cumulative and compounding fashion.

Overheads, which were previously driven constantly upwards, can now be contained by the sharing and dissemination of knowledge, and by growing knowledge connecting knowledgeable people to other knowledgeable people. They can also be brought down by the sharing of technology and resources among players in new enterprise spaces. Added to this is the increased cost saving from collaborating around shared infrastructures.

SIZE AS AN END   Changes in the economics of customer capitalism herald another feature that contradicts the traditional business model's scale logic. With the new model, companies or institutions don't have to be big (in the traditional sense of the word, i.e. number of hard assets or employees) to participate in the positive feedback process that generates increasing returns:

➡ It costs less to be big.
➡ It takes less time to become and act big.
➡ Firms don't have to be big to be price competitive.
➡ They don't have to be big to be global.

➡ They don't have to be big to participate in networking effects.

➡ They don't have to be big to gain from the advantages that a player in an enterprise space gets from the actions and interactions of other players in that enterprise space.

In sum, success leads to size with customer capitalism, not the other way around. Size becomes the end, not the means to the end.

The infinite nature of smart

Coupled with the change in cost structure as products become increasingly smart, with more built-in intelligence and software to get results to customers, fewer resources are needed in a totally integrated experience. The intangibles – ideas, knowledge and information – replace the expensive physical and financial resource-intensive part of the offering, which in his article 'Twelve New Rules for the New Economy' Kelly refers to as *'stuff that requires increasing knowledge'*. There are now microwaves that can surf the Net and find and print out recipes for customers in their kitchens, and printers that photocopy, scan, fax etc. Cars are being created from ultra-lightweight material, substituting mass and scarce resources with smart materials. The accumulated effect of this substitution of intelligence for materials in cars will be vehicles safer than today's that will also require less energy (much of that energy being used now is to move the car, instead of the passenger). Experts believe that soon a car will have more computing power than a typical desktop personal computer.

DOUBLING UP

Thanks to advances in computer technology, products are also beginning to learn like people do. For instance, computers will recognize a user and will turn on and tune in automatically for that person. A car will be able to adjust automatically to the individual preferences and habits – good

MULTIPLE TRAITS AND TASKING

and bad – of each driver, and protect them, based on these habits, gathering value along the way. A drug will be able to adjust according to the metabolism of the individual's body.

Multiple traits are already being built into offerings, such as Monsanto's seeds, meaning that from one physical product several customer outcomes are possible. In addition, many functions can be performed by single products. Ever present with customers are mobile phones, which can provide more than just telephony services. They can multiple task – delivering personal number and access services, navigation services, banking services, video-conferencing, car and road guidance news and cash, as well as linking the customer into the Internet. And a computer mouse can act as a mobile phone today. To take another example of multiple tasking, thanks to Java's computing language and Mondex's MULTOS multiple-application approach, the different ways in which people store, handle and manage their information can now be combined. One card can contain information on credit, debit, health, loyalty and passport, plus it can provide services like shopping or banking, from a variety of terminals.

Such smart offerings relieve customers of the need to keep huge quantities of information in mind. They no longer have to think of many common activities that need doing on their activity cycle, such as having to remember to record, order, fix, improve, replenish, renew, replace and so on. In addition, the more products and services that are linked into an integrated experience, the more savings there are all round in time, money and energy.

A CASE FOR THE ENVIRONMENT There is also the conservation of economic matter to think about. Bob Shapiro of Monsanto argues that getting more for less reduces waste. He has a high environmental component in his new customer capitalism strategy. In his words:

> *The earth can't withstand the systematic increase of material things, but it can support exponential increases in information and knowledge.*

Rather than getting diminishing returns from the use of more finite resources, Monsanto's integrated crop concept endeavors to increase the productivity of farms while reducing waste:

> *We can genetically code a plant to repel insects. That means we don't have to spray the plants with pesticides (up to 90 percent of what is sprayed on crops today is wasted!) ... the key is growth in value without having to multiply the scarce 'stuff'.*

Cash is more important than profit

The marginal cost of producing units of products and services is no longer the focal point in the financial algorithm of the new enterprise. Nor is it what gives the new enterprise its competitive advantage. So what is?

Enduring revenue streams take center stage, for which a firm needs to get customer lock-on. To build this customer lock-on requires investment in the relational, intellectual and infrastructural assets that forge new markets and provide ongoing platforms for extension and growth for those that already exist.

GENERATING HIGH-QUALITY VALUE STREAMS

In a strategy based on customer capitalism, cash flowing from the time value of customers – call it high-quality value streams – is ascendant over profits made on each unit. So the prime concern for the modern enterprise is how to get the customer lock-on from an installed base, ever expanding, ever lucrative, to obtain the value streams that generate the free cash to invest and to reward shareholders, investors and employees.

PART TEN
SCORING TO WIN

CHAPTER 29
PRICING FOR TIME

REVENUES AND CASH GENERATION ARE ALL ABOUT WHO GETS what, where and when, in the customer activity cycle. Some activities in the customer activity cycle attract more revenues and cash, others less. But generally, the customer value streams are increasingly coming from the 'pre' and 'post' stages, which is where the high-ground results are being produced.

Sharing the total value pool

With customer capitalism, total potential equals that pool of revenues extracted by participating players in enterprise spaces which directly interface with customers, or develop for or supply to those which do in a particular market space. For example, in the *renal sufficiency* sub-market space, all parts of the offering to get extended life to end users, from early diagnosis into PD and HD dialysis, through transplant into end-stage care (which could be over a period of 30 years), equals the total value pool at any given moment in time. In the *risk assurance farming* market space, it is all of the offerings that ensure that farmers get maximum agricultural and financial results, from decisions on what to make through all climate, crop and cash-managing activities. In the *electronic global networking capability* market space, the total potential equals the revenue of all the activities: consulting, systems integration, installation, training, maintenance and repair. It also includes updates and the various products and services to develop, deliver and support as well as constantly upgrade the offering to get the appropriate and lifelong results for customers.

What percentage of that value pool a Baxter, Monsanto, IBM or any of their collaborators captures depends on what activities it dominates in a given market space. Intuitively, we know that the more activities it is involved in, the greater the interplay of the positive loops and possibility for customer lock-on and increasing returns. But note: with the principles of customer capitalism, extracting as much value as possible doesn't mean charging or making as much as possible on every discrete unit or single product or service produced. That was the scenario with traditional capitalism when the focus was on margins per unit.

This is because:

➡ With **traditional capitalism**, the profitability of each discrete product, service, unit, division etc. was all important.
➡ With **customer capitalism**, it is the profitability that comes from the time value of the customer that matters.

To charge or not to charge

The fact that every division, country, unit, product or service had to be profitable in the past was a by-product of the way that corporations were structured for accounting purposes. With customer capitalism the logic is quite different. In the *lifelong event cash management* market space over a customer's life, for instance, Virgin Banking has defied traditional organization. It doesn't engage in the duplicated expenses of, nor make money from, every single product or service in the customer's experience, as was the case when firms and industries each did their own thing in disparate silos. What Virgin Banking favors is not the profitability of each unit, division, product or service, but the overall or lifelong profitability of individuals or households. The emphasis is on superior value at low delivered cost for customers over time. It is from this achievement that the customer value streams for reinvestment and reward distribution come.

Does every single product or service offered in the customer activity cycle have to be charged for? What if the corporation decides to provide a product or service to avoid a value gap, but elects not to charge? Then the extra cost must be funded by one or more of the following:

FUNDING THE
VALUE GAP

➡ increased revenues obtained through the time value of customers (economies of stretch)
➡ prevalence so that investment costs can be spread over greater customer numbers (economies of spread)
➡ knowledge gained and transferred into longer, more cost-effective customer relationships and wider market opportunities (economies of skill)
➡ the elimination of duplications, waste or activities that add costs, rather than produce the customer value through the increased use of networked technology (economies of sweep).

You may recall that Baxter gives away its training at £1000 a patient. However, the customers who are trained get better results on the therapy and stay on treatment longer, thus more bags are sold. Apparent reduced margins are therefore not really reduced margins, rather they are an investment for which Baxter gets longer-term commitments, lower renewal costs and greater depth, width and diversity of customer spend. This is why by year-end 1998 Baxter's sales and profits were both up (although unit profit margins were down). And what it refers to as 'therapy transfer', which is the percentage of people lost to death, HD or transplant, went down for PD from nearly 50 percent in 1996 to 37 percent.

Its home care service is not a profit center in the traditional accounting sense of the word – but does that make it a failure? On the contrary, it has given the company its edge, entry and brand stretch into competitive HD treatment and other services and drugs related to total renal patient care at home at low marginal cost. This has widened the corporation's potential share of the renal sufficiency value pool, as well as increasing the overall size of the value pool. Additionally, getting into HD has enabled Baxter Renal to spread its investment costs over an even longer period with customers.

And as we discussed, many of the services that Virgin Atlantic offers are not charged for, but are factored into the customer lock-on effects that produce opportunities for greater revenue from the longevity, depth, width and diversity of spend on the one hand, and on the other the economies of skill, stretch, sweep and spread by which positive disproportionate rewards have been gained.

The total value equation

PAYING CUSTOMERS BACK   Whether or not the corporation charges for all or some offerings, and how it charges, depend on many factors. What's important is that to get the positive feedback looping mechanism operative and customers to lock on, total gain for these customers must be pushed up over the activity cycle, while total costs must be pulled down (see Figure 16 for a conceptual visual).

Let's take an example. Peapod customers get a 24-hour, personalized shopping service and everything else we have mentioned, for which they pay a price. This is basically an amount for the software applications that enables them to access Peapod. They also pay a monthly fee, a delivery fee and a 5 percent surcharge on the order. But, and here's the important point, this cost is more than offset for them by savings they make over their total activity cycle. They get more information about products, which helps them make better decisions on what to buy so that they waste less; they

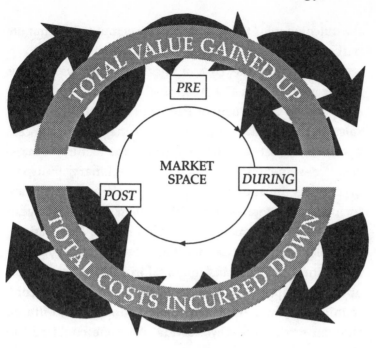

Figure 16 The total value equation

save money using more coupons than they normally do.
They also do more comparison shopping and less impulse
purchasing, and save time, money and energy from not
using any transport.

While this sounds intuitively simple, it runs contrary to
the well-established buying and selling pattern of classical
management. Here, the attempt was to cut the cost of the
core item, not to look at total costs and gains, because the
concern was not with results but with the discrete core
items, and keeping the cost of these items as low as possible, to sell as much as possible. This was not solely a corporate habit, I hasten to add. Many customers compared
prices of the core items – renal bag for renal bag, loan for
loan, personal computer for personal computer, seed for
seed – so as to cut down on their up-front costs. In fact, professional buyers were rewarded for just that. Result: they
acquired the core items at the cheapest price but didn't get

the outcome, plus the cost of this turned out to be a minute part of their overall expense.

For instance, the cost of the renal bag was always higher for Baxter's PD treatment compared to the HD competitors' prices bag for bag, which lost Baxter a lot of sales in the old days. But looking at the therapy process and its total costs as a whole changes the picture, if materials, consumables, depreciation of machinery, transport of patients in and out of the hospitals and so on are included. The total cost for HD is then £29,140 per year, while the PD treatment totals only £17,520. This statistic, first calculated by Baxter and then corroborated by health authorities, has been instrumental in getting a total therapy pricing approach accepted by the renal customer community and the new Baxter Renal UK approach diffused through Baxter Renal worldwide. And one could add to that a series of opportunity costs, such as the cost to hospitals of poor treatment due to inappropriate or slow diagnosis, the cost of late treatment and of complications setting in as a result, the costs of district nurses and other services to the community, and the social and professional cost to patients of being out of circulation for three days a week if on HD.

The unfounded assumption that is rectified by customer capitalism is that if up-front costs of the core items are as low as possible then total costs will be low. For example, research shows that the actual personal computer, i.e. the hardware, is only 5 percent of a corporate customer's total cost of networking capability. The rest is software and service expenses incurred through the customer activity cycle. Farmers are always looking to save on up-front cost of seeds or seed treatments, but these costs are minuscule compared to losing a crop or a field for lack of preventive treatment. The same can be said about the cost of bearings compared to the cost of downtime for an after-market customer, as SKF discovered.

In the US, the new 'Measured Response Treatment Plan', involving innovative, interactive, digital data-based diagnosis and minimal access surgery, pioneered by Imperial College, University of London, means that patients paying insurance can now get treatments early on that give them better results for a longer period. It costs them more initially, but makes the total treatment much less expensive in the long term. For instance, due to the *new way of diagnosing and monitoring*, a person can get special surgery to a knee when the ailment first becomes obvious, which, together with ongoing monitoring and care, can give many pain-free years and avoid the need for an expensive artificial knee later on.

Charging for results

The total value approach so central to customer capitalism is a long way from pricing for core items of discrete products and services transacted, based on the cost of the last unit made or the next unit coming on to the production line. This was what the old school called efficiency pricing.

Though there may be weird and wonderful mechanisms for collecting mounds of data on these costs, for both tangible and intangible resources, customer capitalism permanently changes the thinking structure and the model. The new enterprise can neither price on fixed costs (because it has nothing to do with the number of units made) nor price on marginal costs (because these are less and less relevant). In addition, it dare not price to cover investments in the short term without risking long-term gains.

Pricing must increasingly relate to results – what customers get out of products and services, rather than what the firm puts into them. Pricing must also increasingly relate to the total customer experience, not just transactionally at the moment when ownership of the core items changes hands.

The new enterprise not only extracts value differently through its pricing, but it extracts its share of value at different times. Let's look at some examples. To get a sustainably lucrative crop investment to farmers, Monsanto is approaching pricing completely differently. First, with all the knowhow invested up front, the tendency could easily have been to capture as much as possible, as quickly as possible, as is the habit in most bulk manufacturing industries. Monsanto is charging at the output end of the crop concept, i.e. when something concrete is achieved.

Second, with traditional thinking, Monsanto would have charged for the physical entities. Now its object is to extract value in any of several forms of fee, gain share or payment systems from the intangibles, which is what produces the real value. These intangibles – the software in the seed and seed treatments and their knowhow services – are replacing the tangible scarce resources and materials, to produce higher yields.

In the not-too-distant future, the enterprise will probably begin charging when the biogenetic seeds begin to behave in a particular way: when the 'switch' occurs that tells the seed to trigger the trait for wheat to produce lower starch for bread makers, or to adapt in some way to an impending storm. Alternatively, it could depend on which of the multiple traits is switched on, and how often, to suit the individual (or changing) needs of that particular farmer or circumstance over a growing cycle.

The same goes for cars. Today's cars are also endowed with multiple traits. A standard model can be upgraded electronically by a customer inserting a smartcard into a slot in the vehicle to get any feature they want, say a four-wheel drive to go into the mountains on weekends, or an open sunroof on a nice warm day, or sporty power for a quick drive through the country. A customer is thus paying 'per drive' and for the use of the car's multiple traits, rather than buying or owning the product. This is in exactly the same

way that they will increasingly pay-per-view for a personalized TV channel service.

Shifting from 'ownership' to 'usership'

The new enterprise is also increasingly charging for use,
rather than for the physical object itself, which, in a way, is
what Monsanto is doing (and why intelligent seeds cannot
be reused without some payment arrangement). Bob
Shapiro, Monsanto's CEO, asks this provocative question:
'Why should anyone want to own anything anyway?'

Not all customers want to own, say, a carpet (do they?).
What many increasingly want is to walk on a hygienic,
clean, nice-looking carpet and have it replaced when necessary. Similarly, in many of the world's advanced countries,
the car is no longer the status symbol it once was. Many
drivers no longer want to pay for owning a car, but rather
for using it. Renault in France, for example, offers a package
of services as part of the initial leasing price. It is effectively
'lending' customers the car, freeing them of all of the usual
hassles of ownership over the contract, and charging for
that lending and the care and the services. (The only thing
the driver has to do is pay for the gas!) Renault believes that
not only do customers get more value over the life of the
vehicle this way, but it also costs them less and Renault
plans to gain by using this approach to become a permanent
feature over the customer's entire driving life.

PAY
AS YOU
'LEND'

Though a good deal of investment has been made in the
multimedia technology that Toyota intends to offer customers, the money to be had is not going to come from the
extra margin on high-tech terminals, which will eventually
be copied and become regular, low-cost features. Instead, it
will come from customers using the system, subscribing to
the Nihon Mobile Broadcasting Corporation (NMBC) for
Internet TV, video, sound and e-mail services personalized
to suit their own needs.

Not all people want or can wait for a book or information in traditional form. What many want is simply to read the book and use the information. Previously, publishers of books, magazines and journals got the material together and printed it. The product went through the distributors which delivered it to stores, which went through whatever was necessary to get it to readers, usually using the 4P formula of product, price, place and promotion. Increasingly, customers want to be freed of this lengthy linear chain process and traditional capitalism mentality. With personal computers overtaking traditional forms of printing, and the World Wide Web providing a global information and distribution channel, customers will increasingly be paying for use of the information and knowledge, rather than actually owning the book, magazine or trade journal.

Already bookstores and publishers are merging. Online Originals, a London-based venture created by an American author and book lover, is a publishing company that operates solely on the Internet, distributing book-length works in digital form, using e-mail for both orders and delivery. The company looks for authors to write innovative, thought-provoking fiction or non-fiction works, in both English and French. It then does all of the traditional publishing work on the manuscript, and sells it on the Net to an increasingly growing installed base of interested readers. The company charges $7 (£4) per book and gives authors 50 percent of the order revenues.

Web site information services are struggling with the question of how customers pay and for what. Most well-known journals and newspapers, like *The Economist*, *New York Times*, *Financial Times*, *Wall Street Journal*, *El Mundo* (Spain), *Der Standard* (Austria), *Les Echos* (France) and *Corriere della Sera* (Italy), to name but a few, recognize that they need a Web site to complement their print copies, both for their own users and to grow the overall market.

Their real concern is how to sell their tangible products, but at the same time shift customers on to Web sites. Up to now, newspapers have been reluctant to put up stories on the Net before they publish in hard print for fear of scooping themselves. (The 'Clinton affair' certainly taught us that a breaking story does not have to be disseminated by the traditional players or media.)

The experience of journals and newspapers reflects the new challenge: the trick is not to try to continue to control copies of the content-static core items. In their case it's to tell the story to their installed customer base with the kinds of personalized content and contact that add the value that each customer wants in whatever media that customer chooses. This thereby makes them lock on to the organization as lifelong subscribers, generating for the corporation the positive disproportionate gains of the new economy.

London-based *Financial Times* (FT), part of the Pearson group, is leading the way in the *global electronic business and financial information management* market space and in the process consolidating its stature as a provider of broad coverage, analysis and comment for key business and financial decision makers. Beyond just a Web site:

➡ The company can personalize to suit individual needs, e.g. a customer can search by sector, company, industry, publication, region or according to specific need like a competitive analysis for a marketing manager.
➡ It has over 5000 information sources on which customers can draw (many of which were considered competitors previously), ranging from authoritative news journals and news wires, to trade journals, company information industry reports, country analyses and market research.
➡ The search can be done by customers or by FT's Business Research Centre, which offers an extensive team of people who provide information on both UK and international business issues, ranging from basic enquiries to in-depth research.

In other words, as opposed to customers simply buying and owning a copy of a paper, journal or newspaper, they pay to use the information they need – from whatever source is relevant. And the finding, linking and making the various bits of information relevant is FT's value add.

PAY
IF YOU
KEEP

Lego, also, isn't just about owning the physical core items any more. Kids now use virtual technology software to build their own imaginary models on screen, which they program themselves (even creating their own programs), in any manner they want. And customers can watch and listen to a piece of music as often as they like on the Global Music Network. They only have to pay if they want to keep a record of the performance, which can either be downloaded from the net or mail-ordered from GMN.

CHAPTER 30
VALUING FOR INCREASING RETURNS

KONUSUKE MATSUSHITA, THE FOUNDER OF THE MATSUSHITA
Panasonic empire, once asked his top management to draw
up a 200-year plan. One of the Hopi Indian tribes in North
America has a rule: when a chief makes a decision, he has
to think seven generations ahead. Neither of these is
intended to test forecasting skills. Rather, both aim to make
a strong statement – namely, that what we do today should
be considered for the long term.

To the new enterprise, 200 years or seven generations
into the future is certainly over the top. However, look at
how today's corporate leaders and investors rate performance and you will see the minds and spirits of customer capitalism beginning to make their mark. Horizons are getting
much longer. Gone are concerns with history, the traditional capitalism approach, because it has been recognized
that in times of fast change, data about the past is no indicator of future potential. It tells nothing about whether the
corporation has the ability to create new markets that
haven't existed before. Neither does it say whether firms
can originate for rapidly changing environments, nor follow
the natural progression of new customer patterns. There is
also no reflection of whether a corporation possesses the
new thinking structures that sense and 'see' new market
opportunities, or how well they absorb information and
learn about customers, rather than just buying their way
into growth.

Even more importantly, the past tells executives and
investors nothing about the ability of the enterprise to

HORIZONS
GET LONGER

attract customers and collaborators, and whether adequate investments in relational, infrastructural and intellectual assets are being made to give and get the value needed for the accumulated customer capital that leads to long-term shareholder wealth.

Investors call a new tune

But that is what we now need. Investors are hungry today for information that will tell them about the potential of a corporation tomorrow. The worth of a corporation will not be judged by adding up historical profits. Instead, an investor wants to be able to judge a corporation by its prospects for creating and competing in exciting new markets, and whether it has what it takes to sustain competitiveness in futures yet to be defined. This is more important that what appears in its conventional financial documents.

Investors are looking differently at established corporations, turned entrepreneurial, in addition to supporting small start-ups going beyond the obvious. These are companies creating new playing fields – Auto-by-Tel and Amazon are yet to make profits in the conventional accounting sense, but both are changing the fabric of their industries and are poised for an upward increasing returns path. When Amazon went public late in 1997, it had huge demand for its stock despite its lack of profits and owning nothing tangible. When it initially offered its stock on the market, the price was $18, by the end of that year it had shot up to $59. And by late 1998, it had reached almost $300 (before the stock split), its market capitalization was almost five times that of Barnes & Noble and it was making over 25 percent of its sales from expansion activities. Although no one can tell what decisions it will make in the future which might alter the success it has achieved so far, the fact is that perception of future value potential, based on what it had made happen in the marketplace and the response it obtained, is what drove Amazon's popularity up and up. This same future customer value stream potential is what got it the $75 million credit facility from a consortium of banks, led by Deutsche Morgan Grenfell, to execute its new millennium strategies despite the fact that it had not shown a conventional positive bottom line.

This is part of a giant shift on the part of shareholders and investors to look at prospects for the long term rather than make a quick buck, to look to future potential instead of past profits, which is why many of Microsoft's shareholders continue to buy up shares even though they are not getting dividends. What they want is to keep their money in the company, where they believe that they will continue to enjoy the exponential returns they cannot get from conventional financial institutions, even those considered to be doing well by conventional standards.

In addition, this is why, though Microsoft's earnings have been less than GE's, its market value has been greater – an apt reflection that perceptions of corporate wealth are shifting as we move from the traditional capitalism model to customer capitalism.

This brings us to the last principle of customer capitalism, deeply contrasting the traditional and new model (see Table 13). In the past, wealth was seen as solid and calculable and the market wanted immediate returns on specific and quantified investments and assets, so corporations obliged and scored accordingly. **Today what is needed is market creation and the amassing of a competitive advantage that is unbeatable, with plenty of potential for growth and wealth generation**. Do we know how to score for that?

COUNTING THE
UNCOUNTED

We need new valuers

We can certainly not score with tools inherited from traditional capitalism. Several factors have contributed to that situation:

	TRADITIONAL CAPITALISM PRINCIPLES	CUSTOMER CAPITALISM PRINCIPLES
1 **AIM**	Maintaining the status quo	Fundamentally transforming
2 **LEADERS**	Replicating and improving products and/or services	Finding new ways of doing things for and with customers
3 **INNOVATION**	Inventing new technologies	Originating for and with customers
4 **OBJECT**	Optimizing margins on unit transactions	Maximizing the time value of customers
5 **MEANS**	Increasing market share in product/service categories	Dominating activities in market spaces
6 **VALUE**	Making and moving more core items	Linking benefits in an ongoing integrated experience
7 **TARGET**	For markets and average customer	For individual customers in an ever-increasing, ever-lucrative installed base
8 **UNIT OF COMPETITION**	By units/companies/countries/industries	With win–win for all contributing players in new enterprise spaces
9 **RESOURCES**	Relying on the scarce tangibles	Relying on the abundant intangibles
10 **SCORE**	To make set ROI, ROA ROC targets	Creating market and accumulating a sustainable advantage

Table 13 Principles of traditional and customer capitalism

The fetish with hard assets

Part of the reason that Japan has not been a dominant player in the fast, vast software industry is because most banks there still require real property as collateral. Since the only software houses that can raise that kind of hard asset are part of the larger *keiretsu* structures, the most innovative entrepreneurs have been left out, killing what could have been a thriving, worldwide opportunity for Japan.

This fetish with hard assets is a worldwide malady. When Richard Branson tried to raise cash in the late 1980s because his company was growing so fast, he was asked to produce hard assets as tangible proof of his creditworthiness. Nothing could have been further from his mind. With no tangible assets to speak of, the only thing Branson and his directors could do was to begin systematically to buy their homes to finance their new initiatives. Then, some time during the Gulf War when the whole airline industry was in recession, Branson wanted to be the first to install 14-channel, seat-back movie screens throughout his Virgin Atlantic aircraft at a cost of about $20 million. He was refused a loan from banks for this, but offered $4 billion to buy new aircraft (hard assets). In the end, he had to resort to getting Boeing and Airbus to include the screens as part of the aircraft order!

Inside vs outside information

Another part of the problem is that financial information collected by corporations has primarily been about events inside the company rather than what is going on in the marketplace. According to acclaimed management guru Peter Drucker, this can count for 90 percent or more of information. This degenerative tendency is still largely the case. As Drucker observes, even the most sophisticated techniques, like activity-based accounting, the balanced scorecard and economic value added (EVA), are internally focused tools, based on inside rather than outside information.

LACKING EXTERNAL INFORMATION

According to Drucker, top management's poor supply of crucial external information, even where it is easily obtainable, was demonstrated in the 1998 collapse of the Asian economies:

> *This collapse was predictable at least a year ahead of time. The only question was what would trigger it and where it would start. But otherwise it was clearly foretold in public statistics on the size and composition of various countries' debts, and on their balances of payment. Yet most big companies – American as well as Japanese – were totally surprised and unprepared for it. All their information was inside information, despite their sizeable stakes in these countries.*

The orientation of the financial accounts

FINANCIAL ACCOUNTS ARE NOT ENOUGH

An additional problem is that, traditionally, we've looked at corporations through balance sheets. These financial accounts were supposedly a picture of a company's state at a moment in time, the proxy for corporate performance and worth. However, this is increasingly not the case. In the 1960s and 1970s, about 25 percent of the discrepancies in stock price changes could be attributed to differences in reported earnings, but by the 1980s and 1990s the figure had dropped to less than 10 percent.

Many people now acknowledge that conventional financial accounts are just ill suited to report items considered to be today's engine for growth and sustained competitiveness. They show everything that is hard and owned – assets and liabilities – and the difference in value between the two is assumed to be net worth. However, this so-called worth says nothing at all about the firm's worth in terms of its ability to create and capture value in new and growing environments. American Airlines loses money from the hard assets on its balance sheets, the planes for instance, but it earns millions from SABRE, its reservation and ticketing service, which is not on its books.

Being patently wrong

Many of the patents registered on the balance sheet, taken to be important assets with old logic and indicators of a firm's innovative capacity, were often not what created the new markets. True, they were documented representations of what corporations knew, but they were not indicative of what they could (or would) do with that knowledge.

In fact, it has been found that a significantly negative correlation exists between how many software patents were granted to a company in the last few decades and how many were turned into real new market opportunities. Microsoft and Lotus have relatively few software patents compared with, say, IBM, AT&T, Xerox, Hitachi and Toshiba.

The problems with book value

Moreover, in no way did the balance sheet's book value of assets reveal a corporation's future potential to give and extract lifelong customer value. This is demonstrated over and over again by the growing disparity between book value and market valuation, a gap now known as Tobin's Q, after James Tobin, the Nobel Laureate professor of economics at Yale University, consistently bearing out that the hard core items – be they computers, planes, buildings or money in the bank – can't in and of themselves create wealth or make a firm successful in the long term. It also takes account of the ascendancy of the intangibles – the ideas and knowledge that people have, the skills to use this knowledge and the information they hold to produce superior customer value – over the tangible assets in a corporation's worth.

In fact, as Skandia's Leif Edvinsson points out, a damaging paradox is actually built into the fetish with hard assets and book value. The more a company invests in what could make it market rich in the future, the more it is penalized: profits go down, reflecting adversely on the balance sheet. In addition, traditional (technological) R&D (which tends to be expensed on balance sheets since it is difficult to

TOBIN'S Q

determine future paybacks) is the very investment that brings in the long-term and exponential rewards, as are investments in customer relationships and knowhow, which do not appear at all on most balance sheets. All should be amortized over time and treated like any other investment that adds to market capitalization.

Are you measuring performance?

Today's investor communities increasingly recognize these modern problems and paradoxes and they are rapidly changing their perception of corporate worth, scoring to reflect a firm or institution's accumulation of the kinds of relational, intellectual, infrastructural assets that will take it successfully into a future built on customer capital. This is indeed necessary if those generating the new wealth are to get the funds they need to make the relevant investments. This may be a sweeping statement and it's probably happening at differing rates in different parts of the world, but in general that's the direction.

Testament to this is that many of the corporations, such as British Airways, with the highest tangible assets are not the ones which are the most highly valued today. In contrast, look at those that have many intangibles, innovating with the new business model for customer origination, such as Microsoft, Monsanto, Virgin, Intel, Amazon or Skandia: these companies are most highly valued. (As an aside: the combined market value of Detroit's big three is dwarfed by Microsoft today. And the market value of the 4000-odd, small, start-up software companies in Silicon Valley, with no tangible assets worth mentioning, approached that of the entire French stock market as 1997 drew to a close.)

A lot of effort is being put into trying to quantify the intangible assets and score corporations more accurately on these and other unquantifiables that do not appear on conventional balance sheets. Canadian Imperial Bank of

Commerce (CIBC) is an example. It has a knowledge-based lending group that has calculated new ways of defining creditworthiness for knowledge-intensive companies, based on strength of customer relationships, new innovations, rewarding policies, growth in knowledge, customers' collaborative projects and so on, instead of just counting up how much real estate or hard assets they own.

Typically with traditional capitalism, scores on performance were designed as lag indicators and so were reflective in nature and therefore very different from what we need today. They measured and tracked for an era of management who understood and were reliant on scarce, tangible resources. Now we need scores based on the true intangible value producers. Previously, scores drove share price, which could be artificially maneuvered by cutting back on long-term potential. Today, scores must take into consideration that new ventures or investments, pursuing opportunities for the future, can easily push earnings down initially. Previously, scores drove companies to reach high returns on financial capital to raise yet more financial capital. But financial capital is not scarce these days, or it shouldn't be.

Gary Hamel warns of the persistent dangers of scoring a corporation based on the wrong criteria. He suggests that whatever financial theory might say, it is unwise in these times for a company to be content with any of the conventional or even more modern scores, like a high growth rate or positive 'economic value added' (EVA) – earning more before interest than your weighted cost of capital – if unconventional competitors are capturing the majority of new wealth generated by shifts in business and the economy. There are many semiconductor companies that earn more than their cost of capital, for instance, and have a high EVA, but it is still Intel that has captured most of the new wealth in semiconductors' share of the overall value pool in that market space.

EVA vs CAPTURING THE NEW WEALTH

While IBM's return on invested financial capital was more than 17 percent in 1996 and its share price was going up rapidly, its actual share of wealth in the overall electronic computing value pool had plummeted from 45.95 percent to just 14.2 percent in a decade. IBM was slow to articulate the *global electronic networking capability* market space, and to recognize that within it people would want total mobility. It didn't see that work and leisure needs would increasingly merge, and that customers would want more integrated offerings cutting across IBM's businesses instead of more disintegration. This, of course, created a value gap in its product, service and skill portfolio, depriving the company of millions of customer dollars, which were gobbled up by unconventional rivals and start-ups that are now firmly entrenched.

However you put it, what we have to learn, and learn quickly, is that rather than look at the firm's ability to raise the share price or other short-term indicators of its success, top management and the investment community need to gauge a corporation's ability to create potential for future growth and exponential wealth. For this they need to invest in growth spending, which may mean forgoing immediate gain initially until increasing returns kick in, and scoring more accurately to reflect this. The new enterprise asks these four questions:

ASK THESE
QUESTIONS

➡ What new opportunities have been or are likely to be created in market spaces
  - existing?
  - emerging?
  - imagined?
➡ What share of the total value pool does our corporation have/want to get?
➡ Have we accumulated/will we have the assets
  - relational?
  - infrastructural?

– intellectual?

to dominate activities within these market spaces and so lock on customers?

➡ Will the new market and economic dynamics produce the exponential gains from customer value streams and free cash flows needed for new investments and investor rewards?

New value reporting

Conventional accounting fails in every way to quantify the worth associated with the company's ability to produce superior customer value, let alone to attribute this to its market value. Moreover, data like revenue and profit are still so highly aggregated as to give little clue to the individual customer sources of success or failure. Because of this, we will see more and more of a change in accounting. Increasingly, techniques are being developed to account for lifelong customer value. These provide a quantified and balanced set of performance measures to help companies make decisions on investments in long-term market prospects and tell the public about their ability to do so. Part of these new techniques consists of calculating and quantifying the present cash value of future revenues over a customer's expected lifetime. Using the principles of customer capitalism, these future revenues accelerate, are enhanced and are less volatile, plus they have a larger residual value at the end of a contract or period.

CUSTOMER VALUE = MARKET VALUE

Some companies are trying to change balance sheets so that they no longer show fixed assets and financial capital but instead show the new, true revenue-generating relational, infrastructural and intellectual assets. These are what create the possibilities for building and accumulating customer capital at an exponential rate, and what get the positive disproportionate rewards due to high-quality cash streams from the new economies of skill, stretch, sweep and spread.

BUILDING NEW BALANCE SHEETS

Skandia, for instance, is renowned for having created new ways to describe intangibles and measure them in among the overwhelming mass of routine financial information. It creates a supplement to its annual reports which shows growth trends for these assets, and which assists investors in their appreciation of their value. This also gives them an instrument to manage and develop future growth more effectively. In addition, the supplement looks at ratios to see the direction that these intangible assets are taking and whether or not they are being leveraged, rather than just adding up how many of them there are.

Monsanto, which is being valued today on its potential for future growth without investors knowing exactly what that future or growth might be, is also accounting in its corporate statements for difficult-to-measure new factors. Bob Shapiro expects exponential growth from discontinuity in biotechnology. What Monsanto has in order to achieve success in sustainable agricultural farming is now being quantified in its accounts, having previously been off the balance sheet.

Wanted: giving and getting customer value

More important than the calculations or figures themselves is that new accounting systems enable what sounds like a simple idea – the giving and getting of lifelong customer value – to be transformed into robust working practice. When customer origination is treated as a long-term 'investment', with future and exponential growth potential and compounding value all round, it enables people having to lead enterprises or growth projects in both public and private sectors to sell new ideas to the powers that be, as they would for any other investment.

THE LUXURY OF BEING PRIVATE?   Perhaps privately owned companies are just better off, as Richard Branson has so often suggested. In the 1980s he decided to take Virgin public. Shares quoted on the stock exchange brought many financial benefits, but restricted him to such an extent that he bought the company back, to *'achieve over months rather than decades'* – his point being that he wanted to take his time and not be forced into quick results. In Branson's own words:

> *One of the luxuries I have been able to enjoy in my years of running companies is that 99 percent of the companies I have run are private. Short-term taxable profits with good dividends are a prerequisite of public life. Avoiding short-term taxable profits and seeking long-term capital growth is the best approach to growing private companies.*

Nearly two decades later, Branson has gone back to the market to try again, but this time with a different, more enlightened investor community who have begun to accept the notion that he has helped personify – that it takes more than short-term profits to drive stocks up and more than a high share price to continuously create markets and durably compete within them.

Columbus in the new world

Where does all this leave us? With a new business model based on increasing returns that can never be remotely like the one of the past. Short-term economic constructs and horizons based on calendar time gone forever. Linear chains and static recipes for strategy and marketing simply not working any more. New requirements for risk and reward that need roles and behavior never before considered and a new understanding of the role of market leaders. No one able to succeed alone. A need to evaluate and score differently and a need for new definitions of competitiveness, industry and monopoly. The stakes much higher than ever, and less margin for error. And no one exempt. All companies and institutions irrespective of industry or size are inexorably bound up with the need to build strategies based on lifelong customer value so that they can leverage from the new market and economic dynamics of customer capitalism – unless they want to become commodity suppliers, and slip deeper and deeper into diminishing returns...

Of course, for those of you who accept the proposition and promise of customer capitalism, there is always the problem of getting buy-in from those around you. Brian Arthur warns that the danger is that the old order has been so well entrenched, that the people who challenge it are often assumed to be what is wrong, not the thinking itself. When colleagues challenge you (as they will) and ask you what they can get from moving from the old business model they know and understand so well to customer capitalism, still to be played out, tell them what Andy Grove, chairman of Intel, said. Early on, he was tackled about his return on investment for his new Internet ventures and he replied: *'Are you crazy? This is Columbus in the New World ... What was his ROI?'*

REFERENCES, NOTES AND POINTS OF DEPARTURE

Prologue

This is based on a case study entitled 'Amazon.com: Marketing a New Electronic Go-between Service Provider', by Sandra Vandermerwe and Marika Taishoff, The Management School, Imperial College, 1998 (available, with bibliography and references, from the European Case Clearing House at Cranfield University).

Other quotes from 'Amazon.com: the Wild World of E-commerce', *BusinessWeek*, December 14, 1998.

Chapter 1

Page 2: Statistic on corporate margins going up while total shareholder value went down from Gary Hamel, 'Strategy Innovation and the Quest for Value', *Sloan Management Review*, Winter 1998, volume 39, number 2.

Page 3: *Fortune* 500 list of 1970 where today companies no longer appear is from Robert E. Johnston , Jr. and Soren M. Kaplan, 'Harnessing the Power of Strategic Innovation', www.ideascope.com. This is an American statistic. In Europe the situation is slightly different, a lot having to do with many of the large companies having been, until very recently, government owned. Hence most are still in existence but, of the top 20, seven are worth less today than the accumulated capital invested in the business and, according to some analysts, 'Continental firms have consistently failed to earn the true cost of their capital' (*The Economist*, 23 November 1996, Survey of Business in Europe).

Page 4: For a managerial discussion of lock-in from a product-based perspective see, for example, Brian Arthur, 'Increasing Returns and the World of Business', *Harvard Business Review*, July/August 1996; an interview by Joel Kurtzman, 'Thought Leader: Brian Arthur', in *Strategy and Business–Booz, Allen & Hamilton*, Second Quarter, 1998. In 'The Delta Model: Adaptive Management for a Changing World', *Sloan Management Review*, Winter 1999, Arnoldo Hax and Dean Wilde suggest system (product) lock-in as one of three alternative competitive strategies. Also see *Information Rules* by Carl Shapiro and Hal Varian, Cambridge, MA: Harvard Business School Press, 1998.

Page 8: Amazon quote by publisher from David Streitfeld, 'Paper Money on the Net: Amazon.com Rewrites Bookselling Script', *International Herald Tribune*, 11–12 July 1998.

Page 17: The traditional economic model of diminishing returns also worked on a loop mechanism. But with classical economics the negative loops (so called) that were operative meant that any major change or unexpected action was rejected by market forces, which reverted the system to its original (or another) equilibrium state, the conditions for the 'perfect state of competition'. It was assumed that the equilibrium point was a point that the market should (and would always) revert to – costs and prices would reach this point and thus no one could succeed indefinitely. This, it was argued, was the best outcome possible given that the resources that characterized classical economics were scarce, and thus needed to be allocated most efficiently.

Page 18–20: The positive loops of increasing returns reward innovation and change. These loops reinforce rather than resist. But they reinforce upward as well as downward. Hence those who succeed, succeed still more, while those who fail do so still more. This book argues that success – and therefore increasing returns – comes to those who work with the principles of customer capitalism.

Page 18: For more on the new economics of increasing returns and positive feedback loops as a characteristic of increasing returns, see, for instance, work by economists in the field such as Brian Arthur and Paul Romer: Brian Arthur, in his article 'Increasing Returns and the World of Business', *Harvard Business Review*, July/August 1996; and an interview by Joel Kurtzman, 'Thought Leader: Brian Arthur', in

Strategy and Business–Booz, Allen & Hamilton, Second Quarter, 1998. For Romer's work, see for instance 'An Interview with Paul Romer', by Joel Kurtzman, in *Strategy and Business–Booz, Allen & Hamilton*, First Quarter, 1998, Internet edition; Paul Romer, 'Increasing Returns and Long Run Growth', *Journal of Political Economy*, October 1986; 'Increasing Returns and New Developments in the Theory of Growth', National Bureau of Economic Research, Working Paper 3098, September 1989.

Page 19: Complex adaptive systems are being studied by a variety of disciplines, from physics and mathematics to economics and biology. The research and papers of the Santa Fe Institute, based in Santa Fe, New Mexico, whose members include a number of Nobel Prize winners, are a good starting point for understanding complexity theory in this context.

Page 20: Kevin Kelly's quote is from his book *New Rules for the New Economy*, London: 4th Estate, 1998, page 26.

Page 22: Customer capital was defined by Hubert Saint-Onge (professor of knowledge management at the Canadian School of Management) as the value of a firm's franchise, its ongoing relationships with the people or organizations to which it sells. It is cited by several authors, including Thomas A. Stewart in his book *Intellectual Capital: The New Wealth of Organizations*, London: Nicholas Brealey, 1997, as one of several categories of assets (usually human, structural and customer capital). With customer capitalism, the building and accumulating of customer capital form the overall aim.

Chapter 2

Page 24: Much has been written in both the academic and more mainstream press about Amazon. For a sampling, see: 'A Fable Concerning Ambition: Would Britain's Leading On-Line Booksellers Have Done Better in the US?', *The Economist*, 21 June 1997; 'Amazon com. Plans Net Ad Extravaganza', *Marketing Week*, 17 July 1997; Anthony Bianco, 'Virtual Bookstores Start to Get Real', *BusinessWeek*, 27 October 1997; Tim Clark, 'Why the Street Loves Amazon.com', CNETNews.com, 8 April 1998; Soumitra Dutta, Stephen Kwan and Arie Segev, 'Strategic Marketing and Customer Relationships in Electronic Commerce', INSEAD Working Paper, 1997; Paul Farrow, 'OnLine Booksellers', *Precision Marketing*, 20 October 1997; John Gapper, 'Internet Stores May Give Lift to Book Sales', *Financial Times*, 6 November 1997; Lucy Kellaway, 'Billionaire Nerd on His Own Bandwidth', *Financial Times*, 13 November 1998; Suresh Kotha, 'Competing on the Internet: The Case of Amazon.com', *European Management Journal*, April 1998; Madeline Lyons, 'Hesitate and Profits Slip Through the Net', *Irish Times*, 6 March 1998; Alice Rawsthorn, 'Webs for Bookworms: Retailer's On-Line Sales Speak Volumes', *Financial Times*, 2 August 1997; Richard Waters and John Labate, 'Brought to Book: The Internet Retailing War is Turning Into Struggle Over Distribution', *Financial Times*, 10 November 1998; *BusinessWeek* Cover Story: 'Amazon.com', 14 December 1998; 'Barnes & Noble: A Better Stock Play?', *BusinessWeek*, 14 December 1998.

Chapter 3

Page 29: The quote and other information on Borders from, among others, 'Interview with Bob DiRomualdo, Borders: Book Lover With a Fresh Shelf Life', by Alice Rawsthorn, *Financial Times*, 2 September 1998.

Page 31: Information on Encyclopaedia Britannica from Philip Evans and Thomas Wursten, 'Strategy and New Economics of Information', *Harvard Business Review*, September/October 1997. See also Elizabeth Gardner, 'Britannica Online: Too Pricey?', *Web Week*, vol. 1, no. 7, November 1995, and Robert Shepard, 'Encyclopaedia Britannica to Go Online', *Net Week: The Internet letter*, January 1994.

Page 31: *The Asian Wall Street Journal* quote from 'The Stark Truth of Moore's Law', by Rich Karlgaard, *The Asian Wall Street Journal*, 28 May 1998.

Page 32: More on the dramatic growth of Cisco, and the strategies it has employed in the past few years, is documented by Glenn Rifkin, 'Growth by Acquisition: An Interview with Cisco CEO John Chambers', in *Strategy and Business–Booz, Allen & Hamilton*, Second Quarter, 1997, Internet edition, and John Byrne, 'Cisco: The Corporation of the Future', *BusinessWeek* Special Issue: The 21st Century, 31 August 1998. Cisco as one of most admired companies from Evyn Brown, 'America's Most Admired Companies', *Fortune*, 1 March 1999.

Page 32: Statistics on the growth rates in multimedia data traffic over the Internet from 'Attackers vs. Incumbents: The Battle for Value in an IP-Networked World', by James Seaberg, Jeff Hawn, Goktekin Dincerler, Cristofer Eugster and Nagendra Rao, *McKinsey Quarterly*, volume 4, 1997.

Chapter 4

Page 33: Some of the information on Mondex from Christopher Westland, Mandy Kwok, Josephine Shu, Terence Kwok and Henry Ho, 'Electronic Cash in Hong Kong', *Focus Theme*, volume 7, no.2, 1997.

Page 35: Peapod information from speech by Tim Dorgan, President, Peapod Interactive, at the AMA Attitude and Behavior Conference on 'Exploring New Research Opportunities via On-Line Shopping', January 1996. More on Peapod can be found in Joseph Pine, Don Peppers and Martha Rodgers, 'Do You Want to Keep Your Customers Forever?', *Harvard Business Review*, March/April 1995.

Page 35: Research on the dislikes people have about grocery shopping from Julie Bird, 'How and Where People Shop: 48% Rate Convenience as Highest Above Price', *Precision Marketing*, 24 February 1997.

Page 36: Understanding of European attitudes to Internet shopping from reports jointly done by KPMG Management Consultants and The Oxford Institute of Retail Management, Templeton College, Oxford. For instance: *Home Shopping Across Europe: Experiences and Opportunities*, April 1997, and *The Internet: Its Potential and Use by European Retailers*, June 1996.

Page 37: The Netscape executive quote from Michael Cusumana and David Yoffie, *Competing on Internet Time: Lessons from Netscape and its Battle with Microsoft*, New York: Free Press, 1998.

Page 38: Microsoft expecting to get 25% of its revenues from media holdings in the near future from Christopher Harper, *And That's the Way it Will Be*, New York: New York University Press, 1998.

Chapter 5

Page 41: Two articles on the ongoing battle between Reuters and Bloomberg: Ben Potter, 'Battle of the Small Screens', *Daily Telegraph*, 14 February 1998, and Helen Dunne, 'Bloomberg is Just Mind-Boggingly Good', *Daily Telegraph*, 14 February 1998.

Page 42: Bloomberg's quote and some of the information on Bloomberg's strategy from Michael Bloomberg, *Bloomberg by Bloomberg*, New York: John Wiley & Sons, 1997, pages 53–4.

Page 45: The quote from Amazon's VP of product development on involving customers in designing the perfect site from Amazon.com Press Release: 'Amazon.com Adds Classical CDs to Earth's Biggest Book and Music Store', 9 September 1998.

Page 47: The Tom Peters quote according to Kevin Kelly, *New Rules for the New Economy*, London: 4th Estate, 1998, page 86.

Page 47: Richard Branson's quote on moving on to the Internet from Paul Taylor, 'Virgin Group to Offer Net Shopping Services', *Financial Times*, 18 November 1997.

Page 47: Quote from the Intel manager, like 'Ford getting out of cars', from R.A. Burgelman and A.S. Grove, 'Strategic Dissonance', *California Management Review*, vol. 38, Winter 1996.

Page 48: Intel's move into customers' home through TV or PC discussed by Louise Kehoe, 'Intel Tries to Net TV', *Financial Times*, 10 December 1997.

Page 48: *Time* magazine reference to McDonald's and obsolescence by Bill Saporito, 'Fallen Arches', *Time*, 9 June 1997. A similar assessment of the fast-food giant is to be found in the book by Shona L Brown and Kathleen. M Eisenhardt, *Competing on the Edge: Strategy as Structured Chaos*, Boston, MA: Harvard Business School Press, 1998.

Chapter 7

Page 56: Saturn account from the Harvard Business School Case Study by Anita McGahon and Greg Keller, 'Saturn: A Different Kind of Car Company', 1994, and a follow-up case, 'Saturn Corporation in 1996'. Frederick Reichheld also uses Saturn as a key example in his work on the economics of customer retention, *The Loyalty Effect*, Boston, MA: Harvard Business School Press, 1996.

Page 57: Several articles have examined Wayne Huizenga's strategies for shaking up the used car market. Worth noting are: *BusinessWeek* Online Newsflash, 'Need a Car Loan? Speak to Wayne Huizenga', 6 March 1997; Alex Taylor III, 'Car Wars: Wayne Huizenga vs. Everybody', *Fortune*, 9 June 1997; and Roger Taylor, 'Huizenga Determined to Try Harder', *Financial Times*, 12 August 1997.

Page 57: In addition to interviews, information on Baxter from case study series by Sandra Vandermerwe and Marika Taishoff, 'Baxter A: A Changing Customer Environment'; 'Baxter B: Total Lifetime Customer Strategy'; 'Baxter C: Balancing the Score', Case Studies, The Management School, Imperial College, 1997 (available from the European Case Clearing House at Cranfield University).

Chapter 8

Page 64: Figures about the dissatisfaction with the car purchasing process are from 'Saturn: A Different Kind of Car Company', by Anita McGahon and Greg Keller, Harvard Business School Case Study, 1994.

Page 64: In addition to interviews, information on Auto-by-Tel is from 'Auto-by-Tel Com: Case Study of an EC Application—Report #3, August 1997', by Dr. Rich Magjuka and Digital Services Inc., in FHLBI NewsLink Technology Wire on the Internet; 'Profit Prophet—Driving out the Middleman' by Steve Kelly, from CMP Net—Tech Search/NetGuide, on the Internet; 'Short Take: Auto-by-Tel Awards Millionth Customer' .by Jim Hu, 12/12/97 CNET: News.Com.

Page 66: For more on how market share can be misguided, see James Heskett, W. Earl Sasser and Leonard Schlesinger, *The Service Profit Chain: How Leading Companies Link Profit and Growth to Loyalty, Satisfaction and Value*, New York: Free Press, 1997, who demonstrate that customer loyalty, and not market share, is fundamental to profitability; Bruce Henderson, in his article 'The Origins of Strategy', *Harvard Business Review*, November/December 1989, who queried the validity of market share because it did not define the market; Frederick Reichheld's book *The Loyalty Effect: The Hidden Force behind Growth, Profits and Lasting Value*, Boston, MA: Harvard Business School Press, 1996, focused on the link between customer retention and profitability, as opposed to market share and profitability. Also an article by E. Anderson, C. Fornell and D. Lehmann, 'Customer Satisfaction, Market Share and Profitability: Findings from Sweden', *Journal of Marketing*, July 1994, found a distinct correlation between customer satisfaction and profitability, but not between market share and profitability.

Page 67: The notion of 'market spaces' is not to be confused with that of 'product spaces'. For example, Gary Hamel and C.K. Prahalad in *Competing for the Future* (Boston, MA: Harvard Business School Press, 1994) talk about 'product', or 'white spaces' to get the reader to look to new product opportunities. It is also not to be confused with 'marketspace', a term used by Jeffrey Rayport and John Sviokla to denote cyber-net as opposed to physical space, in their article 'Managing in the Marketspace', *Harvard Business Review*, November/December 1994. For more on market spaces see Sandra Vandermerwe, *The 11th Commandment: Transforming to 'Own' Customers*, London: John Wiley, 1996. Also by the same author, 'Becoming a Customer "Owning" Corporation', *Long Range Planning*, vol. 29, no. 6, 1996.

Page 70: For Qwest and its impact on traditional telephone companies, see David Diamond's article, 'Building the Future-Proof Telco', in *Wired*, May 1998. Also 'Attackers vs. Incumbents: The Battle for Value in an IP-Networked World', by James Seaberg, Jeff Hawn, Goktekin Dincerler, Cristofer Eugster and Nagendra Rao, *McKinsey Quarterly*, volume 4, 1997.

Chapter 9

Page 71: In addition to interviews, discussion on the transformation of Federal Express into a logistics management firm can be found in Todd Lappin, 'The Airline of the Internet', *Wired*, December 1996.

Page 73: In addition to interviews, more information on the RAC from the case study by Sandra Vandermerwe and Marika Taishoff, 'RAC A: Repositioning a Service Brand' and 'RAC B: Using Technology to Reposition a Service Brand', Case Studies, The Management School, Imperial College, 1998 (available from the European Case Clearing House at Cranfield University).

Page 75: The extent to which emerging economies are 'leapfrogging' global patterns in wireless and cellular services is reported in the article 'A Revolution in Interaction', by Patrick Butler, Ted Hall, Alistair Hanna, Lenny Mnedonca, Byron Auguste, James Manyika and Anupam Sahay, *McKinsey Quarterly*, number 1, 1997, which makes the point that the lower-income countries, as they attempt to leapfrog technologies, are registering double the growth rate of high-income nations in the newer wireless and cellular services.

Page 75: The Nicholas Negroponte quote is from Victoria Griffith, 'Fast Forward for the Cyber Evangelist', *Financial Times*, 25 April 1998. For a fuller understanding of Negroponte's views, read his book *being digital*, New York: Alfred Knopf, 1995.

Page 77: For more on Lotus Notes, see for instance Larry Downes and Chunka Mui, *Unleashing the Killer App: Digital Strategies for Market Dominance*, Boston, MA: Harvard Business School Press, 1998. See also the publication by Waite & Co. Consultants, *Beyond Expectations: How Leading Companies are Using Lotus Notes to Jump-Start the I-Net Revolution*, 1997.

Page 78: Winslow Farrell, in his book *How Hits Happen*, New York: Harper Business, 1998, tries to incorporate some of the new ideas of increasing returns, including markets as living systems.

Page 78: Citibank quote from 'Citicorp Faces the World: An Interview with John Reed', *Harvard Business Review*, November/December 1990. For more on Citibank's global ambitions, see Carol Loomis,

'Citicorp's Far-Out Quest for a Billion Customers', *Fortune*, 2 February 1998.

Chapter 10

Page 80: In addition to interviews with Lego executives, some of the information on Lego and the quote from David Blackwell comes from David Blackwell, 'Intelligent as a Brick', *Financial Times*, 27 January 1998.

Page 81: The paragraph on the Italian stroll in the resorts and the blurring of work and play comes from Michael Hobbs, 'Mobile Communication Services in Europe: How Concert Can Change the Game', MBA Thesis, The Management School, Imperial College, September 1997.

Chapter 11

Page 88: Innumerable academic and management books and cases have examined the downfall of IBM in the late 1980s and early 1990s. Worth reading are: P. Carroll, *Big Blues: The Unmaking of IBM*, London: Weidenfeld, 1993; Charles Ferguson and Charles Morris, *The Computer Wars: The Fall of IBM and the Future of Global Technology*, New York: Random House, 1993; Robert Heller, *The Fate of IBM*, New York: Little, Brown, 1993; and D. Quinn Mills and G.B. Friesen, *Broken Promises: An Unconventional View of What Went Wrong at IBM*, Boston, MA: Harvard Business School Press, 1996.

Page 89: An article showing the move from products through services to experiences, although it relates this to how customers are treated as opposed to the results they get, is that by Joseph Pine and James Gilmore, 'Welcome to the Experience Economy', *Harvard Business Review*, July/August 1998.

Page 89: Virgin statistic from 'The Future for Virgin: Will Branson's Cash Keep Flowing if the Music Stops?', Jonathan Ford, *Financial Times*, 13 August 1998.

Page 89: For a detailed explanation of the customer activity cycle as a methodological tool for transformation, see Sandra Vandermerwe, *From Tin Soldiers to Russian Dolls: Creating Added Value Through Services*, Oxford: Butterworth Heinemann, 1993; Sandra Vandermerwe, 'Jumping Into the Customer's Activity Cycle', *Columbia Journal of World Business*, Summer 1993; Sandra Vandermerwe, *The 11th Commandment: Transforming to 'Own' Customers*, London: John Wiley, 1996.

Page 93: Information on Mercedes/Swatch Smart car from 'Smart Move', Brett Fraser, *Daily Telegraph–Motoring Section*, 15 August 1998.

Chapter 12

Page 100: In addition to interviews, data on Lotus Notes and IBM's strategy from 'The Rebirth of IBM', *The Economist*, 6 June 1998.

Page 101: Some of the information on the growing importance of 'pre' and 'post' activities in the total travel experience and information on Expedia from Amon Cohen, 'Your Tickets are in the Ether – Microsoft Aims to Simplify Booking Travel by Computer', *Financial Times*, 25 November 1996.

Page 101: For more on PressPoint, Xerox local newspaper global venture, see Tom Buerkle, 'Newspapers from Home: High Tech Printer Casts an Answer', *International Herald Tribune*, 17 November 1998.

Chapter 13

Page 107: 'Disintermediation' in the wake of the Internet and e-commerce has been handled among others by: Stan Davis and Christopher Meyer, *Blur: The Speed of Change in the Connected Economy*, London: Capstone, 1998; John Hagel and Arthur Armstrong, *Net Gain: Expanding Markets Through Virtual Communities*, Boston, MA: Harvard Business School Press, 1997; and Don Tapscott, *The Digital Economy: Promise and Peril in the Age of Networked Intelligence*, New York: McGraw-Hill, 1995.

Page 111: John Hagel and Jeffrey Rayport, in their article 'The New Infomediaries', *McKinsey Quarterly*, number 4, 1997, describe 'infomediaries' as businesses that make money out of capturing customer information and developing detailed profiles of individual customers for use by third-party vendors. Also see book by John Hagel and Marc Singer, *Net Worth*, Cambridge, MA: Harvard Business School Press, 1999.

Page 111: GE's 'virtual inventory' is described in Michael Treacy and Frederick Wiersema, *The Discipline of Market Leaders: Choose Your Customers, Narrow Your Focus, Dominate Your Market*, New York: Addison Wesley, 1995.

Page 118: Statistics on the dwindling percentage of business to travel agents in the US from Michael Skapinker, 'The Business of Travel – Special report', *Financial Times*, 7 May 1998.

Chapter 14

Page 122: Figures about satisfaction and automobile repurchase rates from Frederick Reichheld, *The Satisfaction Trap*, Bain & Co., January 1993.

Page 123: Reichheld has been instrumental in highlighting the impact of customer retention on financials, for instance in *The Loyalty Effect: The Hidden Force Behind Growth, Profits, and Lasting Value*, Boston, MA: Harvard Business School Press, 1996. For the economics of customer retention, see John Murphy, 'The Art of Satisfaction: Happy Customers Add Directly to the Bottom Line', *Financial Times – Mastering Management*, 1 November 1996. James Heskett, W. Earl Sasser, Leonard Schlesinger, in *The Service Profit Chain: How Leading Companies Link Profit and Growth to Loyalty, Satisfaction and Value*, New York: Free Press, 1997, also look at the financial implications of customers kept and lost.

Page 124: For research on how the cost of retention can lead to diminishing returns, see Robert Blattberg and John Deighton, 'Manage Marketing by the Customer Equity Test', *Harvard Business Review*, July/August 1996.

Page 125: Nigel Piercy's quote from his book, *Market-Led Strategic Change: Transforming the Process of Going to Market*, Oxford: Butterworth Heinemann, 1997, page 42. The quote from the Bain executive is also from this source. Also on this theme see Judith Passingham, 'Grocery Retailing and the Loyalty Card', *Journal of the Market Research Society*, volume 40, number 1, January 1998.

Page 127: For customers potentially beginning to sell information about themselves, see Stan Davis and Christopher Meyer, *Blur: The Speed of Change in the Connected Economy*, London: Capstone, 1998.

Page 127: Jeff Bezos quote from Suresh Kotha, 'Competing on the Internet: The Case of Amazon.com', *European Management Journal*, April 1998.

Page 129: Esther Dyson's quote from 'Mirror Mirror on the Wall', *Harvard Business Review*, September/October 1997. Dyson has also written a book with a series of insights on the implications – not just managerial, but also social, educational and personal – of the new technological paradigm: *Release 2.0: A Design for Living in the Digital Age*, New York: Broadway Books, 1997.

Chapter 15

Page 131: For information on body scanners and virtual clothes and British involvement in this venture, see Clive Cookson, 'Shops get Ready for Invasion of the Body Scanners', *Financial Times*, 4 December 1998.

Page 132: The Gates quote on newspapers from a verbatim transcript of the Newspaper Association of America (NAA) Publisher's Convention, 27 April 1997: 'Bill Gates Addresses American Newspaper Publishers', An E&P Interactive Report, Internet edition.

Page 134: The 'mobility guarantee' offered by Mercedes and valid in 23 European countries is discussed in Jean François Jacquier, 'L'Auto Autrement', *Le Point*, 27 juin 1998.

Page 136: Quote from the Direct Line executive is from Clare Sambrook, 'The City: Direct Line Creator Rings the Changes', *Daily Telegraph*, 28 June 1997.

Page 136: Bezos quotes on personalization from Tim Clark, 'Newsmakers: Jeff Bezos, Turning to a Global Page', CNET News.Com, Internet edition, 8 April 1998, and Lucy Kellaway, 'Billionaire Nerd on his own Bandwidth', *Financial Times*, 13 November 1998.

Page 139: De Mello's quote on Streamline from Britton Manasco, 'Cutting Edge Companies Cultivate Learning Relationships', *Knowledge Inc.*, November 1997, Internet edition. Also see Don Peppers and Martha Rodgers, *Enterprise One-to-One: Tools for Building Unbreakable Customer Relationships in the Interactive Age*, London: Piatkus, 1997.

Chapter 16

Page 142: Johan Roos, Goran Roos, Leif Edvinsson and Nicola Dragonetti, *Intellectual Capital: Navigating in the New Business Landscape*, London: Macmillan Business, 1997, use a sketch on classic S-curve theory to demonstrate that, with the maturity of an industry, returns can go from increasing to diminishing returns.

Chapter 17

Page 151: Data about lagging car sales at dealerships notwithstanding the positive Internet experience for customers is based on a study done by automotive sector consultants J.D. Powers and Associates, and reported in the Forrester Report *On-Line Retail Strategies*, April 1998, Internet edition.

Page 152: Quote from James Moore, *The Death of Competition: Leadership and Strategy in the Age of Business*

Ecosystems, New York: Harper Business, 1996. Another interesting article by Moore is entitled 'The New Corporate Form' in *Blueprint for the Digital Economy: Creating Wealth in the Era of E-Business*, edited by Don Tapscott, Alex Lowy and David Ticoll, New York: McGraw-Hill, 1998.

Page 152: Note the following on 'enterprise spaces'. Several authors have alluded to notions of 'competitive spaces' to indicate going beyond traditional industry boundaries. See, for instance, Gary Hamel and C.K. Prahalad, *Competing for the Future*, New York: Free Press, 1994. James Moore, in *The Death of Competition: Leadership and Strategy in the Age of Business Ecosystems*, New York: HarperBusiness, 1996, refers to 'eco systems', by which he means corporations organically developing together. Kevin Kelly, in his book *Out of Control: The New Biology of Machines, Social Systems, and the Economic World*, New York: Addison Wesley, 1995, and in his article 'The New Biology of Business', in Rowan Gibson (ed.), *Rethinking the Future: Rethinking Business, Principles, Competition, Control & Complexity, Leadership, Markets and the World*, London: Nicholas Brealey, 1997, uses complexity to describe the network as the new competitive entity. In customer capitalism terms these spaces are customer centered, which is what distinguishes the term enterprise spaces as used in this text.

Page 155: For more on Direct Line's links with automotive repair shops see report by Elizabeth Stevens, *Lessons from the Revolution in the Direct Distribution of General Insurance in Europe*, International Financial Consultants Ltd., 1997, Internet edition.

Chapter 18

Page 156: Win–win scenarios are described by several authors in different ways. Kevin Kelly, for instance, talks about players each thriving on each other in his interview in Rowan Gibson (ed.), *Rethinking the Future: Rethinking Business, Principles, Competition, Control & Complexity, Leadership, Markets and the World*, London: Nicholas Brealey, 1997.

Page 156: For more on cooperation, see: Robert Axelrod, *The Complexity of Co-operation: Agent based Models of Competition and Collaboration*, Princeton Studies in Complexity, Princeton: Princeton University Press, 1997; Robert Axelrod, *The Evolution of Co-operation*, New York: Basic Books, 1985; and Matt Ridley, *The Origins of Virtue: Human Instincts and the Evolution of Co-operation*, New York: Viking, 1997.

Page 158: On how networks produce increasing rather than diminishing returns, see Kevin Kelly, 'New Rules for the New Economy: Twelve Dependable Principles for Thriving in a Turbulent World', *Wired*, September 1997.

Page 159: Discussion on Visa from Geoff Mulgan, *Connexity: How to Live in a Connected World*, London: Chatto & Windus, 1997. For Dee Hock quote see Dee Hock, 'The Chaordic Organisation: Out of Control and Into Order', *World Business Academy Perspectives*, volume 9, number 1, 1995, Internet edition.

Page 160: 'Monovation' discussion from Kevin Kelly, *New Rules for the New Economy*, London: 4th Estate, 1998.

Chapter 19

Page 163: The blue tit and robin experiment is described in Arie de Geus, *The Living Company: Growth, Learning and Longevity in Business*, London: Nicholas Brealey, 1997. A complete description of this and similar ornithological experiments is in Jeff Wyles, Joseph Kimbel and Allan Wilson, 'Birds, Behaviour and Anatomical Evolution', *Proceedings of the National Academy of Sciences*, July 1993.

Page 163: The analysis of Kropotkin's 'Darwinian' research in Siberia is from Stephen Jay Gould, *Bully for Brontosaurus: Further Reflections in Natural History*, London: Penguin Books, 1991, 'Kropotkin Was No Crackpot'.

Page 163: For research on collaboration and performance, see joint research project by Andersen Consulting and INSEAD Business School, reported in: 'High Tech Winners Show Raw Speed Doesn't Matter— Exploiting Uncertainty: Hi Tech's High Performers Change the Dynamics of Competition', Andersen Consulting, May 20, 1997, Internet edition.

Page 165: The examples of Bankers Trust in Australia and the Insweb insurance net from Patricia Seybold, 'Coopetition is de Rigour in E-Commerce', Seybold Snapshots Editorial, November 1995, Internet edition.

Page 167: The new German 'super train' is discussed in the *International Herald Tribune*, 'Can Germany Catch the High-Tech Train?', 11 April 1998.

Page 169: The Brandenburger and Nalebuff quote about competing and collaborating simultaneously is from page 38 of their book *Co-opetition*, New York: Doubleday, 1996.

Page 170: Don Tapscott quote from his book *The Digital Economy: Promise and Peril in the Age of Networked Intelligence*, New York: McGraw-Hill, 1996, page 184.

Page 171: Mary Westheimer quote from Brandenburger and Nalebuff, *Co-opetition*, New York: Doubleday, 1996, page 30.

Page 172: For more on the Global Music Network, see 'Click Here for the Future of Music', Norman Labrecht, *Daily Telegraph*, 9 December 1998.

Page 172: NEC's strategy in Japan is fully recounted in Mashima Rieko's 'The Turning Point for Japanese Software Companies: Can They Compete in the Prepackaged Software Market?', *Berkeley Technology Law Journal*, volume 12, issue 2, Fall 1996, Internet edition.

Page 173: Bertelsmann Venture Group, Amazon and NuvoMedia from *BusinessWeek*, 'Coming Soon: The Paperless, Portable Book', 6 July 1998; and Jeff Pelline, 'Bertelsmann Funds Web Book', CNETNews.com, 22 June 1998.

Page 173: Statement from Arno Penzias from 'Talking Networks, Disease, and Yes, Dry Cleaning, With Arno Penzias, Nobel Laureate,' *Fortune*, 8 June 1998.

Chapter 20

Page 180: *Wall Street Journal* quote on Apple from 6 February 1996 edition.

Page 181: Sources for information about IBM's initiatives in school systems world-wide: Italy: *Il Sole 24 ore*, 11 March 1997; Spain: *Pais Madrid*, 8 January 1998 and *Expansion Spain*, 2 January, 1998; Vietnam: *Nation*, 19 April 1994 and *Bangkok Post*, 19 April 1994.

Page 181: For more on IBM's new computer desk, see Louise Kehoe, 'IBM Tries to Tap into Young Minds with Sit in Computer', *Financial Times*, 23 April 1998.

Page 182: That ubiquity is not enough see for instance Brian Arthur, 'Increasing Returns and the World of Business', *Harvard Business Review*, July/August 1996.

Page 182: Some information on McDonald's taken from 'Can This Man Save McDonald's?', Caroline Sellars, *Fortune*, 22 June 1998. See also Jonathan Day and James Wendler, 'The New Economics of Organization', *McKinsey Quarterly*, number 1, 1998.

Chapter 21

Page 186: Jeff Bezos quote from Tim Clark, 'Newsmakers: Jeff Bezos—Turning to a Global Page', CNetnews.com, 8 April 1998.

Page 186: Richard Branson on investments and cash flow from 'The Future for Virgin: Will Branson's Cash Keep Flowing if the Music Stops?', Jonathan Ford, *Financial Times*, 13 August 1998.

Chapter 22

Page 192: For more on electronic cash and Mondex in Hong Kong, see Christopher Westland, Mandy Kwok, Josephine Shu, Terence Kwok and Henry Ho, 'Electronic Cash in Hong Kong', *Focus Theme*, volume 7, no. 2, 1997.

Page 193: More about Minitel, its technology and its market success from INSEAD case studies: Cats Baril and Tawfik Jelassi, 'Establishing a National Information technology Infrastructure: The Case of the French Videotext System Minitel', INSEAD Case Study, 1993; Tawfik Jelassi and Giridhar Murthy, 'Minitel: A Home Retailing Application', INSEAD Case Study, 1993.

Page 194: More on Publicis in a case study, 'Publicis Technology: Advertising Services in Cyberspace', by Sandra Vandermerwe and Rhys Morgan, in *Services Marketing—European Edition*, Christopher Lovelock, Sandra Vandermerwe and Barbara Lewis, London: Prentice Hall, 1999.

Page 197: For more on Netscape's origins and pricing strategy, see Joshua Quittner and Michelle Slatalla, *Speeding the Net: The Inside Story of Netscape and How it Challenged Microsoft*, London: Orion Business Publishing, 1998, and see Kevin Kelly, 'New Rules for the New Economy: Twelve Dependable Principles for Thriving in a Turbulent World', *Wired*, September 1997, Internet edition.

Chapter 23

Page 200: The notion of increasing returns isn't new. But it wasn't until Romer's work, which gave solid evidence of increasing returns in action presented in some structured way, that people began to take it seriously. Mainstream economists (and management theory therefore) had discounted the idea up to then as impractical because it was unmeasureable. For Romer's theories about growth and wealth creation and the role of intangibles, see Paul Romer, 'In The Beginning Was the Transistor', *Forbes ASAP On-Line*, 2 December 1996; Paul Romer, 'Beyond the Knowledge Worker', *Worldlink*, January/February 1995; David Samuels, 'The Adam Smith of Silicon Valley: Economist Paul Romer Preaches the Gospel of Growth', *Worth On-Line*, September 1996.

Page 201: For a comprehensive review of the role of value add through services, and implications, see Sandra Vandermerwe, *From Tin Soldiers to Russian Dolls: Creating Added Value Through Services*, Oxford: Butterworth Heinemann, 1993.

Page 201: SKF's transformation from a manufacturer of bearings into a provider of service-rich 'trouble-free operations' is recounted in the case study by Sandra Vandermerwe and Marika Taishoff, 'SKF Bearings: Market Orientation Through Services', Cases A, B and C, IMD Case Studies, 1990 (available from the European Case Clearing House at Cranfield University).

Page 202: Growth in service revenues even within the high-tech sector by year 2002 is from research conducted by Forrester Research Corporation, and quoted in *Wired*, May 1998.

Page 203: GE's reliance on services recounted in Ram Charan, 'The Rules Have Changed', *Fortune*, 16 March 1998. Also 'GE Capital: Jack Welch's Secret Weapon', *International Business Media Report*, 24 October 1997, Internet edition.

Page 203: On GE's new venture into logistics in Europe, see Charis Gresser, 'GE to Set up Europe Wide Logistics Venture', *Financial Times*, 26 August 1997.

Page 204: The journalist who claimed that Romer 'busted the study of economics wide open' is Kevin Kelly, executive editor of *Wired*, in his article 'The Economics of Ideas', published in *Wired's Hotwired Network*, June 1996, Internet edition. For more, see also his book *Out of Control: the New Biology of Machines*, London: 4th Estate, 1994, and his article, 'New Rules for the New Economy: Twelve Dependable Principles for Thriving in a Turbulent World', *Wired*, September 1997.

Chapter 24

Page 206: Romer and no scarcity remarks from the article by Kevin Kelly, 'The Economics of Ideas', *Wired's Hotwired Network*, June 1996. Also see Paul Romer, 'Idea Gaps and Object Gaps in Economic Development', *Journal of Monetary Economics*, volume 32, 1993; John Wysocoki Jr., 'For Economist Paul Romer; Prosperity Depends on Ideas', *Wall Street Journal*, 21 January 1997.

Page 206: For others on the value of ideas in growth and wealth creation see for instance Arie de Geus, *The Living Company: Growth, Learning and Longevity in Business*, London: Nicholas Brealey, 1997, especially Part I: 'Learning'. See also Thomas Stewart, *Intellectual Capital: The New Wealth of Organizations*, London: Nicholas Brealey, 1997.

Page 206: On the immaterial character of wealth, George Gilder, well-known author, columnist and provocateur on modern-day themes of high-tech, has some interesting thoughts in his article 'The Soul of Silicon', *Forbes ASAP*, 6 January 1998.

Page 206: The birth and evolution of the Internet are well recounted in Geoff Mulgan, *Connexity: How to Live in a Connected World*, London: Chatto & Windus, 1997.

Page 208: Stewart's quote is from page 171 of his book *Intellectual Capital: The New Wealth of Organizations*, London: Nicholas Brealey, 1997. For more on this theme of knowledge see Jonathan Day and James Wendler, 'The New Economics of Organization', *McKinsey Quarterly*, number 1, 1998.

Page 209: The quote on the arithmetic of old capitalism (what the author refers to as the 'goods economy') being different from customer capitalism (what he refers to as the 'knowledge economy') from Thomas Stewart, *Intellectual Capital: the New Wealth of Organizations*, London: Nicholas Brealey, 1997, page 198.

Chapter 25

Page 213: For an interesting discussion on knowhow as 'stock' and 'flow', and the difference between the two, read Liam Fahey and Laurence Prusak, 'The Eleven Deadliest Sins of Knowledge Management', *California Management Review*, volume 40, no. 3, Spring 1998.

Page 214: Charles Handy quote from an interview in *Rethinking the Future: Rethinking Business, Principles, Competition, Control & Complexity, Leadership, Markets and the World*, Rowan Gibson (ed.), London: Nicholas Brealey, 1997, page 30.

Page 215: Some of the information on KPMG from Stephanie Stahl, 'Hire on One, Get 'Em All', *Information Week*, 20 March 1995.

Page 215: Andersen Consulting's approach to harnessing and disseminating 'mindpower' comes partly from

Vanessa Houlder, 'The Power of Knowledge', *Financial Times*, 2 September 1996.

Page 215: Andersen's 'virtual office' in Paris from *Eurobusiness*, 'Virtual Office Reality', February 1996.

Page 219: In addition to interviews, information on managing knowledge at BP from John Cross (BP), Michael Earl, (London Business School), and Jeffrey Sampler, (London Business School), 'Transformation of the IT Function at British Petroleum', SIM 1996 International Paper Award Winner, from the Internet; Stephen Prokesch, 'Unleashing the Power of Learning: An Interview with British Petroleum's John Browne', *Harvard Business Review*, September/October 1997.

Page 219: In addition to interviews, some of the information on managing knowledge at Monsanto comes from Bipin Junnarkan, 'Creating Fertile Ground For Knowledge Management at Monsanto', Ernst & Young Centre for Business Innovation, *Managing Organizational Knowledge*, volume 1, 1997, Internet edition.

Page 221: In addition to interviews, information on Fujitsu from *Value from Knowledge—Managing the Knowledge Perspective: the Top Management Knowledge Agenda*, The Performance Group, London, 1998.

Chapter 26

Page 224: Supplementing interviews on Skandia, information also from: Leif Edvinsson and Michael Malone, *Intellectual Capital*, New York: Harper Business, 1997; Don Marchand, Johan Roos and David Oliver, 'Skandia Assurance and Financial Services: Measuring and Visualising Intellectual Capital', IMD Case Study, 1996; Johan Roos, Goran Roos, Leif Edvinsson and Nicola Dragonetti, *Intellectual Capital: Navigating in the New Business Landscape*, London: Macmillan Business, 1997; Paul Tate, 'Why is Skandia So Successful?', *Information Strategy*, May 1997.

Page 226: For some criticism on the learning curve see Paul Krugman, *Peddling Prosperity: Economic Sense and Nonsense in an Age of Diminishing Expectations*, New York: Norton, 1994, and Frederick Reichheld, *The Loyalty Effect: The Hidden Force behind Growth, Profits and Lasting Value*, Boston, MA: Harvard Business School Press, 1996.

Page 226: Peter Senge wrote his groundbreaking book, *The Fifth Discipline: The Art and Practice of the Learning Organization*, New York: Doubleday, in 1990.

Page 227: James Brian Quinn has long studied the role of knowledge-intensive services in the creation of customer value added, and how companies will have to manage such services. This quote is from his book *Intelligent Enterprise: A Knowledge and Service Based Paradigm for Industry*, New York: Free Press, 1992, page 254, and also from his article, written together with Philip Anderson and Sydney Finkelstein, 'Managing Professional Intellect: Making the Most of the Best', *Harvard Business Review*, March/April 1996. See also his recent book with Jordan Baruch and Karen Anne Zien, *Innovation Explosion: Using Intellect and Software to Revolutionize Growth Strategies*, New York: Free Press, 1997.

Page 227: Shoshanna Zuboff wrote her seminal work, *In the Age of the Smart Machine: The Future of Work and Power*, New York: Basic Books, in 1988.

Page 229: John Browne quote from Stephen Prokesch, 'Unleashing the Power of Learning: an Interview with British Petroleum's John Browne', *Harvard Business Review*, September/October 1997.

Page 231: Data on Citibank's 'model branch' concept is described in the case study series by Sandra Vandermerwe and Marika Taishoff, 'Citibank A: The Tao of Global Consumer Banking'; 'Citibank B: Implementing the Global Tao Pan-Europe and Greece'; Citibank C: Results in Greece', IMD Case Studies, 1994. (available from the European Case Clearing House at Cranfield University).

Chapter 27

Page 233: John Kay, in his *Foundations of Corporate Success*, Oxford University Press, 1993, discusses some of the reasons for diseconomies of scale ultimately setting in as size increases.

Page 233: On high-tech products and especially software, and low production costs, see Brian Arthur, 'Increasing Returns and the World of Business', *Harvard Business Review*, July/August, 1996; also Brian Arthur, *Increasing Returns and Path Dependence in the Economy*, Ann Arbor: University of Michigan Press, 1994; Joel Kurtzman, 'Thought Leader: an Interview with Brian Arthur', *Strategy and Business—Booz Allen & Hamilton*, 2nd Quarter,1998.

Page 236: Information on Toyota from interviews and from Michiyo Nakamoto, 'Japanese Companies Plan Multi-media Service for Cars', *Financial Times*, 28 April 1998.

Page 237: For an interesting discussion on voice recognition technology in cars, see John Griffiths, 'Talking About a New Generation of Clever Cars', *Financial Times*, Weekend Section, 8/9 August 1998.

Page 239: The quote from FedEx VP Michael Janes is from Todd Lappin, 'The Airline of the Internet', *Wired*, December 1996, Internet edition.

Page 241: Paying customers for information see Stan Davis and Christopher Meyer, *Blur: the Speed of Change in the Connected Economy*, London: Capstone, 1998; also see John Hagel and Jeffrey Rayport, 'The Coming Battle for Customer Information', *Harvard Business Review*, January/February 1997.

Page 242: For cost savings in virtual communities, see John Hagel and Arthur Armstrong, *Net Gain: Expanding Markets Through Virtual Communities, Boston*, Boston, MA: Harvard Business School Press, 1997.

Page 242: Lotus and customers helping each other from Thomas Stewart, *Intellectual Capital: the New Wealth of Organizations*, London: Nicholas Brealey, 1997.

Chapter 28

Page 247: Information on ultra-lightweight composition of cars and substitution of knowledge for expensive material from Kevin Kelly, 'New Rules for the New Economy: Twelve Dependable Principles for Thriving in a Turbulent World', *Wired*, September 1997.

Page 248: On the ever-expanding use of mobile phones, see Kevin Duffey, 'Value Added Mobile Services', Logica Consulting White Papers, January 1998, Internet edition.

Page 248: Bob Shapiro's quotes on the environment and knowledge from the interview by Joan Magretta, 'Growth Through Global Sustainability: an Interview With Monsanto's CEO Robert Shapiro', *Harvard Business Review*, January/February 1997.

Chapter 29

Page 256: PCs accounting for only 5% of total networking costs from 'Weighing the Case for the Network Computer', *The Economist*, 18 January 1997.

Page 258: For information on paying per drive see Mark Prigg, 'Smart Card will Activate Car's Optional Features', *Sunday Times*, 29 November 1998.

Page 259: Bob Shapiro query as to why anyone would want to own anything anyway, from Joan Magretta, 'Growth Through Global Sustainability: an Interview with Monsanto's CEO Robert Shapiro', *Harvard Business Review*, January/February 1997.

Page 259: For data on new trends in automobiles in France, see Jean François Jacquier, 'L'Auto Autrement', *Le Point*, 27 juin 1998.

Page 260: For more on Online Originals, see the Web page onlineoriginals.com. Also Tim Jackson, 'Publish and Be Scanned', *Financial Times–Inside Track*, 14 September 1998, and Alice Rawsthorn, 'Online Books Jump off the Page in a Novel Approach to Publishing', *Financial Times*, 23 June 1998.

Page 260: On printed newspapers vs online information services, see Geoffrey Nairn, *Financial Times Survey– FT Information Technology: On-line Newspapers a Challenge for the Printed Page*, 3 December 1997.

Page 260: For some interesting reading on newspapers and the Internet, see also the MBA Thesis by Chris Deavin, The Future of Newspapers on the Internet, Imperial College of Science, Technology, and Medicine, University of London Management School, 1998.

Page 261: Financial Times Electronic Publishing from its Web site, www.ft.com

Chapter 30

Page 264: For some information on new financial measures to better reflect the real worth of companies, see for example Ian Coleman and Robert Eccles, 'Pursuing Value: Reporting Gaps in the UK', Price Waterhouse Paper, London 1997; Philip Wright and Daniel Keegan, 'Pursuing Value: The Emerging Art of Reporting on the Future', Price Waterhouse Paper, London, 1997.

Page 264: The International Accounting Standards Committee (IASC) has also done research on how companies should be accounting for intangibles. For a summary, see Anthony Carey, 'The Real Value of Hidden Assets: The IASC's Proposals on How Companies Should Account for Intangibles', *Financial Times*, 6 November 1997.

Page 265: Microsoft shareholder attitudes from 'Microsoft's Cash Problem', *The Economist*, 26 July 1997.

Page 265: Information on Microsoft's earnings and market value compared to those of GE from 'The Lex Column: Microsoft', *Financial Times*, 17 September 1998.

Page 267: Difficulties faced by Japanese software firms obtaining financing from Mashima Rieko, 'The Turning Point For Japanese Software Companies: Can They Compete in the Prepackaged Software Market?', *Berkeley Technology Law Journal*, volume 12, issue 2, Fall 1996, Internet edition

Page 267: Anecdote on Branson and his directors buying their homes to demonstrate creditworthiness from Tim Jackson, *Virgin King: Inside Richard Branson's Business Empire*, London: HarperCollins, 1995.

Page 267: Peter Drucker comment on measurement tools as being essentially internally focused from 'The Future Has Already Happened', *Harvard Business Review*, September/October 1997. His quote on the Asian collapse from 'The Next Information Revolution', *Forbes ASAP*, 24 August 1998.

Page 268: Statistic on reported earnings accounting for stock price from 'The Old Rules No Longer Apply', Baruch Lev, *Forbes ASAP: Supplement on the Information Age*, 7 April 1997, Internet edition

Page 269: Patent information from 'Negative Correlation of Innovation and Software Patents', revised version of Appendix D of the League for Programming Freedom's Submission to the Patent Office, January 25, 1994, by Gordon Irlam and Ross Williams, Internet edition.

Page 269: James Tobin formulated his theory of investment, which came to be known as 'Tobin's Q', in 1969, in his article 'A General Equilibrium Approach to Monetary Theory', *Journal of Money, Credit and Banking*, November 1969.

Page 270: Data on Silicon Valley and the French stock market, see 'Silicon Valley Forty Years On', *BusinessWeek* , 8 August 1997.

Page 270: More on Canadian Imperial Bank of Commerce's (CIBC) knowledge-based lending approach from Britton Manasco, 'Leading Companies Focus On Managing and Measuring Intellectual Capital', *Knowledge Inc.*, Internet edition, 1997. See also Thomas Stewart, 'Your Company's Most Valuable Asset: Intellectual Capital', *Fortune*, 3 October 1994, which also talks about the initiatives of the CIBC in managing and applying its knowledge base.

Page 271: Hamel's assessment of the danger of using the wrong tools like EVA when firms' percentage of new market deteriorates from Gary Hamel, 'How Killers Count', *Fortune*, 23 June 1997 and Gary Hamel and Al Ehrbar (from Stern Stewart, the consulting firm which launched EVA methods), 'Debate: Duking it Out Over EVA', *Fortune*, 4 August 1997. And for more on this theme see Gary Hamel, 'Strategy Innovation and the Quest for Value', *Sloan Management Review*, Winter 1998, volume 39, number 2.

Page 271: Statistics on Intel and semiconductors from Gary Hamel, 'Strategy Innovation and the Quest for Value', *Sloan Management Review*, Winter 1998, volume 39, number 2.

Page 273: Thomas Stewart, in his *Intellectual Capital: The New Wealth of Organizations*, London: Nicholas Brealey, 1997, offers a comprehensive formula for calculating the net present value of customers over time. See also Frederick Reichheld, *The Loyalty Effect: the Hidden Force behind Growth, Profits and Lasting Value*, Boston, MA: Harvard Business School Press, 1996.

Page 273: An interesting academic article on market-based assets (those off the balance sheet) by Rajendra Srivastava, Tasadduq Shervani and Liam Fahey, 'Market-Based Assets and Shareholder Value: a Framework for Analysis', *Journal of Marketing*, January 1998, provides a conceptual framework of the marketing/ finance interface and elaborates on accelerating and enhancing cash flows.

Page 275: Branson's quote is from a letter he wrote to the editor of *The Economist*, 7 March 1997.

Page 276: Brian Arthur's warning about the persistence of the old guard is from the interview by Joel Kurtzman, 'Thought Leader: Brian Arthur', *Strategy and Business—Booz, Allen & Hamilton*, Second Quarter 1998.

Page 276: The Grove statement about Columbus in the New World from Christopher Anderson, *The Economist: Survey of Electronic Commerce*, May 1997, Internet edition.

INDEX